Exploring Everyday Things with R and Ruby

Sau Sheong Chang

Beijing • Cambridge • Farnham • Köln • Sebastopol • Tokyo

Exploring Everyday Things with R and Ruby

by Sau Sheong Chang

Printed in the United States of America.

Published by O'Reilly Media, Inc., 1005 Gravenstein Highway North, Sebastopol, CA 95472.

O'Reilly books may be purchased for educational, business, or sales promotional use. Online editions are also available for most titles (*http://my.safaribooksonline.com*). For more information, contact our corporate/institutional sales department: 800-998-9938 or *corporate@oreilly.com*.

Editors: Andy Oram and Mike Hendrickson
Production Editor: Kristen Borg
Copyeditor: Rachel Monaghan
Proofreader: Kiel Van Horn
Indexer: Angela Howard
Cover Designer: Karen Montgomery
Interior Designer: David Futato
Illustrator: Robert Romano

July 2012: First Edition

Revision History for the First Edition:

2012-06-26 First release

See *http://oreilly.com/catalog/errata.csp?isbn=9781449315153* for release details.

ISBN: 978-1-449-31515-3

[LSI]

Table of Contents

Preface

Explorers Ahoy!

It's hard to compare intrepid explorers like Ferdinand Magellan, James Cook, and Roald Amundsen with someone, well, like me. While these adventurers braved the elements, wild nature, and unknown dangers to discover new worlds (at least for their civilization), my biggest physical achievement to date would probably be completing a 10-kilometer charity quarter-marathon—walking.

The explorers of old had it good, of course, when it came to choices of unexplored places to stake their claim on. Christopher Columbus only had to sail due west from Europe, and he discovered two entire continents. For us, there are far fewer choices. There isn't much landmass on Earth that is yet unexplored; even the Mariana Trench, the deepest part of the world's oceans, has been conquered.

But explorer I am, and explorer you will be in this book. While much of the known physical world has been conquered (see Figure P-1), the unknown still looms over most of us.

We are all born with a sense of wonder and amazement at the world around us. Many of us just learn to turn it off as we grow older and jaded. I believe this is partly because we don't understand what goes on in the world around us well enough, and thus we don't care either. Click the remote and the TV turns on—why and how does that work? The first time we tried to ask, we were probably given a blank stare or waved away—who cares as long as you can watch the next season of *American Idol*? That soon grows to be our reaction as well.

Figure P-1. The Scott expedition to the South Pole (photo from the Public Domain Review; http://publicdomainreview.org/2012/03/29/remembering-scott)

Well, in this book, I'll take you along winding paths to bring back the original, wide-eyed person you were. We'll find the magic again, and hopefully at the end of the book, you'll continue where we leave off and make your own way in that journey of exploration and discovery.

Data, Data, Everywhere

We are swamped with data every minute and second of our lives. I don't mean this metaphorically, and I am not simply waxing lyrical about big data either.

In fact, we're so swamped that our eyes have evolved and adapted to this fact by shutting off our environment for a very short while every millisecond. In a phenomenon called *saccadic masking*, the brain shuts down during a fast eye movement (a *saccade*) to remove blurred images that come to our retina. Blurred images are not very useful, so the brain discards them, rendering us effectively blind (without us realizing it) during a saccade.

There is much similarity between saccadic masking and the way we process data today. The data comes so fast, so frequently that we often mask it away. There is a lot of data around us that we can extract and analyze to find answers, but the problem has always been *how* to do this.

In the (distant) past, it was always geniuses who had that knack of unlocking secrets with data and insight, along with the serendipitous few who simply stumbled on the answers. Not so anymore. Although intelligence is still a prerequisite, the arrival of computers and programming has elevated us from the more mundane, repetitive, and mind-numbing tasks of processing data to extract nuggets of information.

Only, it hasn't.

At least not for most people, anyway. The exceptions are scientists and mathematicians, who long ago pounced on the tools that enable them to do their work much more efficiently. If you're someone from these two camps, you are likely already taking full advantage of the power of computers.

However, for programmers and many other people, writing computer programs started with providing tools for businesses and for improving business processes. It's all about using computers to reduce cost, increase revenue, and improve efficiency. For many professional programmers, coding is a job. It's drudgery, low-level menial work that brings food to the table. We have forgotten the promise of computers and the power of programming for discovery.

Bringing the World to Us

This book is an attempt to bring back that wonder and sense of discovery. I want this book to uncover things that you didn't know, or didn't understand. I want it to help you discover new worlds within the existing world we see every day. Finally, I want it to enable you to explore the mundane and learn new things through programming and analyzing data.

While sometimes the world we explore in this book is the real world, more often it's not. It's hard to explore the whole wide world with just bits and bytes. So if we can't explore the world we live in, we'll create our own worlds and explore those—in other words, we'll use *simulations*.

Simulations are an excellent way of exploring things that we cannot control. We do this all the time. When we were young, we often created make-believe worlds and lived in them. Doing this enabled us to understand the real world better. We still do this today, through the magic of television (especially serials and soap operas) and movies—where we live through the characters we see on the screen. And for better or worse, simulations like television affect our real lives and even our dreams. For example, a survey by the American Psychological Association found that only 20% of people in their 60s (who grew up before color television was popular) recalled having bright and vivid dreams. However, 80% of people under the age of 30 confirmed that their dreams were in full color.[1]

In this book, we will use simulations to create experiments, isolate factors, and propose hypotheses to explain the results of the experiments. You might or might not agree with the experiments I describe or the hypotheses I suggest, but that doesn't really matter. What I would like you to get out of our journey together is the realization that there is more than business as usual to programming business solutions and processes. What I hope to achieve is for you eventually to design your own experiments, run through them, and discover your own worlds.

Packing Your Bags

So what do you need on this journey of discovery, this grand adventure through programming and analyzing data? Tools, of course. They will be the subject of the next two chapters. These are not the only tools available to you, but they are the ones we will be using in this book.

The two tools we will use are Ruby and R. I've chosen them for specific purposes. Ruby is easy to learn and to read, perfectly suited to explain concepts in human-readable code. I will be using Ruby to write simulations and to do preprocessing to get data. R, on the other hand, is great for analyzing data and for generating charts for visualization.

Although you don't need to be a Ruby or R programmer to be able to appreciate this book, I have assumed a basic understanding of programming. Specifically, I assume you have completed a computer science or related course or have done some simple programming in any programming language.

For the rest of the book, every chapter is more or less self-sufficient. Each chapter explores an idea, starting from the realization that a question exists and then attempting to answer it in either a simulation or some processing that brings out the data. We then analyze this data and make certain conclusions based on our analysis.

The ideas are drawn from diverse fields, ranging from economics to evolution, from healthcare to workplace design (in this case, figuring out the correct number of restrooms in an office). Some ideas are grander than others, and some ideas can be quite personal. The reason for this diversity is to show that the possibilities for exploration are limited only by our creativity.

1. Okada, Hitoshi, Kazuo Matsuoka, and Takao Hatakeyama. "Life Span Differences in Color Dreaming." *Dreaming* 21, no. 3 (2011), 213–220.

Each chapter usually starts off small, and we gradually add on layers of complexity to flesh out its central idea. The hypotheses, conclusions, and results from the experiments surrounding the base idea are incidental. You might, for example, agree or disagree with my conclusions and interpretation of the results. For this book at least, the journey is more important than the results.

With that, we're off! Have fun with the next two chapters, and enjoy the rest of the explorations, intrepid explorer!

Conventions Used in This Book

The following typographical conventions are used in this book:

Italic
: Indicates new terms, URLs, email addresses, filenames, and file extensions.

`Constant width`
: Used for program listings, as well as within paragraphs to refer to program elements such as variable or function names, databases, data types, environment variables, statements, and keywords.

`Constant width bold`
: Shows commands or other text that should be typed literally by the user; also used for emphasis within program listings.

`Constant width italic`
: Shows text that should be replaced with user-supplied values or by values determined by context.

This icon signifies a tip, suggestion, or general note.

This icon indicates a warning or caution.

Using Code Examples

All examples and related files in this book may be downloaded from GitHub (*https://github.com/sausheong/everyday*).

This book is here to help you get your job done. In general, you may use the code in this book in your programs and documentation. You do not need to contact us for permission unless you're reproducing a significant portion of the code. For example, writing a program that uses several chunks of code from this book does not require permission. Selling or distributing a CD-ROM of examples from O'Reilly books does require permission. Answering a question by citing this book and quoting example code does not require permission. Incorporating a significant amount of example code from this book into your product's documentation does require permission.

We appreciate, but do not require, attribution. An attribution usually includes the title, author, publisher, and ISBN. For example: "*Exploring Everyday Things with R and Ruby* by Sau Sheong Chang (O'Reilly). Copyright 2012 Sau Sheong Chang, 978-1-449-31515-3."

If you feel your use of code examples falls outside fair use or the permission given above, feel free to contact us at *permissions@oreilly.com*.

Safari® Books Online

Safari Books Online (*www.safaribooksonline.com*) is an on-demand digital library that delivers expert content in both book and video form from the world's leading authors in technology and business.

Technology professionals, software developers, web designers, and business and creative professionals use Safari Books Online as their primary resource for research, problem solving, learning, and certification training.

Safari Books Online offers a range of product mixes and pricing programs for organizations, government agencies, and individuals. Subscribers have access to thousands of books, training videos, and prepublication manuscripts in one fully searchable database from publishers like O'Reilly Media, Prentice Hall Professional, Addison-Wesley Professional, Microsoft Press, Sams, Que, Peachpit Press, Focal Press, Cisco Press, John Wiley & Sons, Syngress, Morgan Kaufmann, IBM Redbooks, Packt, Adobe Press, FT Press, Apress, Manning, New Riders, McGraw-Hill, Jones & Bartlett, Course Technology, and dozens more. For more information about Safari Books Online, please visit us online.

How to Contact Us

Please address comments and questions concerning this book to the publisher:

O'Reilly Media, Inc.
1005 Gravenstein Highway North
Sebastopol, CA 95472
800-998-9938 (in the United States or Canada)
707-829-0515 (international or local)
707-829-0104 (fax)

We have a web page for this book, where we list errata, examples, and any additional information. You can access this page at:

http://oreil.ly/everyday-things-r-ruby

To comment or ask technical questions about this book, send email to:

bookquestions@oreilly.com

For more information about our books, courses, conferences, and news, see our website at *http://www.oreilly.com*.

Find us on Facebook: *http://facebook.com/oreilly*

Follow us on Twitter: *http://twitter.com/oreillymedia*

Watch us on YouTube: *http://www.youtube.com/oreillymedia*

Acknowledgments

This is the part where I finally get to thank the people who helped me create the book you now hold in your hands. Writing a book is never the sole effort of a lonely author, as I have learned over the years, but the collective work of the author, a professional team, and a community of reviewers and supporters. In no particular order, I would like to thank:

- Mike Hendrickson for agreeing to this rather different type of programming book. It was a wild shot sending in the book proposal and I didn't really expect it to be picked up, except that it was.
- Andy Oram for being patient to a first time O'Reilly author, and arranging really long distance Skype calls halfway around the world, and waking up really early to speak to me every Tuesday evening.
- Kristen Borg, Rachel Monaghan, and the whole production editing team for doing such an awesome and professional job with the book.
- Jeremy Leipzig, Ivan Tan, Patrick Haller, and Judith Myerson for their help in doing the technical reviews and giving great advice. In particular, Patrick Haller, whom I badgered with emails about his comments on my R scripts. Thanks, Patrick!
- Rully Santosa, Chen Way Yen, Ng Tze Yang, Kelvin Teh, George Goh, and the rest of the HP Labs Singapore Applied Research team, to whom I have bounced off countless ideas and have given me innumerable remarks. Special thanks to Rully, Way Yen, and George for their feedback in Chapter 6.

- The Ruby community, especially the Singapore Ruby Brigade, where I made and continue to make good friends with common interests in exploring the world through Ruby. It's a great community to be in, and I relish the (now) annual RedDotRubyConf organized by the ever efficient Andy Croll.

Finally, I would like to dedicate this book to my family, who is my inspiration and my motivation in everything I do. To my lovely wife Wooi Ying, who has been patient yet again (for the third time), thanks for understanding why I simply have to understand everything and how it works. To my soon-to-be teenage son Kai Wen, I hope this book will also be an inspiration to you in being the wide-eyed explorer that I have been all my life.

CHAPTER 1

The Hat and the Whip

Indiana Jones is one of my favorite movie trilogies of all time, and Harrison Ford was a hero to me when I was growing up. Something I always loved about Indy was how he cracked his whip. In fact, I first learned what a bullwhip was watching *Raiders of the Lost Ark*.

The first two movies—*Raiders of the Lost Ark*, and *Indiana Jones and the Temple of Doom*—dealt with Indiana Jones the adult, already fully hardened and cranky. As I watched one movie after another, I wondered about his trademark hat and whip—why the fedora and why on earth a whip?

Finally, all was answered in the third movie of the trilogy, *Indiana Jones and the Last Crusade*. It was one of those satisfying *aha* moments that—although not at all that important in the overall scheme of things—gave Indy an origin, explaining the hat and the whip and why he did what he did.

So what does this have to do with a programming book? Just as the hat and the whip were indispensable tools for Indy, Ruby and R will be our two main tools in the rest of this book. And just as the hat and whip were not conventional tools for archaeology professors doing field work, neither are Ruby and R conventional tools for exploring the world around us. They just make things a whole lot more fun.

Ruby

Each of these tools will need its own chapter. We'll start off first with Ruby and then discuss R in the next chapter. Obviously, there is no way I can explain the entire Ruby programming language in a single chapter of a book, so I will give enough information to whet your appetite and hopefully entice you to proceed to the juicier books that discuss Ruby in more depth.

Why Ruby

One of the first questions you might ask (unless you're a Ruby enthusiast and you already know, in which case you can just nod along) is why did I choose Ruby as one of the two tools used in this book? There are a number of very good reasons. However, there are a couple that I want to focus on, specific to the goals of this book.

First, Ruby is a programming language for human beings. Yukihiro "Matz" Matsumoto, the creator of Ruby, often said that he tried to make Ruby natural, not simple, in a way that mirrors life. Ruby programming is a lot like talking to your good friend, the computer. Ruby was designed to make programming fun and to put the human back into the equation for programming. For example, to print "I love Ruby" 10 times on the screen, simply tell the computer to do exactly that:

```
10.times do
  puts "I love Ruby"
end
```

If you're familiar with C programming and its ilk, like Java, you'll already know that to check whether the variable `a_statement` is true, you need to do something like this (note that in C you will need to use the integer `1` instead of `true`, since C doesn't have a Boolean type):

```
a_statement = true;
if (a_statement == true) {
  do_something();
}
```

While you can certainly do the same in Ruby, it also allows you to do something like this:

```
do_something if a_statement
```

This results in code that is very easy to read and therefore to maintain. While Ruby can have its esoteric moments, it's generally a programming language that can allow someone else to read and understand it easily. As you can imagine, this is a feature that is very useful for this book.

Secondly, Ruby is a dynamic language, and what that means for you as a reader of this book is that you can copy the code from this book, plop it in a file (or the Interactive Ruby shell, as you will see later), and run it directly. There is no messy setting up of makefiles or getting the correct paths for libraries or compiling the compiler before running the examples. Cut, paste, and run—that's all there is to it.

While these are the two primary reasons I used Ruby in this book, if you're keen to understand why many other programmers have turned to Ruby, you can take a look at the Ruby website (*http://www.ruby-lang.org*) or search around the Internet, and you'll find plenty of people gushing over it.

Installing Ruby

Of course, before we can even start using Ruby, we need to get it into our machines. This is generally a simple exercise. There are three main ways of getting Ruby in your platform of choice, depending on how gung-ho you are.

Installing Ruby from source

If you're feeling pretty ambitious, you can try compiling Ruby. This mostly means that you need to have the tools to compile Ruby in your platform, so unless you really want to get serious with Ruby, I suggest that you install it from a precompiled binary, either through a third-party tool or your platform's usual package management tool.

To compile Ruby from source, go to *http://www.ruby-lang.org/en/downloads* and download the source, then compile it using your platform compiler. You can get more information from the same site.

Installing Ruby using third-party tools

Alternatively, you can use one of these popular third-party tools. The recommended approach is to go with the first, which is Ruby Version Manager if you're running on OS X or Linux, and RubyInstaller if you're on Windows.

Ruby Version Manager (RVM). RVM is probably the most popular third-party tool around for non-Windows platforms. A distinct advantage of using RVM is that you will be able to install multiple versions of Ruby and switch to any of them easily. Installing RVM, while not very difficult, is not a single-liner. As of today at least, this is the way to install RVM.

First, you need to have Git and curl installed. Then, issue this command in your console:

```
$ curl -L get.rvm.io | bash -s stable
```

Then, reload your shell by issuing this (or a similar command, depending on your shell):

```
$ source ~/.profile
```

This will allow you to run `rvm`. The next thing you should do is to check whether you have all you need to install Ruby:

```
$ rvm requirements
```

Once you have that, use `rvm` to install the version of Ruby you want. In our case, we'll be using Ruby 1.9.3:

```
$ rvm install 1.9.3
```

After this, check whether the Ruby version you wanted is correctly installed:

```
$ rvm list
```

You should see a list (or at least one) of RVM Rubies installed. If this is your first time installing, there will not be any default Ruby, so you will need to set one by issuing the following command:

```
$ rvm alias create default ruby_version
```

Replace *ruby_version* with the version you've just installed (such as `ruby 1.9.3p125`), and you're done! Check out the RVM website at *https://rvm.io/* for more installation instructions in case you're stuck at any point in time.

RubyInstaller. If you're using Windows, you can't install RVM. In that case, you can either create a virtual machine, install your favorite GNU/Linux distro, and then proceed; or just use RubyInstaller, which is frankly a lot easier. Simply go to *http://rubyinstaller.org/downloads*, download the correct version, and then install it. RubyInstaller includes many native C-based extensions, so that's a bonus. It is a graphical installer, so it's pretty simple to get a fresh installation set up quickly.

Installing Ruby using your platform's package management tool

If none of the approaches listed so far suits you, then you can opt to use your system's package management tool. For Debian systems (and this includes Ubuntu), you can use this command:

```
$ sudo apt-get install ruby1.9.1
```

This will install Ruby 1.9.2. Yes, it's weird.

For Macs, while Ruby comes with OS X, it's usually an older version (Lion comes with Ruby 1.8.7, and the previous versions come with even older versions of Ruby). There is a popular package management tool in OS X named Homebrew, which helps you to replace this with the latest version of Ruby. As you would guess, you'll need to install Homebrew first. Run this command on your console:

```
$ /usr/bin/ruby -e "$(curl -fsSL https://raw.github.com/gist/323731)"
```

Then install Ruby with this simple command:

```
$ brew install ruby
```

Homebrew is actually just a set of Ruby scripts.

Running Ruby

Once you have installed Ruby with any of the preceding methods, it's time to start using it! Unlike compiled languages such as C, C++, or Java, you don't need to have an intermediate step to generate executable files before running Ruby.

There are a few ways of running Ruby code, but the easiest way to get started is probably using the interactive Ruby tool that's built into your Ruby installation. *irb* is a Ruby REPL (read-eval-print loop) application, an interactive programming environment that allows you to type in Ruby commands and have them evaluated in real time:

```
$ irb
ruby-1.9.3-p125 :001 > puts "hello world!"
hello world!
 => nil
ruby-1.9.3-p125 :002 >
```

Note that once you have typed in a Ruby statement (in this case, we are placing the string "hello world!" to the standard output), the statement is evaluated immediately, resulting in "hello world!" being printed on the screen. After that, *irb* tells you the statement evaluates to nil, because the Ruby `puts` statement returns a nil. If you have put in a statement like this:

```
$ irb
ruby-1.9.3-p125 :001 > 1 + 1
 => 2
ruby-1.9.3-p125 :002 >
```

This statement returns `2`, which is the result of the evaluation. *irb* is a tool you will quickly get used to and will be using whenever you're not sure what the result is going to be.

Another common method of running Ruby is to save your code in a file and then run your file through the Ruby interpreter. For example, you could save `puts "hello world!"` to a file named *hello_world.rb*. After that, you can try this command at the console:

```
$ ruby hello_world.rb
hello world!
```

Most of the examples in this book will be run this way.

Requiring External Libraries

While you can probably get away with writing simpler Ruby programs without any other libraries than the ones built into Ruby itself, most of the time you'll need some external libraries to make life easier. Two sets of Ruby libraries come preinstalled with Ruby.

Core
: This is the default set of classes and modules that comes with Ruby, including `String`, `Array`, and so on.

Standard

These libraries, found in the */lib* folder of the Ruby source code, are distributed with Ruby but are not included by default when you run it. These include libraries such as Base64, Open URI, and the Net packages (HTTP, IMAP, SMTP, and so on).

To use the standard libraries and any other libraries other than the Ruby core, you will need to *require* them in your program:

```
require 'base64'
```

In addition to the standard libraries, you will often need to use external libraries developed by the Ruby community or yourself. The most common way to distribute Ruby libraries is through RubyGems, the package manager for Ruby. It's distributed as part of Ruby in the standard library, so you can use it out of the box once Ruby is installed.

Just as *apt-get* and *yum* manage packages on a Linux distribution, RubyGems allows you to easily install or remove libraries and Ruby applications. To be distributed through RubyGems, the library or application needs to be packaged in something called a *gem*, which is a package of files to install as well as self-describing metadata about the package.

Gems can be distributed locally (passed around in a *.gem* file) or remotely through a gem server. A few public gem servers provided gem hosting in the past, including RubyForge, GitHub, and GemCutter, but recently they have been more or less replaced by RubyGems. In RubyGems lingo, gem servers are also known as *sources*. You can also deploy a private gem server where you publish private gems that you prepackage for internal use.

To add sources to your RubyGems installation, you can do this:

```
$ gem sources -add http://your.gemserver.org
```

To install a local gem, you can do the following at the console:

```
$ gem install some.gem -local
```

You can do away with the `-local` option, but doing so will add a bit of time because the command will search the remote sources. Setting the local option tells RubyGems to skip that. To add a gem from a remote source, you can generally do this:

```
$ gem install some_gem
```

You can also install specific versions of a gem like so:

```
$ gem install some_gem -version 1.23
```

To list the gems that you have installed locally, you can do this:

```
$ gem list -local
```

Basic Ruby

With the setup complete, let's get started with Ruby!

Strings

Manipulating strings is one of the most basic things you normally do in a program. Any programming language worth its salt has a number of ways to manipulate strings, and Ruby is no exception. In fact, Ruby has an embarrassment of riches in terms of its capability to manipulate strings.

Ruby strings are simply sequences of characters. There are a few ways of defining strings. The most common ways are probably through the single(') and double(") quotes. If you define a string with double quotes, you can use escape sequences in the string and also perform substitution of Ruby code into the string using the expression #{}. You can't do this inside single-quoted strings:

```
"There are #{24 * 60 * 60} seconds in a day"
=> "There are 86400 seconds in a day"

'This is also a string'
=> "This is also a string"
```

Strings can also be defined using %q and %Q. %q is the same as single-quoted strings, and %Q is the same as double-quoted strings, except that in these cases the delimiters can be anything that follows %q or %Q:

```
%q/This is a string/
=> "This is a string"

%q{This is another string}
=> "This is another string"

%Q!#{'Ho! ' * 3} Merry Christmas\!!
=>"Ho! Ho! Ho!  Merry Christmas!"
```

Finally, you can also define a string using a *here-document*. A here-document is a way of specifying a string in command-line shells (sh, csh, ksh, bash, and so on) and in programming or scripting languages such as Perl, PHP, Python, and, of course, Ruby. A here-document preserves the line breaks and other whitespace (including indentation) in the text:

```
string = <<END_OF_STRING
   The quick brown fox jumps
   over the lazy dog.
END_OF_STRING
=> "   The quick brown fox jumps\n   over the lazy dog.\n"
```

Take note that the delimiter is the string after the << characters—in this case, END_OF_STRING.

Although I can't list everything that Ruby provides for string manipulation in this section, here are a few things it can do:

```
a = "hello "
b = "world"

a + b
=> "hello world"                    # string concatenation (this adds b to a
                                    # to create a new string)

a << b
=> "hello world"                    # append to string (this modifies a)

a * 3
=> "hello hello hello"              # you can repeat strings by simply
                                    # multiplying them

c = "This is a string"              # splitting a string according to a delimiter,
                                    # any space being the default delimiter
c.split
=> ["This", "is", "a", "string"]
```

Arrays and hashes

Just as important as strings, and perhaps sometimes even more so, is being able to manipulate data structures. The two most important data structures, which you'll meet very often in this book (and also in Ruby programming), are arrays and hashes.

Arrays are indexed containers that hold a sequence of objects. You can create arrays using square brackets (`[]`) or using the `Array` class. Arrays are indexed through a running integer starting with 0, using the `[]` operator:

```
a = [1, 2, 'this', 'is', 3.45]
a[0]  #  1
a[1]  #  2
a[2]  # "this"
```

There are other ways of indexing arrays, including the use of ranges:

```
a[1..3]  # [2. 'this', 'is']
```

You can also set items in the array using the same operator:

```
a[4] = 'an'
a   # [1, 2, 'this', 'is', 'an']
```

Arrays can contain anything, including other arrays:

```
a[5] = ['another', 'array']
a   # [1, 2, 'this', 'is', 'an', ['another', 'array']]
```

If you're used to manipulating data structures, you might be wondering why I'm discussing only arrays and hashes in this section. What about the other common data structures, like stacks, queues, sets, and so on? Well, arrays can be used for them as well:

```
stack = []
stack.push 1
stack.push 2
stack.push 'hello'
stack   # [1, 2, 'hello']

stack.pop   # 'hello'
stack   # [1, 2]
```

Tons of other methods can be used on arrays; you can find them through the reference documentation on the Ruby website, or even better, by firing up *irb* and playing around with it a bit. A common way of iterating through arrays is using the `each` method:

```
a = ['This', 'is', 'an', 'array']

a.each do |item|
  puts item
end
```

This will result in each item in the array being printed out at the standard output (i.e., the console). In the preceding code, the loop starts with `do` and ends with `end`. It runs for each of the four items in the array; here, we chose the variable `item` to represent the item within the loop. We use vertical bars to surround the variable name `item`. Sometimes, for brevity, we can replace the `do` … `end` with a pair of curly braces {}. This code produces the following results:

```
This
is
an
array
```

Notice that the items in the array are printed in the same sequence in which they are defined.

While arrays have a lot of methods, you should also be aware that `Array` inherits from the `Enumerable` module, so it also implements those methods. We'll get to `Enumerable` shortly.

Hashes are dictionaries or maps, data structures that index groups of objects. The main difference is that instead of having an integer index, hash indices can be any object. Hashes are defined using curly braces {} or the `Hash` class, and indexed using square brackets:

```
h = { 'a' => 'this', 'b' => 'is', 'c' => 'hash'}

h['a']      # "this"
h['b']      # "is"
h['c']      # "hash"
```

Setting an item in a hash also uses the square brackets:

```
h['some'] = 'value'
h   # { 'a' => 'this', 'b' => 'is', 'c' => 'hash', 'some' => 'value'}
```

The *hash rocket* style of assigning values to keys in hashes was changed in Ruby 1.9. While that still works, the new syntax is simpler and more crisp. The following lines of code do exactly the same thing:

```
h = { canon: 'camera', nikon: 'camera', iphone: 'phone'}
# is the same as
h = { :canon => 'camera', :nikon => 'camera', :iphone => 'phone'}
```

There are many ways of iterating through hashes, but here's a common way of doing it:

```
h = { canon: 'camera', nikon: 'camera', iphone: 'phone'}

h.each do |key, value|
  puts "#{key} is a #{value}"
end
```

Just as we used vertical bars earlier to name `item` as the variable to represent items from an array, here we use vertical bars to name two variables. The first represents each key in the hash, and the second represents its associated value. This code produces the following results:

```
canon is a camera
nikon is a camera
iphone is a phone
```

Both `Array` and `Hash` inherit from—that is, are subclasses of—`Enumerable`. `Enumerable` is a module that provides collection classes with a number of capabilities, including several traversal and searching methods, and the ability to sort. A very useful method (we'll get to methods in a bit) in `Enumerable` is the `map` method, which runs through each item in the collection, performs the action given by the block, and then returns a new array with the new values. The input to `map` in the following example is a range of digits (1, 2, 3, and 4), and its output is the square of each input:

```
(1..4).map do |i|
  i*i
end   #[1, 4, 9, 16]
```

The `max_by` and `min_by` methods are also useful. These, as you might have guessed, return the maximum or minimum item in the array:

```
a = ["cat", "horse", "monkey"]
a.min_by {|i| i.length}   # "cat"
a.max_by {|i| i.length}   # "monkey"
```

As before, read up on the available methods in `Enumerable` and try them out in *irb*.

Symbols

Ruby includes the concept of *symbols*, which are constant names. Symbols start with a colon, followed by some kind of name. For example, `:north` and `:counter` are symbols. Symbols are often useful in situations where you need some kind of identifier. Using strings would be overkill since each string you create is a new object. Symbols, once defined, always refer to the same object that was originally created.

Conditionals and loops

If you have done any sort of programming, conditionals and loops in Ruby should look very familiar to you. Ruby has direct and indirect ancestry of C, so its conditional syntax is very similar to C's syntax.

if and unless. The `if` expression in Ruby is pretty similar to that of other languages:

```
if pet.is_a? Dog then
  wag :tail
elsif pet.is_a? Cat then
  meow
else
  do_nothing
end
```

The keyword `then` is optional if every statement is on a new line. The negated and opposite of `if` is `unless`:

```
unless visitor.friend?
  bark :loudly
else
  wag :tail
end
```

Sometimes, when you don't have an `else` statement, you can use `if` and `unless` as *statement modifiers*. Statement modifiers are just that—they modify the statements given that the conditional is satisfied.

```
wag(:tail) if pet.is_a? Dog

bark(:loudly) unless visitor.friend?
```

In the preceding code, the method `wag` will be called if the `pet` object is of the class `Dog`. The method `bark` will be called unless the visitor is a friend.

Finally, just as in C, Ruby recognizes the ternary conditional expression:

```
visitor.friend? ? wag(:tail) : bark(:loudly)
```

This is equivalent to:

```
if visitor.friend? then
  wag(:tail)
else
  bark(:loudly)
end
```

case expression. In Ruby, there are two ways to use a `case` expression. The first is similar to a series of `if` and `elsif` statements:

```
case
when visitor.friend?
  wag :tail
when visitor.postman?
  chase
when visitor.carries :big_juicy_bone
  jump_on visitor
else
  bark :loudly
end
```

The second way is more common, though. Specify a target along with the case, and each `when` clause does a comparison with the target:

```
case visitor.name
  when "Harry" then greet("Hello and welcome!")
  when "Sally" then greet("Welcome my dear!")
  when "Joseph" then greet("They are not here yet")
  else do_not_open_door
end
```

Loops. The two main looping mechanisms in Ruby are `while` and its negated form, `until`. `while` loops through the block zero or more times as long as its condition is true, and `until` does the opposite—it loops through the block until the condition becomes true:

```
while visitor.hungry?
  offer food
end
# is the same as
until visitor.full?
  offer food
end
```

As you can see, both forms do exactly the same thing. So why would you have both ways and not just one? Remember that Ruby can be expressive and often tries to make programs more intelligible. Although both forms are the same, sometimes it's just more natural to do it one way or the other.

Like `if` and `unless`, both `while` and `until` can be used as statement modifiers:

```
offer(food) while visitor.hungry?
# is the same as
offer(food) until visitor.full?
```

Everything Is an Object

Something you will often hear about Ruby is that everything in Ruby is an object. That sounds a bit extreme and is not technically true. Certainly keywords, such as the if-else conditional syntax, are not objects. However, everything that you manipulate within Ruby is an object. Even classes are objects, and so are methods. And everything actually evaluates to an object. Let's see how this works.

Classes and objects

The classic way of creating objects is to instantiate one from a class:

```
class Dog
  attr :breed, :color, :name

  def initialize(name, color, breed)
    @name, @color, @breed = name, color, breed
  end

  def bark(volume=:softly)
    make_a_ruckus(volume)
  end
end
```

If you have done any form of object-oriented programming in other languages, this should be familiar to you. If you haven't done this before, this seems like a bit of a puzzle, but it's easily explainable. The previous code defines a class, which is somewhat like a template from which you create instances or objects. In this example, I defined a `Dog` class, which has attributes like `breed` and `color`, as well as a name for each instance of the class. The keyword `attr` is a method call that helps me create three instance variables (`breed`, `color`, and `name`) along with some standard methods that access these variables. Instance variables in Ruby start with `@`.

The lines that start with `def` define methods. Methods are functions that belong to objects and are called on that object. The example has two methods: `initialize` and `bark`.

`initialize` is a convenience method. Whenever Ruby creates a new object, it will always look for a method named `initialize` and call it. In our `initialize` method, we set up each of the instance variables with a value from the parameter.

The `bark` method, well, simply makes a ruckus. Its definition shows how to assign a default value (`softly`) to an argument if the argument is not passed by the calling method.

So how do we create an object from this `Dog` class?

```
my_dog = Dog.new('Rover', :brown, 'Cocker Spaniel')
```

`my_dog` is a variable that contains an object that has just been instantiated from the `Dog` class, with values sent to the `initialize` method to give the name, color, and breed.

Methods

As mentioned, you can define methods using the `def` keyword, followed by the method name. Method definitions can take in zero or more parameters. If you don't need parameters for your method, you can do away with the brackets altogether:

```
def growl
  make_a_ruckus(:very_softly)
end
```

As you might have noticed from the `Dog` class, you can also set default values to method parameters:

```
def bark(volume=:softly)
  make_a_ruckus(volume)
end
```

In the preceding code, the default value for the volume, which is a parameter, is the symbol `:softly`. If you include a default value in the parameter, when you call the method you can either include the parameter or omit it:

```
my_dog.bark          # in this case dog barks softly
my_dog.bark(:loudly)
```

For methods with multiple parameters, it's common practice to place the parameters with defaults after the ones that do not have defaults. If the parameters without defaults came after the ones with defaults, setting the default would become meaningless because each time the method is called, the parameter must always be given.

Methods always return a value, which can be an array in order to incorporate multiple values. To return a value, you can either specify it directly with the `return` keyword, or simply let the method end, in which case it will return the last evaluated value.

Class methods and variables

So far we've been talking about instances of a class. An earlier example instantiated the my_dog object from the Dog class. Variables and methods really belong to the my_dog object and are called on the my_dog object only. For example, given the previous definition of the Dog class, you can't really do this:

```
Dog.bark
```

Logically speaking, since Dog is the template by which dogs are created, calling the bark method on Dog means asking all dogs to bark! However, in many cases (and if you've done object-oriented programming before, you'll understand what I'm referring to), you will need to call upon methods and even variables that belong to the class instead of the object. How can we do this?

Earlier I said that even classes are objects. What we're doing next is really nothing more than treating a class as an object. To define a class method, simply prefix the name of the method with self:

```
class Dog
  attr :breed, :color, :name

  def self.total_count
    # return the total number of dogs in the system
  end

  # other methods
end
```

self is a keyword that represents the current object (like this in C++ or Java). While we're defining a class, the current object is the class that's being defined. By defining a method with self in the class definition, we're saying we want to add this method to the class itself, not to an instance of the class. In this case, we're adding a method to the Class object that's an instance of the Class class. You'll see a lot of this when we need to define methods that will work on the class itself.

Defining class variables is quite straightforward. Simply prefix the name of variable with @@:

```
class Dog
  @@count = 0
  attr :breed, :color, :name

  def self.total_count
    @@count
  end

  def initialize
    @@count += 1
    # other initialization
  end
```

```
  # other methods
end
```

Notice that the @@count class variable is initialized to zero during the class definition. This is done once only. It would normally be a mistake to initialize a class variable in the initialize method, because the initialize method is called every time a new object is instantiated. This means that the class variable is reset every time a new object is created!

Inheritance

Inheritance is one of the cornerstones of object-oriented programming. Inheritance in Ruby is pretty conventional. To subclass from another class, do this at the class definition:

```
class Spaniel < Dog
  # other definitions
end
```

This creates a subclass named `Spaniel` that inherits everything from the `Dog` class, including methods and variables. This begs the question: if `Spaniel` is the subclass of `Dog`, `Dog` is the subclass of what? You can find out by calling the `superclass` method on the `Dog` class itself. Remember that `Dog` is actually an object, so you can call methods directly on it:

```
Spaniel.superclass      # Dog
Dog.superclass          # Object
Object.superclass       # BasicObject
BasicObject.superclass  # nil
```

As you can see, `Dog` is a subclass of the `Object` class (which is an object—does your head hurt yet?) and `Object` is the subclass of `BasicObject`. As it turns out, that's the end of the line—and it's *not* turtles all the way down.[1]

Now that we have defined the `Spaniel` class, what happens if we call the `bark` method? Since `bark` is not defined in `Spaniel`, it will reach out to its superclass—in this case, `Dog`—and call the same method on `Dog`. Of course, if Ruby can't find `bark` in the `Dog` class, it will continue bubbling up the object hierarchy until it hits `BasicObject`, and then finally throw a `NoMethodError`.

1. From Stephen Hawking's book, *A Brief History of Time* (Bantam):

   A well-known scientist (some say it was Bertrand Russell) once gave a public lecture on astronomy. He described how the earth orbits around the sun and how the sun, in turn, orbits around the center of a vast collection of stars called our galaxy. At the end of the lecture, a little old lady at the back of the room got up and said: "What you have told us is rubbish. The world is really a flat plate supported on the back of a giant tortoise." The scientist gave a superior smile before replying, "What is the tortoise standing on?" "You're very clever, young man, very clever," said the old lady. "But it's turtles all the way down!"

You cannot subclass from more than one superclass. While some languages allow multiple inheritance, Ruby supports single inheritance only. However, Ruby has a mechanism you can use to mimic multiple inheritance: the *mixin* mechanism, using modules.

Modules are simply a way to group methods, classes, and constants to provide a namespace and prevent name clashes. In addition, Ruby enables mixins if you include modules in the class. Because we can include more than one module in a class, we can simulate the effects of multiple inheritance.

Let's take the example of the `Dog` class further by defining a superclass for `Dog` called `Canine`:

```
class Canine
  # some definitions
end

class Wolf < Canine
  # some definitions
end

class Dog < Canine
  # some definitions
end
```

Now, dogs are pets too, so if we want to bunch together some methods and variables for a `Pet` class, how do we make `Dog` inherit methods or variables from `Pet`? We can't do this in Ruby because it is single inheritance. Instead, we can convert `Pet` into a module:

```
module Pet
  def scratch_stomach
    # there's a good boy!
  end
end

class Dog < Canine
  include Pet
  # some definitions
end
```

This way, `Dog` can inherit the methods in `Pet` and `Canine` without violating single inheritance.

An example of a mixin, which you may remember from "Arrays and hashes" (page 8), is that both `Array` and `Hash` classes include the `Enumerable` module.

Code like a duck

Ruby and languages like Python, PHP, and Smalltalk, are well known to be dynamically typed, versus languages like C and Java that are statically typed. Essentially, a language is statically typed if the programmer needs to specify the data type in the code, and the compiler will check and complain if the types don't match. Dynamically typed languages, on the other hand, don't need to specify the data type in the code, and leave type checking to the runtime.

For example, in Java, you need to first declare a variable, then assign it to a value:

```
int count = 100;
```

However, in Ruby, you only need to do this:

```
count = 100
```

You are expected to use the variable properly—that is, if you placed an integer into the variable, you're expected to use it as an integer in your code. When you use `count`, Ruby knows that it's an integer and you're expected to use it as such. However, if you don't, Ruby will automatically cast it to whatever you're trying to use it for. This process is known as *duck typing*.

The idea behind duck typing comes from the duck test: "if it walks like a duck, and quacks like a duck, then it is a duck." What this means is that the type of the object is not determined by the class of the object. Instead, the type depends on what the object can do.

A simple example goes like this. Let's say we define a method named `op`:

```
def op(a,b)
  a << b
end
```

The method takes two parameters and returns a single value. Nowhere in this definition are the parameter types specified. The returned value's type is not specified either. A potential infestation of bugs? Let's see how we use this method. If `x` and `y` are both strings, the return result is also a string. No problem here:

```
x = 'hello '
y = 'world'

op(x,y)
=> 'hello world'
```

If `x` is an array and `y` is a string, the method appends `y` into the `x`, returning an array:

```
x = ['hello']
y = 'world'

op(x,y)
=> ["hello", "world"]
```

If x and y are integers, the method will perform a left-shift bitwise operation, moving binary 1 two positions to the left, resulting in 4:

```
x = 1
y = 2

op(x,y)
=> 4
```

So what does this mean? There are both benefits and drawbacks to duck typing. The most obvious drawback is that we have a method that is inconsistent: if we put different values into the method, we can get wildly different results, and this is not checked anytime before the actual running of the program.

However, the major benefit of this approach is that it results in much simpler code. If you know what you're doing, it can lead to code that is easier to read and to maintain.

Ultimately, duck typing is more of a philosophy than a fixed way of coding in Ruby. If you want to ensure that the op method you defined can be used only for strings, for example, you can always do this:

```
def op(a,b)
  throw "Input parameters to op must be string"
    unless a.is_a? String and b.is_a? String
  a << b
end
```

This will throw an exception if either a or b is not a string.

Shoes

The second part of this chapter will introduce Shoes, a Ruby-based user interface toolkit. Shoes is not commonly used as a UI toolkit, and Ruby itself doesn't have significant strength for building desktop graphical user interfaces. Among the other more popular Ruby UI toolkits (in case you want to get serious later on) are FXRuby, WxRuby, qtRuby, and Tk. If you're looking for something totally cross-platform, JRuby with Swing is a good option, although there are other alternatives to Swing, like SWT and Limelight. For Macs, a good alternative is MacRuby.

However, in this book, we'll be using Shoes.

What Is Shoes?

Shoes is a cross-platform toolkit for writing graphical applications with Ruby. It's entirely and purely Ruby, quite unlike most other toolkits, which are usually Ruby bindings of existing UI toolkits. It's also dead easy, and that's a primary motivation for using Shoes in this book.

Shoes was originally created by why the lucky stiff (yes, that's his name), a rather famous if mysterious Ruby programmer who also draws cartoons and plays music. He is probably most famous for writing *Why's (poignant) Guide to Ruby*, a totally un-programming-book-like book that teaches Ruby programming.

For unknown reasons, _why (as he is also known) removed his Twitter and GitHub accounts suddenly in August 2009 and shut down his personal sites, many of which were popular haunts for Ruby programmers. However, many of his projects, including Shoes, were collected and continued by the Ruby community.

A Rainbow of Shoes

Ruby is red and so is Shoes. Red Shoes is based on C and is the original version of Shoes written by _why. When the community took over after _why left, there were experiments to try out different types of Shoes, and each was "colored" differently.

Red Shoes
: This is the original written by _why, based on C.

White Shoes
: This is called the meta-Shoes, the most generic of all Shoes. It's basically a set of RSpec tests to make sure that all other Shoes are compliant to a standard.

Blue Shoes
: This is built on top of the Qt framework, which is written in C++ and is the original UI framework for Ruby.

Green Shoes
: This is the closest in spirit to Red Shoes because it uses GTK and Cairo's Ruby bindings. It's also one of the most advanced (as of this writing).

Brown Shoes
: This is the version of Shoes written in JRuby and is based on Swing.

In this book, when I refer to Shoes, I am referring to Red Shoes, which in fact is the only version of Shoes that I've run my code against. The standard disclaimer is that the code might not necessarily run properly in any other color Shoes. You're more than welcome to try them out, though!

Installing Shoes

Installing Shoes is usually really easy. If you're using a Mac or Windows, just download it from the Shoes website (*http://shoesrb.com/downloads*) and install it on your platform of choice. *Using* Shoes, however, is not conventional. Unlike most Ruby programs, which can be run through a console, you need to open the Shoes application, then use it to open and run your Shoes program. Alternatively, you can do the following on a Mac, or the equivalent on Windows:

```
$ /Applications/Shoes.app/Contents/MacOS/shoes test_shoes.rb
```

If you're using a variant of Linux, installing Shoes can be a bit more involved. As of this writing, the best way of getting Shoes on the Linux variant of your choice is to build it entirely from source. It's not as difficult as it seems. You do, however, need to install some other libraries it depends on. Here are the steps that are common to all Linux variants:

```
$ git clone git://github.com/shoes/shoes.git
$ cd shoes
$ gem install bundler
$ bundle install
$ rake
```

For more detailed information, you can refer to *https://github.com/shoes/shoes/wiki/Building-Shoes-on-Linux*.

Programming Shoes

One of the main reasons I picked Shoes as the UI toolkit for this book is that it's really simple to create reasonably good graphical interfaces. Because it's Ruby (as opposed to a Ruby binding for another toolkit), the code is typically very readable and easy to understand.

A simple Shoes program looks like this:

```
Shoes.app do
  button("Click me!") do
    alert("Ruby rocks!")
  end
end
```

This produces a simple window with a single button labeled "Click me!" When the button is clicked, an alert dialog box pops up (Figure 1-1).

While Shoes is a simple UI toolkit, there's still lots of stuff in there that is impossible to describe completely in a few sections of a chapter. I'll just go through a couple of basic examples. Let's start by building a simple stopwatch application.

Shoes stopwatch

In this example, I'll show how Shoes can be used to build the very simple stopwatch in Example 1-1.

Example 1-1. Shoes stopwatch

```
Shoes.app height: 200, width: 200 do
  background lightblue
  stack margin: 10 do
    caption strong "Shoes StopWatch"
    flow do
```

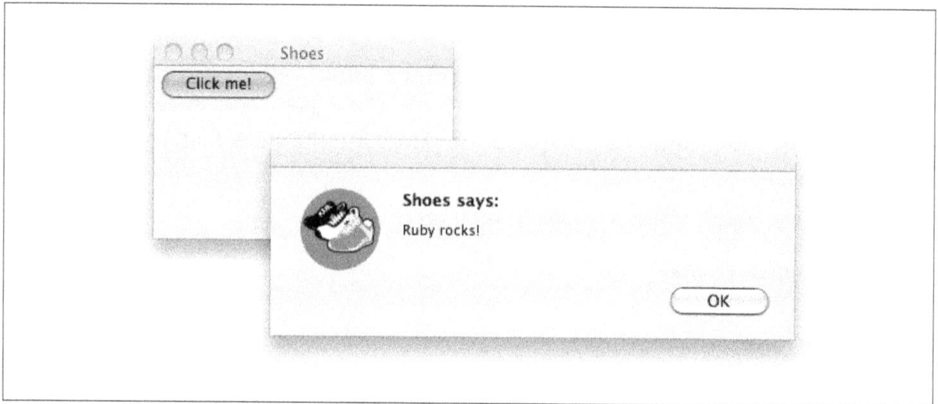

Figure 1-1. Simple Shoes program

```
        button "start" do
          @time = Time.now
          @label.replace "Started at #{@time.strftime '%l:%M:%S %p'}"
        end
        button "stop" do
          @label.replace "Stopped, ", strong("#{Time.now - @time}"),
            " seconds elapsed."
        end
      end
      @label = para "Press ", strong("start"), " to begin timing."
    end
end
```

All Shoes apps must be wrapped by a call to `Shoes.app`. You can optionally set a configuration for the window that starts up. In this example, we set the height and width of the window. The first line in the example sets a background color for the window. This is not always necessary, but notice that the color `lightblue` is predefined in Shoes. There is a list of default colors from the X11 and HTML palette that Shoes predefines with intuitively simple names. If you are inclined to build your own custom colors, you can use the `rgb` method to create them.

Elements in Shoes applications are laid out using *slots*, which are simply containers for elements and other slots. Slots can be also be nested, so you can build quite a complicated layout by nesting slots and elements. There are two common types of slots: *stacks* and *flows*.

Stack
: A stack is a collection of elements that are laid out one on top of another in a column. The stopwatch in Example 1-1 places three items in the stack: a caption text block, a flow slot, and a para text block.

Flow
: A flow slot lays out its elements in a horizontal sequence, one after another, packed tightly. The stopwatch in Example 1-1 places two buttons in a flow, one labeled "start" and the other labeled "stop."

You can also set configuration parameters in the slots. The stack in the stopwatch example uses a margin of 10 pixels.

The `button` element creates a button for the application. If you send in a block of code as shown in the example, the code will be executed when the button is clicked. Alternatively, you can also set the button's click behavior using the `click` method shown later.

Run the previous code, and you'll see the stopwatch in Figure 1-2.

Figure 1-2. Shoes stopwatch

That was quite a conventional user interface application. Let's do something more arty.

Shoes doodler

Let's write a simple doodling application. Example 1-2 is a standard demo application type and not very useful, but it illustrates some basic concepts in Shoes.

Example 1-2. Shoes doodler

```
Shoes.app do
  fill red
  orig_left, orig_top = nil, nil
  animate 24 do
   button, left, top = self.mouse
   line(orig_left, orig_top, left, top) if button == 1
   star(orig_left, orig_top, 5, 15, 5)  if button == 3
   orig_left, orig_top = left, top
  end
 end
```

If anything, this application looks even simpler than the stopwatch!

Let's start by describing the `animate` method. This method starts an animation timer that runs in parallel with the rest of the application. We specify the number of frames per second the loop will be called, so the application will loop endlessly. As you might have guessed, this is an excellent method that can be used in running simulations.

The `self.mouse` method returns an array of three numbers. The first is the number of the mouse button that is clicked. If the mouse button is not clicked, this will be 0. The second and third numbers indicate the left and top positions of the cursor. We take these numbers and assign them according to the variables `button`, `left`, and `top`.

Now when the left button (or button 1) is clicked, we draw a line from where the cursor was positioned originally to where it is now. Because we're looping in an `animate` loop, if we move the mouse around, this will produce the effect of drawing something on the screen.

Similarly, if we click button 3 (usually the wheel button), we will draw a star. And because we specified that all shapes that we draw will be filled with red, we'll be drawing red stars at the position of the cursor. See Figure 1-3 for a sample run.

Figure 1-3. Shoes doodler

Wrap-up

It's impossible to stuff everything about Ruby into a single book, much less a single chapter. What I hope I've done here is introduce you to the language and provide you with a glimpse of what Ruby is able to do. I've skipped many of its more exciting features, including the much-talked-about metaprogramming capabilities. That topic could be and is a whole book on its own. I've also given you a quick introduction to Shoes, a simple but powerful UI toolkit for Ruby, and provided a couple of examples of how to program graphical user interface applications with it. What I've described in this chapter is a good start, and should provide you with enough foundation to explore the rest of the code in this book.

Onward!

CHAPTER 2
Into the Matrix

In the 1999 movie *The Matrix*, Neo and a bunch of other hackers/freedom fighters rebelled against their machine overlords, who imprisoned humans in vats all their lives to use them as batteries. The Matrix itself was a simulated reality that depicted the world as it was in 1999.

The R environment is just like the Matrix (except for the 1999 part). In the R environment, you—like Neo—are the One. You literally control everything in the workspace, and can recall history and see the code. You can manipulate objects in the environment and also source the code. Most importantly, R is built for and has a comprehensive suite of matrix operations that allows you to perform matrix programming with ease.

In this chapter, you will be learning about all of these topics. By the end of this chapter, although you might not be the One, you will certainly be able to fly on to the rest of the book.

Introducing R

Programmers are trained in logic, and our daily work mostly involves controlling and moving bits and bytes around. So when we're faced with a chunk of data and asked to do something with it, our reactions usually involve either bolting for the nearest exit or stuffing the data into a relational database and running `SQL SELECT` statements on it.

I'm exaggerating, of course. Most, if not all, data scientists are also programmers, and you can hardly get away with data analysis without doing some programming work.

However, not all programming platforms and languages are suitable for data analysis and manipulation. There are a number of languages built for this rather specialized purpose, including MATLAB and S, as well as packages like SAS and SPSS. One particular programming language we're going to use extensively in this book is R.

R is a free software programming language and environment for statistical computing and graphics. It was originally created by Ross Ihaka and Robert Gentleman at the University of Auckland, New Zealand, though it is now maintained by the R Development Core Team. R is named partly after the first names of its creators and partly as a play on the name of S. In fact, R is often considered the GNU version of S.

According to Rexer's Annual Data Miner Survey in 2010, R has become the data mining tool used by more data miners (43%) than any other tool.

R offers a powerful and appealing interactive environment for exploring data, and using that interactive environment is part of its appeal. The other reason why R is getting increasingly popular is that it is free. The existing batch of tools for data analysis—S, MATLAB, SPSS, and SAS—can be quite expensive, and R is a cost-effective way to achieve the same goals. Also, R has a very vibrant and active community of domain experts and developers, including statisticians and data scientists who contribute many very useful packages that enhance its overall capabilities.

R is available in most major platforms, and installing it is quite straightforward. Just visit the R website (*http://www.r-project.org/*), download the necessary binaries or installer for your platform, and then install it accordingly. If you're using Linux, you can use the platform's package management system to install R or download a precompiled binary. Alternatively, you can compile R for your platform, though it's not advisable or necessary because R has binaries for most platforms already.

In this book, we will be using R version 2.14.2.

Using R

R comes with a bunch of stuff, including a nice graphical user interface. Now, if you were expecting something visual and drag-and-drop (or seeing some digital rain), you will be sorely disappointed because the GUI is the R environment and is a console. Yes, that's right—you have to type stuff in.

The user interface for Windows and Mac OS X is quite similar and is the actual application that you start up. Alternatively, for Mac OS X and Linux, you can start R from the terminal:

```
$ R
```

This will give you the R console on your normal command line. Notice that it's a capital R. To start up the same user interface on Linux, you can do this:

```
$ R -g Tk &
```

This starts up R running in its own window in the background. The `Tk` refers to a graphic library used for the GUI.

There are also plenty of other unofficial R user interfaces, such as R Commander and RStudio. RStudio has a very nice R environment that runs on the server but is accessible through the browser. Another alternative is to integrate the R interpreter with your favorite text editor. There are plenty of choices; just choose one that you're most comfortable with and let's move on to the next section.

The R Console

Whichever way you choose to eventually use R, you will inevitably end up with the console. The console is likely the tool that you will be using most often when exploring R. When you get into the user interface, you will see something like Figure 2-1. For the rest of the chapter, you should cut and paste (whenever you can) or type the code into the console to try it out for yourself. You'll find that it makes a lot more sense than simply reading it.

Let's run through a simple example of interacting with the console. For this example, we will use the height and weight of a sample group of women.[1]

At the very bottom of the console is a small > sign. This is the command prompt for the R console. Let's type in something:

```
> height <- c(58, 59, 60, 61, 62, 63, 64, 65, 66, 67, 68, 69, 70, 71, 72)
```

The `c()` function creates a *vector* (an ordered collection of numbers) of heights (in inches), whereas the `<-` assigns the vector to a variable named `height`. Next, we do the same with the weight (in pounds):

```
> weight <- c(115, 117, 120, 123, 126, 129, 132, 135, 139, 142, 146, 150,
            154, 159, 164)
```

Now that we have data, let's do something with it. Let's say we want to find the average height of this group of women:

```
> mean(height)
[1] 65
```

The answer is 65, but notice the number 1 in square brackets just before the answer. This means the index of the first item displayed on the returned row is 1. If there are more items and the returned value needs to wrap the line, the new row will begin with another number in square brackets, indicating the index of that item.

1. Taken from the American Society of Actuaries' Build and Blood Pressure Study.

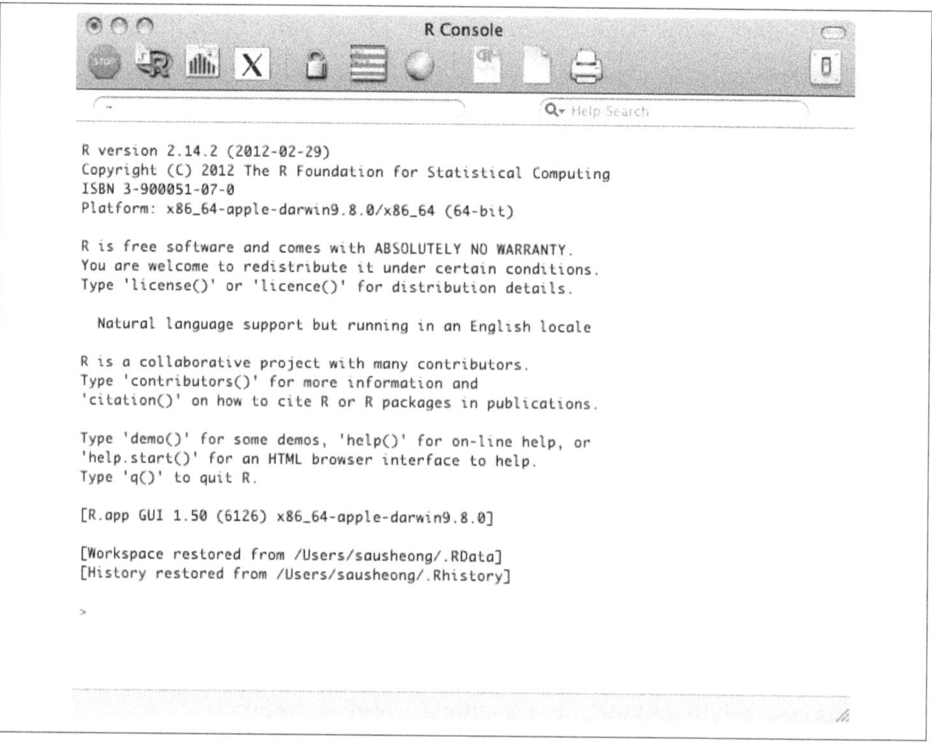

Figure 2-1. R console from the user interface

Let's get back to our example. If we want to get the standard deviation of the weight, we can use the `sd()` function:

```
> sd(weight)
[1] 15.49869
```

Let's say now we want to find whether the weight of the women is related to their height. To do this, we use the `cor()` function, which finds the linear correlation between the women's weight and height:

```
> cor(weight, height)
[1] 0.9954948
```

We find that there is very strong linear correlation; in fact, it is almost 1 to 1. Finally, to visualize this correlation, we can run a plot on these two vectors:

```
> plot(weight, height)
```

This draws a scatterplot that shows how the two vectors are related (Figure 2-2).

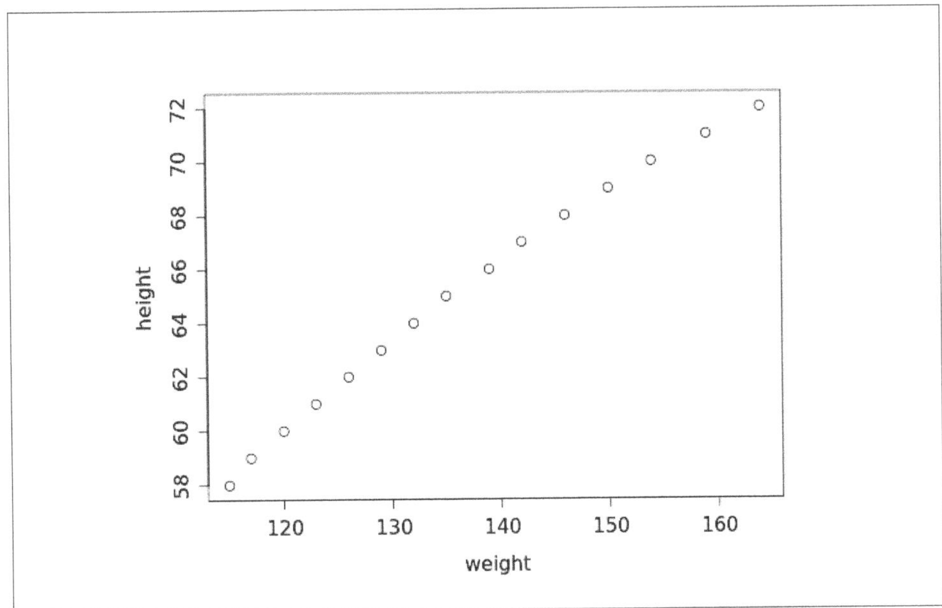

Figure 2-2. Scatterplot of weight versus height

Sourcing Files and the Command Line

Everything in the previous section was typed into the console and executed line by line. If you already have all the code written down, you're probably not too interested in cutting and pasting to the console. There are a couple of alternatives that run the code from a file.

The first is to use the R console and the `source()` function. Let's say you have a file named *weight_n_height.R* with the code in Example 2-1.

Example 2-1. Weight and height source file

```
height <- c(58, 59, 60, 61, 62, 63, 64, 65, 66, 67, 68, 69, 70, 71, 72)
weight <- c(115, 117, 120, 123, 126, 129, 132, 135, 139, 142, 146, 150, 154,
            159, 164)
print(mean(height))
print(sd(weight))
print(cor(weight, height))
plot(weight, height)
```

Notice that we need to explicitly print the output to the console now. The output looks like Figure 2-3.

An alternative to sourcing the file from the R console is to run it in batch mode from the command line:

```
$ R CMD BATCH weights_n_heights.R
```

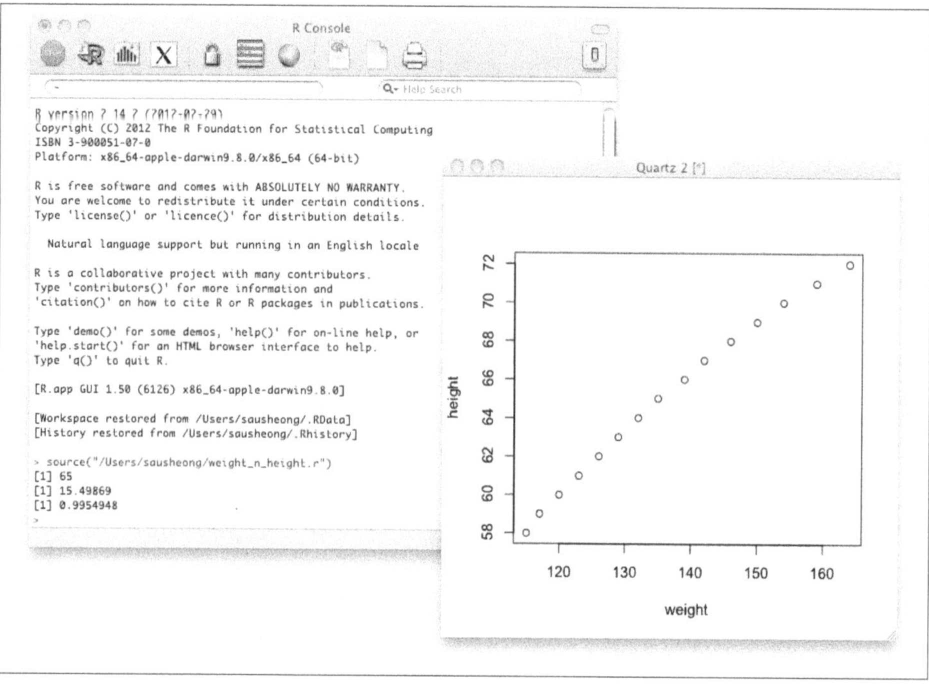

Figure 2-3. Output from sourcing the R file

The command creates a file named *weight_n_height.Rout* containing the complete output from running the batch command, including the header from starting up R, as shown in Example 2-2.

Example 2-2. Output from running R in batch mode

```
R version 2.14.2 (2012-02-29)
Copyright (C) 2012 The R Foundation for Statistical Computing
ISBN 3-900051-07-0
Platform: x86_64-apple-darwin9.8.0/x86_64 (64-bit)

R is free software and comes with ABSOLUTELY NO WARRANTY.
You are welcome to redistribute it under certain conditions.
Type 'license()' or 'licence()' for distribution details.

  Natural language support but running in an English locale

R is a collaborative project with many contributors.
Type 'contributors()' for more information and
'citation()' on how to cite R or R packages in publications.

Type 'demo()' for some demos, 'help()' for on-line help, or
'help.start()' for an HTML browser interface to help.
Type 'q()' to quit R.
```

```
[Previously saved workspace restored]

> height <- c(58, 59, 60, 61, 62, 63, 64, 65, 66, 67, 68, 69, 70, 71, 72)
> weight <- c(115, 117, 120, 123, 126, 129, 132, 135, 139, 142, 146, 150, 154,
            159, 164)
> print(mean(height))
[1] 65
> print(sd(weight))
[1] 15.49869
> print(cor(weight, height))
[1] 0.9954948
> plot(weight, height)
>
> proc.time()
   user  system elapsed
  0.261   0.043   0.331
```

How about the scatterplot? A separate PDF file named *Rplots.pdf* is created, containing the same scatterplot as before.

Packages

An R package is a set of related functions and help files, bundled together. It is very similar to a gem in Ruby or libraries in C or C++. Normally, all functions within a single package are related: for example, the `stats` package contains functions for statistical analysis. As with Ruby, there are a few public repositories of packages. The largest is CRAN (Comprehensive R Archive Network; *http://cran.r-project.org*). CRAN is hosted by the R Foundation (the same organization that is developing R) and contains 3,646 packages as of this writing. CRAN is also mirrored in many sites worldwide.

Another public repository is Bioconductor (*http://www.bioconductor.org*), an open source project that provides tools for bioinformatics and is primarily R-based. While the packages in Bioconductor are focused on bioinformatics, it doesn't mean that they can't be used for other domains. As of this writing, there are 516 packages in Bioconductor.

Finally, there is R-Forge (*http://r-forge.r-project.org*), a collaborative software development application for R. It is based on FusionForge, a fork from GForge (on which RubyForge was based), which in turn was forked from the original software that was used to build SourceForge. R-Forge has 1,244 hosted projects as of this writing. It differs from CRAN and Bioconductor in that anyone can start up a project in R-Forge, and it doesn't necessarily need to end up with an R package.

Installing packages

To use a package, you first need to install it into R. This process is very similar to installing a gem in Ruby. There are a number of ways to do it, just as many as there are ways of using R.

If you're using the R console user interface, you can always use the package installer from the menu. The exact menu path to the item varies, but you should always get some sort of window that helps you to explore and search for packages on CRAN (Figure 2-4).

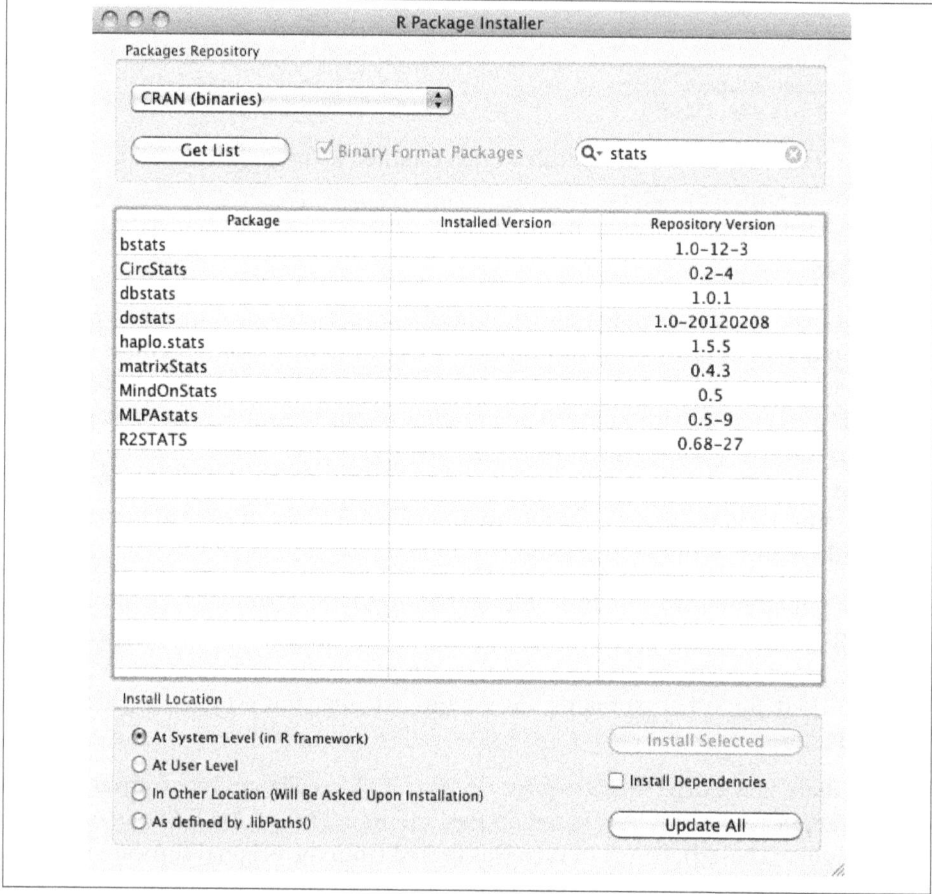

Figure 2-4. Package installer window in Mac OS X

Alternatively, you can install R packages directly through the R console. The following example installs the `tree` package:

```
> install.packages('tree')
Installing package(s) into '/Users/sausheong/Library/R/2.14/library'
(as 'lib' is unspecified)
trying URL 'http://cran.cnr.Berkeley.edu/bin/macosx/leopard/contrib/2.14/
            tree_1.0-29.tgz'
Content type 'application/x-gzip' length 158835 bytes (155 Kb)
opened URL
==================================================
downloaded 155 Kb


The downloaded packages are in
 /var/folders/0W/0WaBiTP9GcGX4vyLiy95Yk+++TI/-Tmp-//RtmpUbNCUX/
   downloaded_packages
```

If you want to find out what the available installed packages are, you can also use the command:

```
> installed.packages()
```

This will tell you all about the packages that have been installed, including where they were placed, which license they are under, and which version you have installed.

Using packages

Once you have installed the package you want, using it is quite simple. To load the package into R, just enter the following line of code before you start using any functions from that package:

```
library(tree)
```

Note that when you first install the package, the name of the package is a string, but once it is installed, you can use the package name directly.

Programming R

R code is essentially a series of *expressions* (in Ruby, they would be called statements). Expressions consist of objects and functions and are separated by a new line or a semicolon. R is an object-oriented language, meaning that everything in R that you interact with is an object, has a type, and belongs to a class. Even functions are objects of the class `function`:

```
> height <- c(58, 59, 60, 61, 62, 63, 64, 65, 66, 67, 68, 69, 70, 71, 72)
> class(height)
[1] "numeric"
> mean(height)
[1] 65
> class(mean)
[1] "function"
```

Variables and Functions

Variable assignment in R is interesting because the language offers a few different assignment operators. The `<-` is the most common assignment operator, and can be used anywhere. The `->` operator is exactly the same as `<-`, but with the variable and the value reversed:

```
x <- 1
# is the same as
1 -> x
```

The `=` assignment operator can be used only at the top level (directly from the console). Using it within a function scopes the variable within that function only. For example:

```
> mean(x = 1:10)
[1] 5.5
> x
Error: object 'x' not found
```

The variable `x` is scoped within the `mean()` function only. However, if we use `<-` instead, `x` will be defined at the user workspace and is available outside of the function:

```
> mean(x <- 1:10)
[1] 5.5
> x
 [1]  1  2  3  4  5  6  7  8  9 10
```

Functions in R are objects that accept input and return output. All work in R is done by functions, even setting variables, looping, conditionals, and so on. Just to prove a point, let's consider this very simple expression:

```
> a <- 1
> a + 1
[1] 2
```

The addition operator `+` is actually a function. This means we can call it like a function:

```
> `+`(a,1)
[1] 2
```

In the preceding example, we surrounded the `+` with backticks in order to evaluate it as what it really is—a function. Of course, we would normally not need to invoke an operator as a function, but it's useful to know that R treats operators that way. Defining a function is simple and follows a familiar format:

```
my_function <- function(x,y) {
  x + y
}
```

The body of the function doesn't really need to be in separate lines, and the curly braces aren't even necessary if the body is just a single expression. Once `my_function` has been defined, you can use it:

```
> my_function(1,2)
[1] 3
```

You can set default values in the function when creating it:

```
my_function <- function(x,y=5) {
  x + y
}
```

If you have default values, you don't need to specify all the arguments. This syntax is quite similar to Ruby's:

```
> my_function(1,2)
[1] 3
> my_function(1)
[1] 6
```

To return a value from a function, you can use the `return` keyword. If you don't execute an expression with `return`, R will return the last evaluated expression, just as in Ruby.

Note that because functions are also objects, you can always pass a function into another function as the argument. An example of this is how you use the `sapply()` function. The `sapply()` function accepts a list and a function, then applies the function to every element of that list and returns the result (if you are familiar with Ruby, this is the same as the `map` method in the `Enumerable` module):

```
> l <- c(1,2,3,4,5)
> sapply(l, my_function)
[1]  6  7  8  9 10
```

Conditionals and Loops

Conditionals in R are similar to those of Ruby (and most other languages):

```
x <- 10
if (x > 20) {
  print("x is greater than 20")
}
else {
  print("x is less than 20")
}
```

That's all there is to it.

R has three forms of loops. The first is `repeat`, which, as the name implies, repeats a particular expression or series of expressions. `repeat` doesn't stop until it hits a `break` keyword, which means if you forget to insert a `break` somewhere, it'll loop forever:

```
> x <- 0
> repeat { if (x > 10) break else {print(x); x <- x + 1}}
[1] 0
[1] 1
```

```
[1] 2
[1] 3
[1] 4
[1] 5
[1] 6
[1] 7
[1] 8
[1] 9
[1] 10
>
```

We need to break down the long `repeat` expression from the outside in to understand it. Within the outermost braces is an `if-else` expression: `if (x > 10) break else {print(x); x <- x + 1}`. You now may be able to see that the inner set of braces is part of the `else` clause: `print(x); x <- x + 1`. The semicolon separates the clause into two parts. The first is a `print` statement, and the second increments `x` so that the condition that terminates the loop, `x > 10`, is eventually satisfied.

R has a `while` loop as well:

```
> x <- 0
> while (x < 10) {print(x); x <- x + 1}
[1] 0
[1] 1
[1] 2
[1] 3
[1] 4
[1] 5
[1] 6
[1] 7
[1] 8
[1] 9
>
```

Finally, R has `for` loops, which iterate through each item in a vector or a list:

```
> x <- 0
> for (x in 1:10) print(x)
[1] 1
[1] 2
[1] 3
[1] 4
[1] 5
[1] 6
[1] 7
[1] 8
[1] 9
[1] 10
>
```

The colon creates a vector, passing each integer from 1 to 10 to the loop.

Data Structures

As you might have guessed, data structures are a critical part of R, and there are lots of them. This section goes through a few key ones. Let's start with the most basic data structure, a vector.

Vectors

A vector is a one-dimensional array that holds numeric, character, or logical data. It's the most basic data structure and the one that is most frequently used. The easiest way to create a vector is through the combine function, `c()`:

```
> height <- c(58, 59, 60, 61, 62, 63, 64, 65, 66, 67, 68, 69, 70, 71, 72)
```

Here, `height` is a numeric vector. Note that there can be only one type in a vector: numeric, character, or logical. Unlike in Ruby arrays, you cannot mix the types in a vector.

As we saw in the previous section, you can also create vectors using the `:` operator:

```
> 1:10
 [1]  1  2  3  4  5  6  7  8  9 10
```

Another way of creating a vector is through the `seq()` function, which lets you specify the step increment of the sequence:

```
> seq(0,100,by=10)
 [1]   0  10  20  30  40  50  60  70  80  90 100
```

To get the length of the vector, you can use the `length()` function:

```
> v <- 1:10
> length(v)
[1] 10
```

You can reference elements of vectors using square brackets, `[]`:

```
> v <- seq(0,100,by=25)
> v
[1]   0  25  50  75 100
> v[2]
[1] 25
> v[3]
[1] 50
> v[2:4]
[1] 25 50 75
> v[c(2,4)]
[1] 25 75
```

Note that the index of the vector starts with 1 instead of 0, unlike most programming languages, including Ruby. You can also specify a range of returned values. In the previous example, we requested the second through fourth items in the vector, which returns another vector. You can also pick and choose which items to return in the vector if you provide another vector as the index.

Another way to reference vectors is through double square brackets, `[[]]`. While a single bracket can return multiple values, double brackets will always return only a single value:

```
> v[[3]]
[1] 50
> v[[3:4]]
Error in v[[3:4]] : attempt to select more than one element
```

Lists

A list is a vector with names for each item. While you can refer to each item by the index, as we just did with vectors, you can also refer to the item by its name. In addition, the items don't need to be of a single type, and each item can be a different object. This means you can also create an arbitrary data structure using a list:

```
> peter <- list(name='Peter', age=30, glasses=TRUE)
> peter
$name
[1] "Peter"

$age
[1] 30

$glasses
[1] TRUE
```

You can see that the name of each item is preceded by a `$`. You can then reference each item in the list by its position or its name:

```
> peter[1]
$name
[1] "Peter"
> peter$name
[1] "Peter"
> peter[['name']]
[1] "Peter"
> peter[['na']]
NULL
> peter[['na',exact=FALSE]]
[1] "Peter"
```

You can also reference the item using the double square brackets notation. If you set the `exact` parameter to `FALSE`, you can even use part of the item name.

Matrices

A matrix is a two-dimensional array. Just like vectors, matrices can hold elements only of the same type. Create a matrix using the `matrix()` function:

```
> m <- matrix(1:20, nrow=5, ncol=4)
> m
     [,1] [,2] [,3] [,4]
[1,]    1    6   11   16
[2,]    2    7   12   17
[3,]    3    8   13   18
[4,]    4    9   14   19
[5,]    5   10   15   20
```

This example shows how to create a 5×4 matrix. By default, the matrix is populated by column, which is why the running numbers go from top to bottom. If you want to populate by row, you need to specify that with the `byrow` parameter:

```
> m <- matrix(1:20, nrow=5, ncol=4, byrow=TRUE)
> m
     [,1] [,2] [,3] [,4]
[1,]    1    2    3    4
[2,]    5    6    7    8
[3,]    9   10   11   12
[4,]   13   14   15   16
[5,]   17   18   19   20
```

To access a matrix, use square brackets again. The following example extracts elements from the matrix we just defined:

```
> m[10]
[1] 18
> m[3,4]
[1] 12
> m[3:5]
[1]  9 13 17
> m[3:5,2:3]
     [,1] [,2]
[1,]   10   11
[2,]   14   15
[3,]   18   19
```

If you provide only one number within the brackets, R will count by row and column to return the item with the specified number. In the previous example, therefore, `m[10]` indicates the 10th item in the matrix, in a running sequence column-wise. *It doesn't matter whether you created the matrix by row.* If you specify both numbers, the item returned is based on *`matrix[row, column]`*. So, in the previous example, `m[3,4]` returns the item at row 3 and column 4. If you provide a single vector, as before, it will return a vector according to the range. You can also provide two vectors, in which case the returned result is a matrix. In the previous example, `m[3:5,2:3]` returns the matrix from the third through fifth rows and the second through third columns.

In addition, you can give names to each row and each column using the `dimnames()` function. You can set them when you create the matrix or afterward:

```
> dimnames(m) <- list(c('a','b','c','d','e'), c('p','q','r','s'))
> m
   p  q  r  s
a  1  2  3  4
b  5  6  7  8
c  9 10 11 12
d 13 14 15 16
e 17 18 19 20
```

The first parameter passed to the `list()` function is a vector of the row names. The second is a vector of the column names.

Arrays

An array is an extension of the vector to more than two dimensions. Just as the matrix is created with the `matrix()` function, the array is created with the `array()` function:

```
> a <- array(1:24,c(2,3,4))
> a
, , 1

     [,1] [,2] [,3]
[1,]    1    3    5
[2,]    2    4    6

, , 2

     [,1] [,2] [,3]
[1,]    7    9   11
[2,]    8   10   12

, , 3

     [,1] [,2] [,3]
[1,]   13   15   17
[2,]   14   16   18

, , 4

     [,1] [,2] [,3]
[1,]   19   21   23
[2,]   20   22   24
```

This example creates an array with the dimensions of four sets of two rows by three columns. Accessing items in the array follows the same patterns as before. The first dimension within square brackets refers to the row, the second to the column, and the third to the set:

```
> a[10]
[1] 10
```

```
> a[2,3,]
[1]  6 12 18 24
> a[1,2,3]
[1] 15
> a[,2,3]
[1] 15 16
> a[,,3]
     [,1] [,2] [,3]
[1,]   13   15   17
[2,]   14   16   18
> a[,2,]
     [,1] [,2] [,3] [,4]
[1,]    3    9   15   21
[2,]    4   10   16   22
```

Note that if you have a single number in the square brackets, it means that you're specifying the *n*th item in the array. If you have more than one number within the square brackets, you are providing the dimensions, and this means you need to provide all the dimensions (leaving it blank returns all the values within that dimension). For example, to extract all the numbers in column 2, use `a[,2,]`. Also, as in the matrix, you can set the names of each dimension in an array.

Factors

Values can be *nominal*, *ordinal*, or *continuous*. Nominal values are labels that describe a category. For example, nominal values can be the colors "green," "blue," and "red." There is no particular order to these values.

Ordinal values are also labels and describe a category, but they are ordered sequentially. For example, "poor," "average," and "good" are three ordinal values. While they are not quantifiable, their order implies that "average" is better than "poor," and "good" is better than "average."

Lastly, continuous values are simply sequences of values that also represent a quantity. For example, 1, 2, and 3 are continuous values.

In Ruby, we represent nominal values with symbols, continuous values are simply numbers, and ordinal values are objects that implement the `Comparable` module. In R, nominal and ordinal values are represented by *factors*. We create factors using the `factor()` function:

```
> colors <- c('green', 'red', 'blue')
> factor(colors)
[1] green red   blue
Levels: blue green red
> results <- c('poor', 'average', 'good')
> factor(results)
[1] poor    average good
Levels: average good poor
```

By default, factor levels for character data are created in alphabetical order. However, we can set the order of the levels when creating the factors:

```
> factor(results, order=TRUE, levels=results)
[1] poor    average good
Levels: poor < average < good
```

Data frames

The data frame is the data structure we will be using most often in this book, and in fact it is one of the most frequently used data structures in R. A data frame is a list that contains multiple named vectors of the same length. It's a lot like a spreadsheet or a database table, but don't be fooled into thinking that it's the same thing. While most of us use spreadsheets by row, and certainly database tables have records by row, data frames are constructed by columns.

To create data frames, use the `data.frame()` function. Let's see how we create a data frame to represent the league table for the top eight teams in the English Premier League (EPL) as of March 4, 2012:

```
> team <- c('Man City', 'Man Utd', 'Totenham', 'Arsenal', 'Chelsea',
          'Newcastle', 'Liverpool', 'Stoke')
> home_wins <- c(14, 10, 10, 9, 8, 7, 4, 6)
> home_draws <- c(0, 1, 2, 2, 2, 4, 8, 4)
> home_losses <- c(0, 2, 1, 2, 3, 2, 1, 4)
> away_wins <- c(7, 9, 6, 6, 5, 5, 6, 4)
> away_draws <- c(3, 3, 3, 2, 5, 3, 1, 2)
> away_losses <- c(3, 1, 4, 6, 4, 5, 6, 7)
> league_table <- data.frame(team, home_wins, home_draws, home_losses,
                             away_wins, away_draws, away_losses)
> league_table
       team home_wins home_draws home_losses away_wins away_draws away_losses
1  Man City        14          0           0         7          3           3
2   Man Utd        10          1           2         9          3           1
3  Totenham        10          2           1         6          3           4
4   Arsenal         9          2           2         6          2           6
5   Chelsea         8          2           3         5          5           4
6 Newcastle         7          4           2         5          3           5
7 Liverpool         4          8           1         6          1           6
8     Stoke         6          4           4         4          2           7
```

To get a subset of the data frame, use the square brackets notation:

```
> league_table[c('team','home_wins')]
       team home_wins
1  Man City        14
2   Man Utd        10
3  Totenham        10
4   Arsenal         9
```

```
5   Chelsea         8
6 Newcastle         7
7 Liverpool         4
8     Stoke         6
```

To refer to a specific column, specify it by name:

```
> league_table$team
[1] Man City  Man Utd  Totenham  Arsenal  Chelsea  Newcastle  Liverpool  Stoke
Levels: Arsenal Chelsea Liverpool Man City Man Utd Newcastle Stoke Totenham
```

To find specific values based on criteria from other columns, you can use the square brackets notation again. In the following example, we find out which teams have scored more than eight away goals:

```
> league_table$team[league_table$home_wins > 8]
[1] Man City Man Utd  Totenham Arsenal
Levels: Arsenal Chelsea Liverpool Man City Man Utd Newcastle Stoke Totenham
```

You can also use more than one column. In this next example, we find out which team has more away wins than home wins:

```
> league_table$team[league_table$away_wins > league_table$home_wins]
[1] Liverpool
Levels: Arsenal Chelsea Liverpool Man City Man Utd Newcastle Stoke Totenham
```

That seems pretty long, and frankly, a bit difficult to read. We can simplify the code a bit using the `with()` function, which takes in a data frame (or a list or some environment), and use that as a basis for evaluating the rest of the expressions:

```
> with(league_table, team[away_wins > home_wins])
[1] Liverpool
Levels: Arsenal Chelsea Liverpool Man City Man Utd Newcastle Stoke Totenham
```

Sometimes we get our data from multiple sources and end up with multiple data frames. If you want to merge the data frames horizontally (i.e., add new columns), use the `merge()`function. Let's say we now have the points for each team in the table in a separate vector. First, we need to create a data frame with the name of the team and the corresponding points in the table:

```
> pts <- c(66, 61, 53, 49, 46, 43, 39, 36)
> points <- data.frame(team, pts)
> points
       team pts
1  Man City  66
2   Man Utd  61
3  Totenham  53
4   Arsenal  49
5   Chelsea  46
6 Newcastle  43
7 Liverpool  39
8     Stoke  36
```

To merge the two data frames, use the `merge()` function specifying that they are linked by the team name:

```
> league <- merge(league_table, points, by='team')
> with(league, league[order(-pts),])
       team home_wins home_draws home_losses away_wins  ...  pts
4  Man City        14          0           0         7  ...   66
5   Man Utd        10          1           2         9  ...   61
8  Totenham        10          2           1         6  ...   53
1   Arsenal         9          2           2         6  ...   49
2   Chelsea         8          2           3         5  ...   46
6 Newcastle         7          4           2         5  ...   43
3 Liverpool         4          8           1         6  ...   39
7     Stoke         6          4           4         4  ...   36
```

In our `with()` function, using the `order()` function, we reorder the data frame in our output, sorting it by the points in decreasing order. By default, the sorting order is ascending. If we prepend the sorting variable (`pts` here) with a minus sign, it will sort by descending order.

If now we want to add in another row, we can use the `rbind()` function. Let's say we have another data frame with the next two EPL teams:

```
> another_table
       team home_wins home_draws home_losses away_wins  ...  pts
1 West Brom         6          2           8         6  ...   35
2   Norwich         5          4           4         4  ...   35
```

To add this data frame vertically, use the `rbind()` function:

```
> rbind(with(league, league[order(-pts),]), another_table)
        team home_wins home_draws home_losses away_wins  ...  pts
4   Man City        14          0           0         7  ...   66
5    Man Utd        10          1           2         9  ...   61
8   Totenham        10          2           1         6  ...   53
1    Arsenal         9          2           2         6  ...   49
2    Chelsea         8          2           3         5  ...   46
6  Newcastle         7          4           2         5  ...   43
3  Liverpool         4          8           1         6  ...   39
7      Stoke         6          4           4         4  ...   36
9  West Brom         6          2           8         6  ...   35
10   Norwich         5          4           4         4  ...   35
```

Importing Data

Typing in all that data can be pretty tedious. R packages often come with data, so if you want to explore and play around with data, the best thing to do is probably to load up an R package using the `library()` function. For example, the `ggplot2` package has a dataset of fuel economy data from 1999 and 2008 for 38 popular car models:

```
> library(ggplot2)
> mpg
   manufacturer                model displ year cyl      trans drv cty hwy ...
1          audi                   a4   1.8 1999   4   auto(l5)   f  18  29 ...
2          audi                   a4   1.8 1999   4 manual(m5)   f  21  29 ...
3          audi                   a4   2.0 2008   4 manual(m6)   f  20  31 ...
4          audi                   a4   2.0 2008   4   auto(av)   f  21  30 ...
5          audi                   a4   2.8 1999   6   auto(l5)   f  16  26 ...
6          audi                   a4   2.8 1999   6 manual(m5)   f  18  26 ...
7          audi                   a4   3.1 2008   6   auto(av)   f  18  27 ...
8          audi           a4 quattro   1.8 1999   4 manual(m5)   4  18  26 ...
9          audi           a4 quattro   1.8 1999   4   auto(l5)   4  16  25 ...
10         audi           a4 quattro   2.0 2008   4 manual(m6)   4  20  28 ...
11         audi           a4 quattro   2.0 2008   4   auto(s6)   4  19  27 ...
12         audi           a4 quattro   2.8 1999   6   auto(l5)   4  15  25 ...
13         audi           a4 quattro   2.8 1999   6 manual(m5)   4  17  25 ...
14         audi           a4 quattro   3.1 2008   6   auto(s6)   4  17  25 ...
15         audi           a4 quattro   3.1 2008   6 manual(m6)   4  15  25 ...
16         audi           a6 quattro   2.8 1999   6   auto(l5)   4  15  24 ...
17         audi           a6 quattro   3.1 2008   6   auto(s6)   4  17  25 ...
18         audi           a6 quattro   4.2 2008   8   auto(s6)   4  16  23 ...
19    chevrolet  c1500 suburban 2wd   5.3 2008   8   auto(l4)   r  14  20 ...
20    chevrolet  c1500 suburban 2wd   5.3 2008   8   auto(l4)   r  11  15 ...
21    chevrolet  c1500 suburban 2wd   5.3 2008   8   auto(l4)   r  14  20 ...
22    chevrolet  c1500 suburban 2wd   5.7 1999   8   auto(l4)   r  13  17 ...
23    chevrolet  c1500 suburban 2wd   6.0 2008   8   auto(l4)   r  12  17 ...
24    chevrolet            corvette   5.7 1999   8 manual(m6)   r  16  26 ...

...other data truncated
```

Importing data from text files

To work with your own data, you have a couple of choices. The easiest is probably to get the data into a delimited text file—for example, CSV—and use the `read()` function to read the file into a data frame. Here's how you can import a CSV file into a data frame:[2]

```
> epl <- read.csv('english_premier_league_data.csv')
> epl
    Div     Date    HomeTeam     AwayTeam FTHG FTAG FTR HTHG HTAG HTR    ...
1    E0 13/08/11   Blackburn       Wolves    1    2   A    1    1   D    ...
2    E0 13/08/11      Fulham  Aston Villa    0    0   D    0    0   D    ...
3    E0 13/08/11   Liverpool   Sunderland    1    1   D    1    0   H    ...
4    E0 13/08/11   Newcastle      Arsenal    0    0   D    0    0   D    ...
5    E0 13/08/11         QPR       Bolton    0    4   A    0    1   A    ...
6    E0 13/08/11       Wigan      Norwich    1    1   D    1    1   D    ...
7    E0 14/08/11       Stoke      Chelsea    0    0   D    0    0   D    ...
8    E0 14/08/11   West Brom   Man United    1    2   A    1    1   D    ...
9    E0 15/08/11    Man City      Swansea    4    0   H    0    0   D    ...
```

2. For the EPL data, I took the CSV from *http://www.football-data.co.uk/data.php*.

```
10   E0 20/08/11       Arsenal  Liverpool  0  2  A  0  0  D   ...
11   E0 20/08/11 Aston Villa  Blackburn  3  1  H  2  0  H   ...
12   E0 20/08/11       Chelsea  West Brom  2  1  H  0  1  A   ...
13   E0 20/08/11       Everton        QPR  0  1  A  0  1  A   ...
14   E0 20/08/11    Sunderland  Newcastle  0  1  A  0  0  D   ...
15   E0 20/08/11       Swansea      Wigan  0  0  D  0  0  D   ...
16   E0 21/08/11        Bolton   Man City  2  3  A  1  2  A   ...
17   E0 21/08/11       Norwich      Stoke  1  1  D  1  0  H   ...
18   E0 21/08/11        Wolves     Fulham  2  0  H  2  0  H   ...
19   E0 22/08/11    Man United  Tottenham  3  0  H  0  0  D   ...
20   E0 27/08/11 Aston Villa     Wolves  0  0  D  0  0  D   ...
21   E0 27/08/11    Blackburn    Everton  0  1  A  0  0  D   ...
22   E0 27/08/11       Chelsea    Norwich  3  1  H  1  0  H   ...

...other data truncated
```

Importing data from a database

If your data is in a relational database, you can use the `DBI` set of packages to extract it. Let's say you have a MySQL database with a database named `epl` and a table named `league`.[3] This contains the EPL data as before. To connect to the database, we need to install the packages:

```
> install.packages(c('DBI', 'RMySQL'))
Installing package(s) into '/Users/sausheong/Library/R/2.14/library'
(as 'lib' is unspecified)
trying URL 'http://cran.cnr.Berkeley.edu/bin/macosx/leopard/contrib/2.14/ \
            DBI_0.2-5.tgz'
Content type 'application/x-gzip' length 390206 bytes (381 Kb)
opened URL
==================================================
downloaded 381 Kb

trying URL 'http://cran.cnr.Berkeley.edu/bin/macosx/leopard/contrib/2.14/ \
            RMySQL_0.9-3.tgz'
Content type 'application/x-gzip' length 5857481 bytes (5.6 Mb)
opened URL
==================================================
downloaded 5.6 Mb


The downloaded packages are in
 /var/folders/0W/0WaBiTP9GcGX4vyLiy95Yk+++TI/-Tmp-//RtmpIb2HF7/ \
 downloaded_packages
```

Once we have the packages, we can start to connect to the database:

```
> con <- dbConnect(MySQL(), host='localhost', dbname='epl', user='root',
                   password='root')
```

3. Basically, I created a MySQL database and imported the data from the CSV I mentioned earlier into the table.

This is a good one-shot operation, but if you have a few databases and tables to connect, it can become a chore. Instead of specifying the username and password as well as the database each time you connect, you can add a *$HOME/.my.cnf* file, which contains information on how to connect (see Example 2-3). Note the initial dot on the filename.

Example 2-3. .my.cnf file

```
[epl]
user = root
password = root
database = epl
host = localhost
```

Then you can issue a shorter expression to connect:

```
> con <- dbConnect(MySQL(), groups='epl')
```

The `groups` parameter connects you to the `epl` section in the configuration file (the section within the square brackets in the *.my.cnf* file). You can include multiple sections in the file to let you connect to multiple databases.

Once you have connected, you can start issuing SQL queries. In our case, we want to grab all the data from the `epl` data and massage it ourselves to find the information we want:

```
> league <- dbGetQuery(con, 'select * from league')
> dbDisconnect(con)
[1] TRUE
```

This creates a data frame named `league` that has all the rows and columns in the database. You would probably not want to do this if you have a lot of data in the database. Instead, you would likely extract a sample and process the data bit by bit. In our case, though, there's not a whole lot of data, so we simply take everything (our results show up as shown in Figure 2-5 in the console). Note that we should play nice and disconnect from the database after we get our data. Otherwise, R will keep that connection live, and you'll soon run out of connections.

What we want to do next is use our newfound data frame powers and find out how many wins each team in the league has scored. If we were doing this in SQL, it would not be as easy as it sounds. However, with R it is a piece of cake:

```
> wins <- with(league, {
+   home_wins <- HomeTeam[FTHG > FTAG]
+   away_wins <- AwayTeam[FTAG > FTHG]
+   sort(table(home_wins) + table(away_wins), decreasing=T)
+ })
>
> print(data.frame(wins))
           wins
Man City     20
Man United   19
```

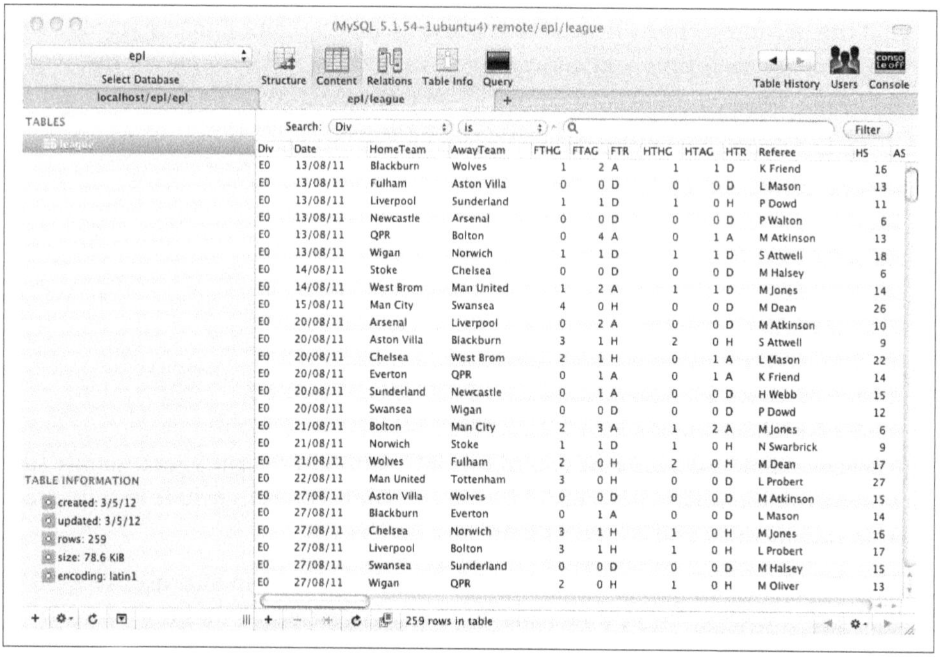
(MySQL 5.1.54-1ubuntu4) remote/epl/league
epl
Select Database
localhost/epl/epl
Structure Content Relations Table Info Query
epl/league
Table History Users Console
TABLES
Search: Div is
Filter
Div Date HomeTeam AwayTeam FTHG FTAG FTR HTHG HTAG HTR Referee HS AS
E0 13/08/11 Blackburn Wolves 1 2 A 1 1 D K Friend 16
E0 13/08/11 Fulham Aston Villa 0 0 D 0 0 D L Mason 13
E0 13/08/11 Liverpool Sunderland 1 1 D 1 0 H P Dowd 11
E0 13/08/11 Newcastle Arsenal 0 0 D 0 0 D P Walton 6
E0 13/08/11 QPR Bolton 0 4 A 0 1 A M Atkinson 13
E0 13/08/11 Wigan Norwich 1 1 D 1 1 D S Attwell 18
E0 14/08/11 Stoke Chelsea 0 0 D 0 0 D M Halsey 6
E0 14/08/11 West Brom Man United 1 2 A 1 1 D M Jones 14
E0 15/08/11 Man City Swansea 4 0 H 0 0 D M Dean 26
E0 20/08/11 Arsenal Liverpool 0 2 A 0 0 D M Atkinson 10
E0 20/08/11 Aston Villa Blackburn 3 1 H 2 0 H S Attwell 9
E0 20/08/11 Chelsea West Brom 2 1 H 0 1 A L Mason 22
E0 20/08/11 Everton QPR 0 1 A 0 1 A K Friend 14
E0 20/08/11 Sunderland Newcastle 0 1 A 0 0 D H Webb 15
E0 20/08/11 Swansea Wigan 0 0 D 0 0 D P Dowd 12
E0 21/08/11 Bolton Man City 2 3 A 1 2 A M Jones 6
E0 21/08/11 Norwich Stoke 1 1 D 1 0 H N Swarbrick 9
E0 21/08/11 Wolves Fulham 2 0 H 2 0 H M Dean 17
E0 22/08/11 Man United Tottenham 3 0 H 0 0 D L Probert 27
E0 27/08/11 Aston Villa Wolves 0 0 D 0 0 D M Atkinson 15
E0 27/08/11 Blackburn Everton 0 1 A 0 0 D L Mason 14
E0 27/08/11 Chelsea Norwich 3 1 H 1 0 H M Jones 16
E0 27/08/11 Liverpool Bolton 3 1 H 1 0 H L Probert 17
E0 27/08/11 Swansea Sunderland 0 0 D 0 0 D M Halsey 15
E0 27/08/11 Wigan QPR 2 0 H 1 0 H M Oliver 13
TABLE INFORMATION
created: 3/5/12
updated: 3/5/12
rows: 259
size: 78.6 KiB
encoding: latin1
259 rows in table

Figure 2-5. English Premier League table

```
Tottenham     16
Arsenal       14
Chelsea       13
Newcastle     12
Liverpool     10
Everton        9
Norwich        9
Stoke          9
Sunderland     9
West Brom      9
Fulham         8
Swansea        7
Aston Villa    6
Bolton         6
Blackburn      5
QPR            5
Wolves         5
Wigan          4
```

We use the `with()` function to reduce typing. First, we find all the home wins, which is essentially a vector of team names, where the full-time home goal (`FTHG`) is greater than the full-time away goals (`FTAG`). Next, we do the same with the away wins, but since the team is away we have to reverse `FTHG` and `FTAG` to find them. After that, we get the table of counts for both the home and away wins and add them together. Finally, we sort the answer and return it as an object of class `table`, which is an array of integer values, with the names of each item in the array corresponding to the team name.

To print it out nicely in two columns, we convert it into a data frame before printing it to the screen.

Charting

Part of R's great power is its ability to generate beautiful charts easily. In this section, we'll first take a look at the default built-in features for creating charts in R, then quickly move on to a powerful R package for generating charts, called `ggplot2`.

Basic Graphs

Out of the box, R provides very comprehensive charting and graphics capabilities through its `graphics` package. Before we jump into this package, we need to set up the output. Normally, graphics output from R goes to the default graphics device. If you create any graphics (and this includes, of course, charts) without invoking the graphics device first, the default graphics device will be automatically opened. But you can also open the device manually on Windows by calling the `windows()` function. On Linux and other Unix-like systems, the device can be opened with `X11()`, and on Mac OS X it can be opened with `quartz()`. To close the device, use the `dev.off()` function.

Alternatively, if you want to output the chart to a file, you can use `pdf()`, `png()`, `jpeg()`, `bmp()`, `win.metafile()`, and other functions to set the output file format. The main parameter to these functions is the name of the file to write to.

In this book, we will be creating PDF files. This is how we will create charts:

```
pdf('some_file_name.pdf')
# do some chart plotting
dev.off()
```

Plotting charts

The workhorse of the graphics package is the `plot()` function. Calling `plot()` actually redirects it to the correct function according to the input parameters. Most of the time, however, if you call `plot()` with a set of numbers, it will create a scatterplot.

Let's take the data we got earlier from the EPL. If we plot against this, we will get a scatterplot (shown in Figure 2-6):

```
> wins <- league_table$home_wins + league_table$away_wins
> plot(wins)
```

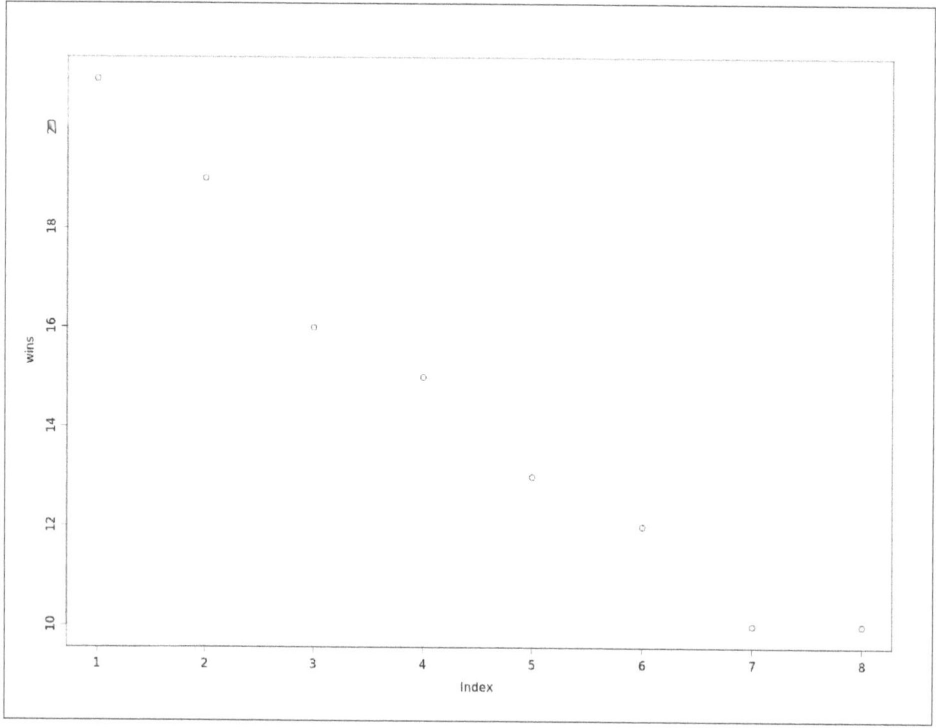

Figure 2-6. Plotting the wins

This, of course, is not very useful or pretty. Charting in R works by layers. After you create the plot (by calling the `plot()` function), you can add a new layer with new information on it. For example, the next expression adds the names of the various teams next to the points:

```
> text(wins, team, pos=4)
```

This is a little better, but it still doesn't give us very good information (Figure 2-7).

Let's try something else:

```
> wins <- league_table[c('home_wins','away_wins')]
> data <- t(as.matrix(wins))
> barplot(data, names.arg=league_table$team, legend=c('home', 'away'))
```

Instead of adding the home and away wins, we subset the data frame and keep only the home and away wins. Then we convert this data frame into a matrix. We want to stack the home wins and the away wins, so we need to transpose the matrix using the `t()` function. Finally, we use the `barplot()` function to plot a stacked bar chart. In the `barplot()` function, we set the names of the axis to be the team names, and also create the legend to represent the home and away goals scored (Figure 2-8).

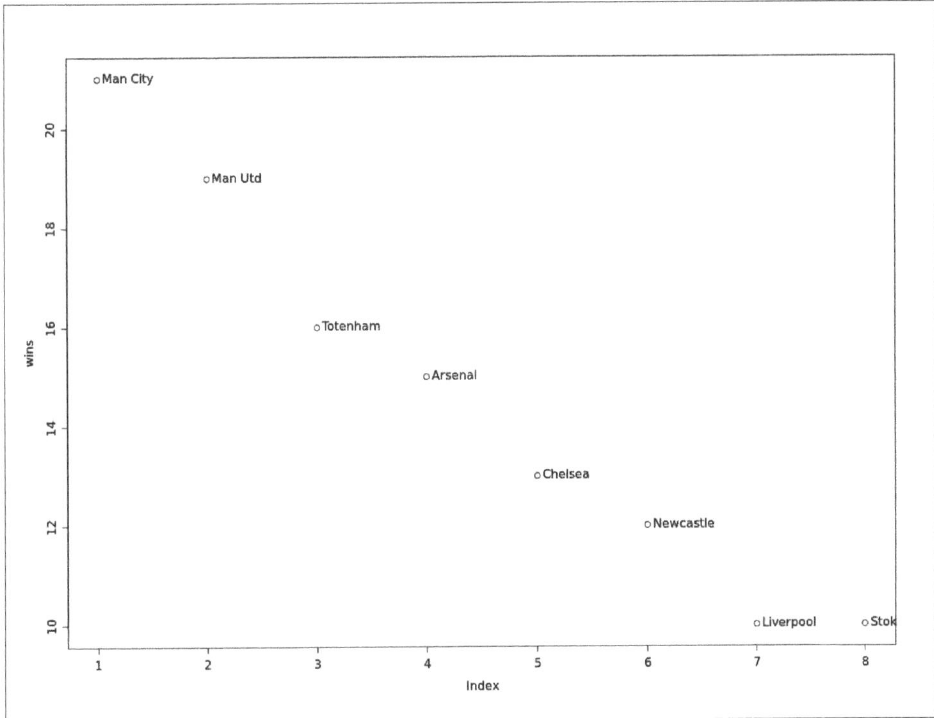

Figure 2-7. Labeling the teams

Because of the way the charts are drawn in layers, we can specify certain parameters before we even start plotting, although nothing will show up until `plot()` (or an equivalent) is called. To do this, we use the `par()` function. For example, to set the background of the chart to a specific color (in this case, gray), we can do this:

```
> par(bg="gray")
```

The functions are quite easy to use, but are also quite rich in features. However, the basic concepts remain the same. There is a whole book on R graphics if you need more depth, but for this book, we won't go any deeper than this. Instead, we'll be using `ggplot2`, a powerful and comprehensive graphics library for R.

Introducing ggplot2

The `ggplot2` package was created by Hadley Wickham to implement the ideas from Leland Wilkinson's book *The Grammar of Graphics* (Springer). The package provides an alternative and powerful way of creating charts and plots with R. `ggplot2` is based on the idea of composing plots using multiple layers that can be stacked on top of one another. It has a relatively small set of primitive components that can be combined in various ways to generate many types of charts.

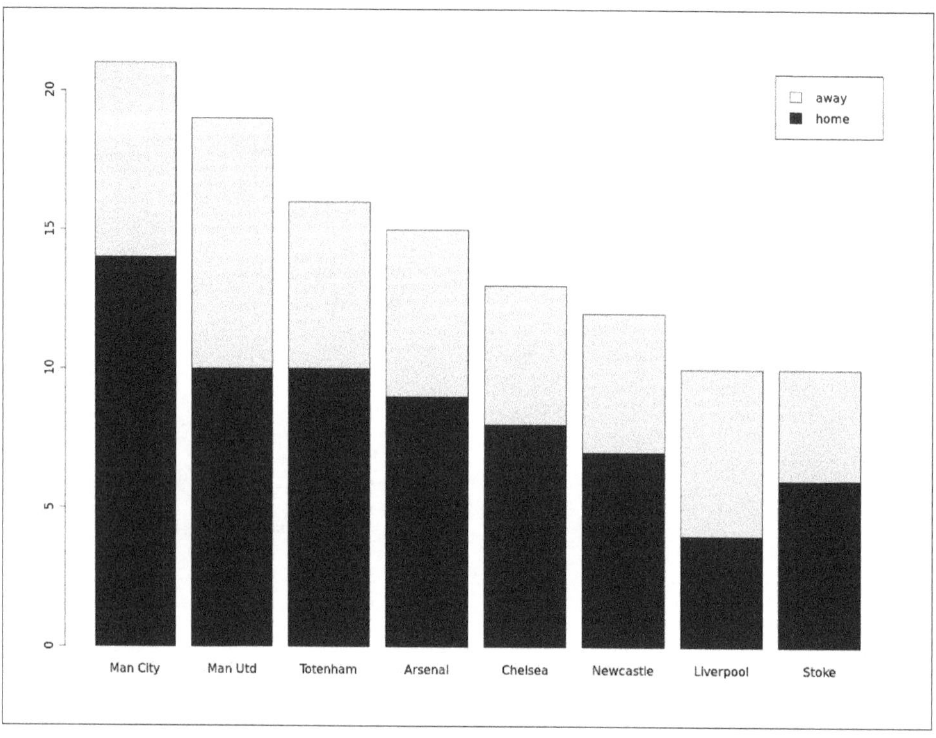

Figure 2-8. Plotting home versus away goals

The Grammar of Graphics

The Grammar of Graphics is a book written by Leland Wilkinson, a statistician and computer scientist who created SYSTAT, the statistics and statistical graphics software package. In his book, Wilkinson explained that statistical graphics are mappings from data to aesthetic attributes of geometric objects, which can be statistically transformed and drawn on a coordinate system. To generate the same plot for different subsets of data, faceting is used. Aesthetic attributes include properties such as color, shape, and size, whereas geometric objects can be points, lines, bars, and so on.

In this section, I'll be introducing `ggplot2` as an alternative graphics package to draw plots. In fact, most of the R scripts in this book will use `ggplot2`.

qplot

A quick way to start using ggplot2 is with qplot, which is short for "quick plot." qplot essentially provides a convenient way to assemble basic plots with a single line, but is really not representative of the power of ggplot2. It is designed to be similar to plot() to provide a level of comfort and familiarity to people who are more used to that function.

Let's look at how qplot works. In the next example, we will be using the fuel economy dataset mpg (miles per gallon), which is included as part of the ggplot2 package. We looked at the dataset briefly in "Importing Data" (page 46).

This dataset records the make, model, class, engine size, transmission, and miles per gallon on the highway and in the city for a number of cars from 1999 to 2008. We want to find out whether the engine size affects the fuel economy of the car, so we use qplot to chart the engine size (displ) against the mileage on the highway:

```
> qplot(displ, hwy, data=mpg)
```

With this single line, we can get a good indication of the answer (Figure 2-9), which, as we've expected, is that the mileage (on the y-axis) goes down as the engine size (on the x-axis) increases. However, you might notice that this isn't always the same. Some cars with large engines in fact have pretty decent fuel economy. Which ones? Let's answer that:

```
> qplot(displ, hwy, data=mpg, shape=factor(year))
```

We take the factor for the year (otherwise, it will be considered as a continuous value) and map it as a third variable (Figure 2-10).

As you can clearly see, the fuel economy of the cars in 2008 has improved over those in 1999.

Using the grammar

While qplot is a quick way of using ggplot2, the strength in ggplot2 lies in its grammar and in creating the plots by adding up layers. When we use qplot, it does a lot of things for us, including creating the plot object and adding up the layers we want on that plot. If we do this ourselves, we have more flexibility and control with each layer.

Plot

To create the plot manually, we initialize a plot using the ggplot() function:

```
> p <- ggplot()
```

There is nothing to see until we add layers, but we'll get to that in a minute. The ggplot() function takes in two parameters, the first being the data to be used and the second being the aesthetic mapping.

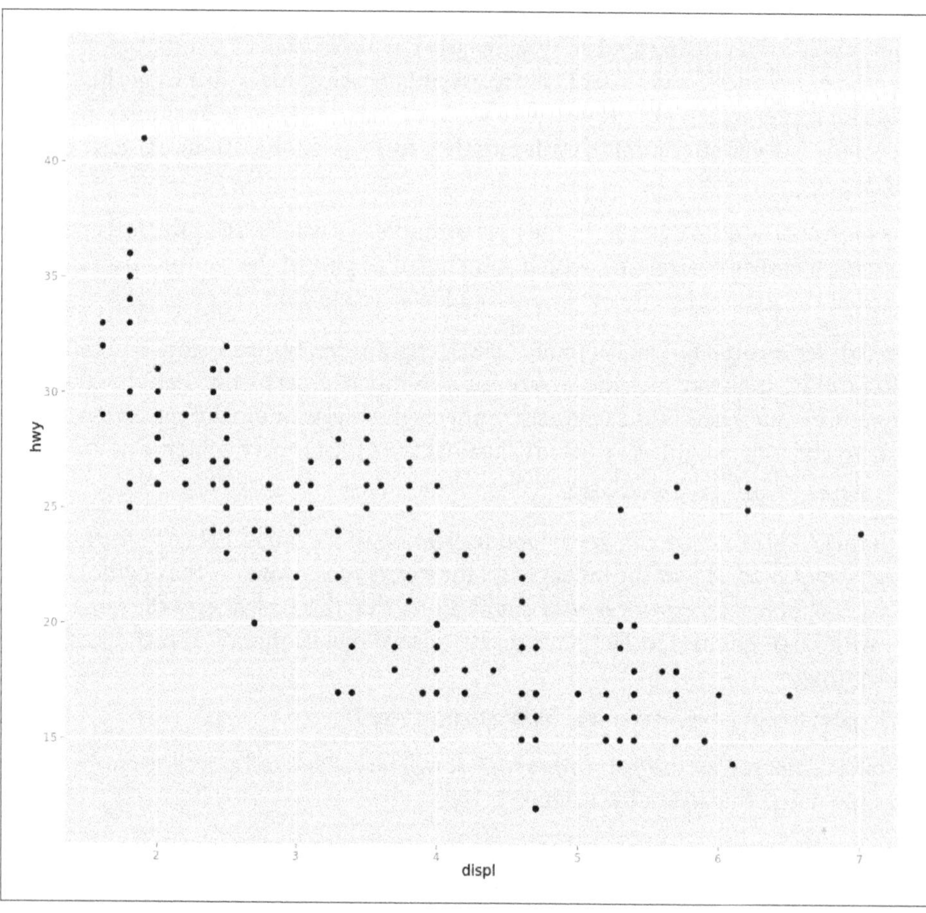

Figure 2-9. Using qplot to chart the engine size versus the mileage on the highway

The data that you send into `ggplot()` must be a data frame. If you set the data and the aesthetic mapping, this will be used throughout the rest of the plot. However, you can also optionally leave any of these out, and set them at each layer. The aesthetic mapping is created using the `aes()` function, which again we will get to momentarily.

We can add each layer on top of the initial plot using the + operator, which in object-oriented fashion is overloaded for the plot object that is created:

```
> p <- p + layer(geom='point')
```

This adds a new scatterplot layer on top of our initial plot. A layer consists of five components:

Data
: The data to be used in this plot

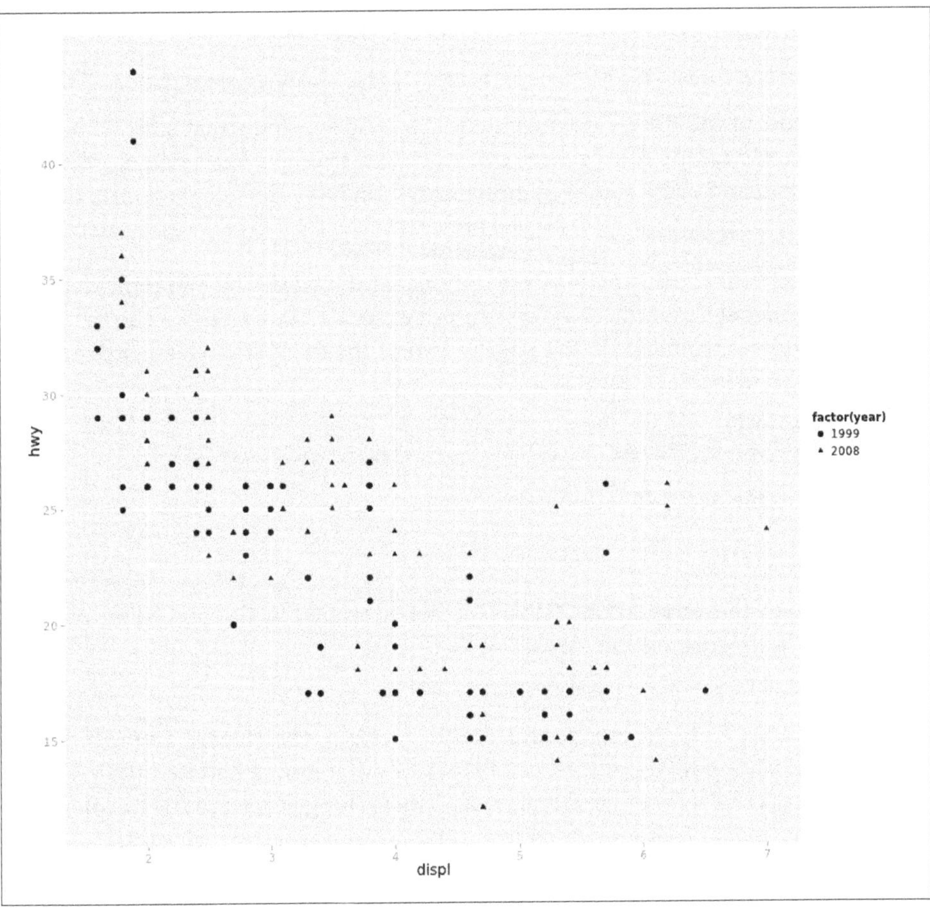

Figure 2-10. Adding a third dimension to the plot

Aesthetic mapping
: A mapping of the data to what we want to see on the plot

Statistical transformation (stat)
: Transforms the data—for example, getting the count and the mean

Geometric object (geom)
: Controls the type of plot to be created—for example, scatterplots and histograms

Position adjustment
: Applies minor tweaks to the positions of the elements within a layer—for example, setting the fill, jittering to avoid overplotting, and stacking bars in bar charts

The `layer()` function takes in a number of parameters that correspond to the components in the grammar:

```
layer(geom, geom_params, stat, stat_params, data, mapping, position)
```

However, most of the time, for convenience, we use shortcuts that start with either `geom` or `stat`. We can do this because every geometric object has a default statistical transformation, and every statistical transformation has a default geometric object:

```
> p <- p + geom_point()
```

The parameters for these functions are optional and include the mapping, data, position, and parameters for the `geom` or `stat`. For example, if we were to redo the earlier plot, this is how it would look. We specify two of the five parameters: `data` and the `aes()` function mentioned earlier:

```
> p <- ggplot()
> p + geom_point(data=mpg, aes(displ, hwy, shape=(factor(year))))
```

We'll focus on the `aes()` function next.

Aesthetics

Aesthetics map the way data is displayed. For example, in the preceding plot, we specified the following aesthetics:

```
aes(x = displ, y = hwy, shape = (factor(year))
```

This maps the x-axis to the engine size and the y-axis to the mileage on the highway, and also indicates that we want to use shapes to differentiate between the years. As shown earlier, x and y don't need names, and we no longer need to refer explicitly to the dataset we're using either, which makes typing and reading a bit easier.

Statistical transformation

Statistical transformations, or stats, transform the data and produce another dataset that can be used for plotting. For example, `stat_bin` (used to create histograms) produces a dataset that includes the count and the density of the observations in each bin. This output can be used in the plot as well.

To show how `stat_bin` can be used, we'll take another dataset that has more data points. We'll use the movies dataset, which comprises movie information and user ratings from IMDB, the Internet Movie Database. This dataset includes information like the title, year of release, budget, length in minutes, and average user rating in IMDB. We'll chart the number of movies made over a period of 90 years or so:

```
> p <- ggplot(movies)
> p + stat_bin(aes(year, ..count..))
stat_bin: binwidth defaulted to range/30. Use 'binwidth = x' to adjust this.
```

When we run this, `ggplot2` reminds us that it has assigned a default bin width[4] and tells us that if we want to change the default, we can set it with `binwidth`. The output of the previous command is shown in Figure 2-11.

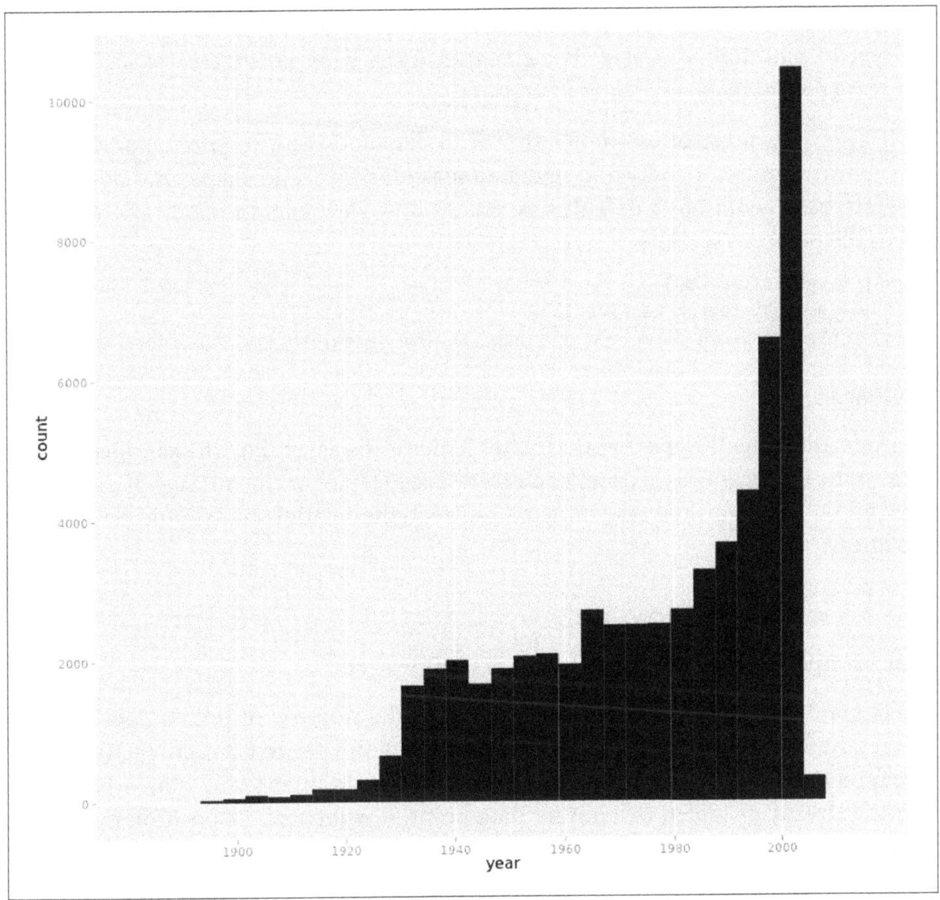

Figure 2-11. Movies produced per year

We can see that there is an explosion in the number of movies made in the past few years. Notice that we have used the year in the aesthetic mapping, but we have also used a funny-looking variable that looks like `..count..`. The variable between the two instances of `..` is one of the outputs of the stat that was run.

4. When you make a histogram, you're actually making a bar chart that shows how many data points fit within a certain range. That range is the *bin width*. In this case, we're looking at the year where the movie was first screened, and the range of years is from 1893 to 2005. The default bin width is then (2005–1893)/30, which is around four years. This means the range is 1893–1897, followed by 1898–1902, and so on.

Note also that we didn't specify any geometric object for this chart. We don't need to, because stat_bin uses the histogram geometric object by default.

Geometric object

The geometric object, or geom, performs the actual rendering of the layer and defines the type of plot that is created. For example, using geom_point creates scatterplots, whereas geom_histogram creates histograms.

Each geom has a set of aesthetics that it understands and requires. For example, geom_point requires x and y and understands color, size, and shape aesthetics. As in the stats, each geom has a default stat. Here's how we create the same chart that we did in the previous section:

```
> p <- ggplot(movies)
> p + geom_histogram(aes(year))
stat_bin: binwidth defaulted to range/30. Use 'binwidth = x' to adjust this.
```

Adjustments

Position adjustments apply tweaks to the elements in a layer. For an example, let's get back to the fuel economy dataset and create a scatterplot of the mileage of cars in the city and on the highways. As you would expect, the relationship should be more or less linear:

```
> p <- ggplot(mpg)
> p + geom_point(aes(cty, hwy))
```

That's simple enough, and Figure 2-12 is what we get.

Looks good, but if you take a closer look at it, the number of points doesn't seem correct. In fact, the points are overlapping, so we don't get an accurate picture of the actual relationship. ggplot2 provides a function to add jitter to the plot—that is, if a point is already occupied by another data point, it will tweak its position by a bit to prevent plotting over the same place:

```
> p <- ggplot(mpg)
> p + geom_point(aes(cty, hwy), position='jitter')
```

Jittering the position gives a more accurate representation of the data (Figure 2-13). However, there's a danger of *overplotting*—having too much data on the chart. If we had a dataset like the movies dataset we used in the previous section, we probably wouldn't be able to make much sense of the plot (pun intended)!

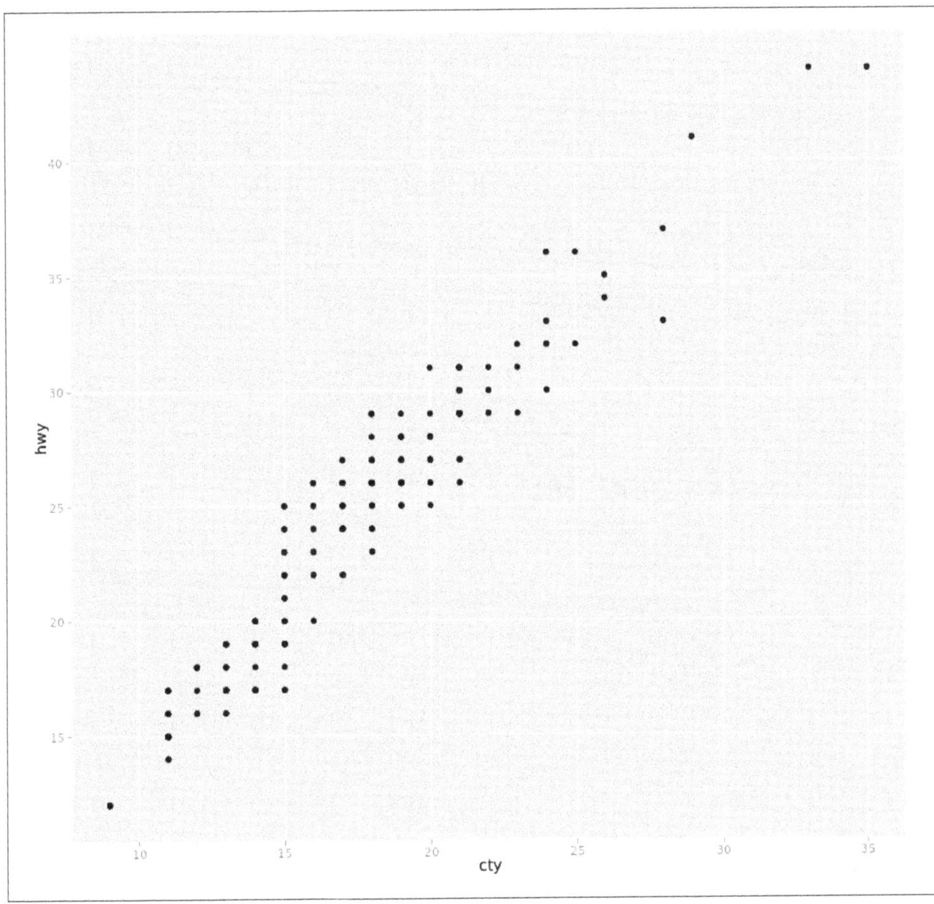

Figure 2-12. Relationship between mileage in the city and mileage on highways

Wrap-up

This chapter was a whirlwind tour of the R language and environment. I did not cover large parts of what R can do, especially its statistical capabilities, but I described enough to take us through the rest of the book. R is a very powerful language, and if you're into data and statistical analysis, it should be an important part of your toolbox. In this chapter, I've talked only briefly about using R, the basics of R programming, and charting with the base R graphics package and the `ggplot2` package.

To learn more about R programming, I recommend one or both of these books:

- *R in a Nutshell*, by Joseph Adler (O'Reilly)
- *R in Action*, by Robert Kabacoff (Manning)

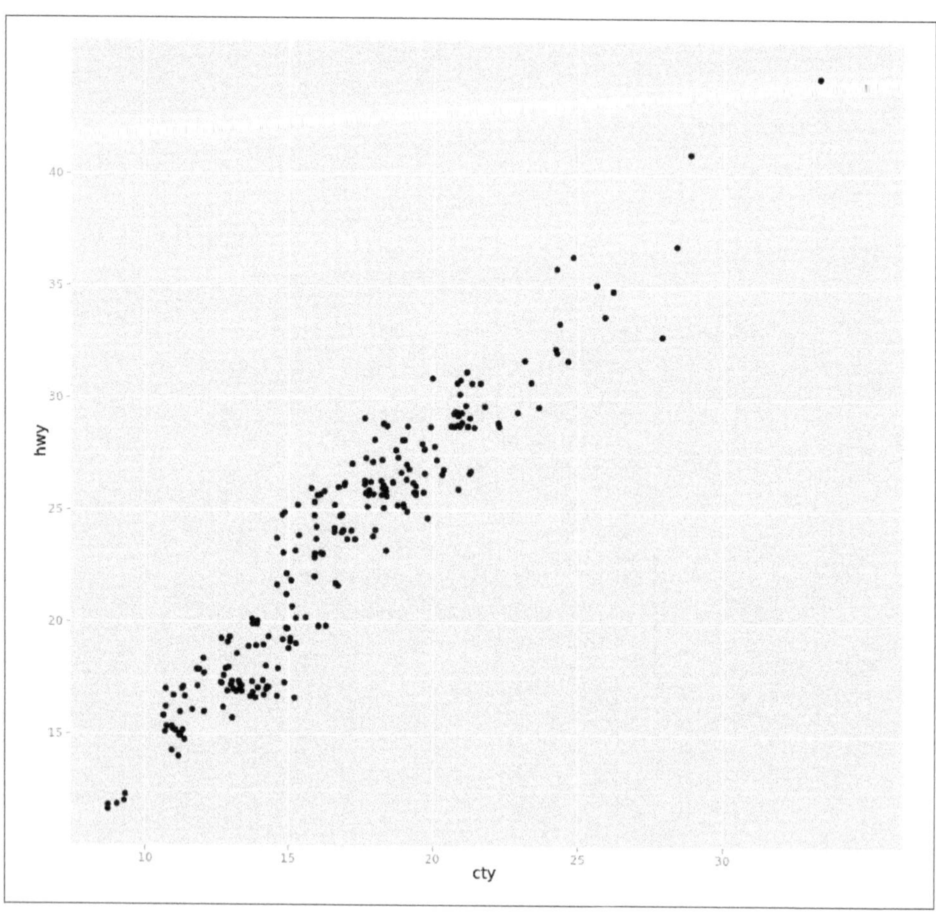

Figure 2-13. Jitter plot

To learn more about creating charts in R or graphics in R, check out these books:

- *ggplot2: Elegant Graphics for Data Analysis*, by Hadley Wickham (Springer)
- *R Graphics*, by Paul Murrell (Chapman & Hall/CRC)

Now that you're finally ready and equipped with the tools, the rest of the book is all fun and games in exploring the world around us!

CHAPTER 3

Offices and Restrooms

It started with a lunch conversation that slowly turned into a coffee break mini-debate. You see, I had just moved into a new job and my first task was to hire engineers to staff my team. Although the final numbers were not absolute, 70 was bandied around for the population of the office. We had half a floor, plenty of space really, but the bone of contention was focused on more delicate facilities (i.e., the restrooms).

The problem was that the whole floor shared a single pair of restrooms (one for the men and another for women) with the gents having two toilets and three urinals. I was totally convinced that with 70 people in the office, we would reach bladder or bowel apocalypse, an absolute disaster in the waiting. My other colleagues were less worried—they noted that the other floors seemed to be doing fine. It wasn't as if we could do anything about it: no one was about to magically add new restrooms for us, no matter how long the queue was or how loudly we shouted. But I was curious in a general sense: what algorithm determines the number of restrooms per square meter of occupancy?

The first thing any respectable research engineer would do, of course, is to search for the answers online. I did enthusiastic searches on building regulations in Singapore for information on the ratio of people to the number of restrooms but found none. However, the United Kingdom has some interesting regulations covered by the Health and Safety Executive (HSE). HSE is the UK's national independent watchdog for work-related health, safety, and illness and has published a number of regulations regarding health and safety in the workplace. One of its regulations gave exactly the recommendation I was looking for (as shown in Table 3-1).

Table 3-1. UK Health and Safety Executive recommended restroom facilities (adapted from http://www.legislation.gov.uk/uksi/1992/3004/schedule/1/made)

Number of employees	Number of toilets	Number of urinals
1–15	1	1
16–30	2	1
31–45	2	2
46–60	3	2
61–75	3	3
76–90	4	3
91–100	4	4

Well, the numbers that I anticipated having seemed to fit those of the UK regulations, but these were just regulations. I had no idea how realistic they were or how the HSE came up with those numbers. Still, that gave me a base reference point. Time to whip out the tools.

The Simple Scenario

To determine the correct people-to-restrooms ratio, we have to devise a model of how restrooms are used by people in the office.

At any point in time, anyone in the office can enter the restroom. The choice of each person entering the restroom normally doesn't cause anyone else to enter or not enter the same restroom. So, at a simple level, the usage of restrooms in an office can be modeled as a *Poisson process.* A Poisson process, named after famous mathematician Siméon-Denis Poisson, is a random process in which events occur continuously and independently of each other. This fits nicely into a simple model of restroom usage where the events are the acts of people entering and using the restroom, then leaving.

We also need to find out how many times the average person needs to urinate in a day. It turns out that our bladder will signal us to make a trip to the restroom when it fills up to about 200 milliliters.[1] Combined with the information that the average urine output of an adult is 1.5 liters a day,[2] this means that we need to go about eight times a day (24 hours), or once every three hours on average. The normal working hours in my company are 8:30 a.m. to 5:30 p.m., which is nine hours, so this means that on average employees go to the restroom three times during the course of the workday.

1. Culley C. Carson III and Tracy Irons-Georges, eds., *Magill's Medical Guide*, vol. 3 (Englewood Cliffs, NJ: Salem, 1998).

2. "Water: How much should you drink every day?", Mayo Clinic (*http://www.mayoclinic.com/health/water/NU00283*).

Naturally, this is not realistic because it is only a model. In real life, more people will use the restrooms during and after lunchtime, but let's ignore that for the moment. We'll revisit it later in a more complex model.

To keep the model simple, we set the lowest time unit to one minute. This means someone in the office decides whether to go to the restroom every minute within the 9 hours in the office, or 540 minutes. Coupled with an average of 3 times in 540 minutes, it also means the probability that a person will go to the restroom every count of the minute is 3/540. In the case of urinating, my estimate is that a person will be able to complete the necessary job within one minute on average and vacate the restroom.

Our simple model accounts for only the usage of the men's restroom. Being an engineering research outfit, we have a pretty bad ratio of male to female engineers, so there aren't going to be problems in the women's restroom anytime soon. Bladder apocalypse is strictly for men. Following on with this assumption, we consider only the urinals and take it that the toilets are off-limits in this exercise.

Something else we ignore in this model is human physiology. Under most circumstances, the need to urinate after going to the restroom drops to zero immediately and slowly increases until the next time we need to go again. To keep things simple, we will ignore this as well.

Armed with this model, we can now try to simulate restroom usage in a computer program using a technique called the *Monte Carlo simulation method.* This is a very fast and effective way of finding out answers when it is difficult or impossible to derive algorithms to describe systems. In a way, it's a very pragmatic technique to getting to answers. The steps are rather straightforward and mechanical:

1. First we model the process or system.
2. Then we randomly create inputs and pass them into the model. The model is normally written as a computer program because otherwise the volume of input makes processing unfeasible.
3. The model generates the output, given the inputs.
4. Finally, we analyze the output to find the answers we want.

The Monte Carlo simulation method is named after the famous casino in Monaco. The name was coined by scientists working in the Manhattan Project in the 1940s. Monte Carlo methods are often used in simulating physical and mathematical systems by repeatedly using random samplings. Effectively, this means randomly generating numbers and using the uncertainty and randomness to model the systems we want to investigate.

The simulation can often be iterative, as we refine the model to better represent the system. This means tweaking the model until we get good answers. How do you know when an answer is good? This really depends on what you want to achieve. In this chapter, this means first finding out whether having 70 people in the office creates a high risk of bladder apocalypse.

> Remember that all models are wrong; the practical question is how wrong do they have to be to not be useful.
>
> —George Edward Pelham Box

Let's look at how we can use Monte Carlo simulation with our model.

Representing Restrooms and Such

As the necessary underlying code for the simulations, I wrote a few base classes that represented the restrooms, the facilities (putting it more delicately) in the restrooms, and the people in the office who will be visiting the restrooms.

I started off with the `Restroom` class, as shown in Example 3-1.

Example 3-1. Restroom class

```
class Restroom
  attr_reader :queue
  attr_reader :facilities

  def initialize(facilities_per_restroom=3)
    @queue = []
    @facilities = [] # the facilties in this restroom
    facilities_per_restroom.times { @facilities << Facility.new }
  end

  def enter(person)
    unoccupied_facility = @facilities.find { |facility| not facility.occupied?}
    if unoccupied_facility
      unoccupied_facility.occupy person
    else
      @queue << person
    end
  end

  def tick
    @facilities.each { |f| f.tick }
  end
end
```

All code examples may be downloaded from GitHub (*https://github.com/sausheong/everyday*).

The `Restroom` class represents the restroom and has two readable attributes—a queue of people waiting to enter the restroom, and a list of facilities (read: urinals) in the restroom. During its creation, we initialize the `Restroom` object with an empty queue as well as create a given number of facilities, defaulting to three.

The `Restroom` object has two methods that can be called on it. The first is `enter`, which looks for the next available facility and lets the person (passed in as a parameter) occupy it. If there are no unoccupied facilities, the person is placed on the queue.

The second method, `tick`, simply goes through each facility and calls on the `tick` method in that facility. This is how we count down the time. The `tick` method in the `Facility` class is described shortly.

The `Facility` class, shown in Example 3-2, represents a single facility in the restroom.

Example 3-2. Facility class

```
class Facility
  def initialize
    @occupier = nil
    @duration = 0
  end

  def occupy(person)
    unless occupied?
      @occupier = person
      @duration = 1
      Person.population.delete person
      true
    else
      false
    end
  end

  def occupied?
    not @occupier.nil?
  end

  def vacate
    Person.population << @occupier
    @occupier = nil
  end
```

```
  def tick
    if occupied? and @duration > @occupier.use_duration
      vacate
      @duration = 0
    elsif occupied?
      @duration += 1
    end
  end
end
```

This is a slightly more complex class and has two attributes, both of which are accessible only to the internal methods. The `occupier` attribute holds the person currently using the facility. If the facility is unused, the `occupier` attribute is assigned nil. The second attribute is `duration`, which indicates how long the facility has been used by the current occupier. I'll clarify the use of this attribute momentarily.

There are four methods in this object. The first, `occupy`, which was called in our `Restroom` class, checks whether the facility is occupied and assigns someone to the facility if it isn't. The `duration` is then increased by one count, and the person occupying the facility is removed from the restroom queue. A `true` or `false` is returned according to whether the facility is successfully occupied or not.

The second method, `occupied?`, simply checks whether the facility is occupied.

Just as the `occupy` method allows a person to occupy a facility, the `vacate` method removes him from the facility and adds him back into the overall population.

The last method in the `Facility` class is `tick`, as mentioned previously. This method keeps track of the passing of each discrete period of time. In our simulation, each tick is equivalent to a minute in the real world. The `tick` method performs two tasks. If the current occupant of the facility has been in it for too long, he will be vacated. If not, the `duration` attribute is incremented.

The last class in our trio of base classes is the `Person` class, demonstrated in Example 3-3.

Example 3-3. Person class

```
class Person
  @@population = []
  attr_reader :use_duration
  attr_accessor :frequency

  def initialize(frequency=4,use_duration=1)
    @frequency = frequency
    @use_duration = use_duration
  end

  def self.population
    @@population
  end
```

```
  def need_to_go?
    rand(DURATION) + 1 <= @frequency
  end
end
```

This is a simple class like `Restroom`, but with three attributes. The first is the `population` attribute, a class variable that stores the entire population of the simulation. The second is `use_duration`, a read-only attribute that describes how long the person takes to use the facility. The third is `frequency`, an attribute that describes how many times the person will use the facility over the duration of the simulation. This, as explained before, is 9 hours or 540 minutes, which is stored as a constant named `DURATION`. For example, if someone's `frequency` is 3, then our model says that he will visit the restroom 3 times within a period of 540 minutes.

There is only one interesting method here: `need_to_go?`. This method will return true if the person needs to use the restroom. We take a random number from 1 to 540 and check if it is less than or the same as the frequency. If it is, the method returns `true`.

What this method really asks is "what is the probability of the person needing to go at this point in time?" In our simulation, the answer is 3/540. For the probability-minded among you, this is equivalent to drawing from a bag of marbles labeled 1 to 540 and finding a marble numbered 1, 2, or 3.

We place all three classes into a file named *restroom.rb* to be used in our simulation, and we're ready to roll.

The First Simulation

We start off with the simple model, the one where we assumed the rate of people visiting the restroom to be constant throughout the period. The simulation code has two separate parts:

1. Run through the simulation and store the gathered data temporarily.
2. Write this data into a comma-separated value (CSV) file.

Comma-Separated Value files

The comma-separated value (CSV) format is a file format in which tabular data (numbers and text) is stored in a plain-text form that can be easily written and read in a text editor. CSV is widely supported and is popularly used to move tabular data between programs. Most spreadsheet programs, such as Excel and Numbers, support CSV. Consequently, many programming languages come with libraries that easily produce and consume the data in CSV files.

Many of the scripts in this book generate raw observation data in CSV format. Once generated, we can quickly review it for correctness in a text editor or a spreadsheet program before we load it up in our R scripts for further analysis.

In the simulation in Example 3-4, we will take the queue size as the only data point. Let's step through the code line by line.

Example 3-4. Simulation script 1 (varying population size)

```
require 'csv'
require './restroom'

frequency = 3
facilities_per_restroom = 3
use_duration = 1
population_range = 10..600

data = {}
population_range.step(10).each do |population_size|
  Person.population.clear
  population_size.times { Person.population << Person.new(frequency, use_duration) }
  data[population_size] = []
  restroom = Restroom.new facilities_per_restroom
  DURATION.times do |t|
    data[population_size] << restroom.queue.size
    queue = restroom.queue.clone
    restroom.queue.clear
    unless queue.empty?
      restroom.enter queue.shift
    end
    Person.population.each do |person|
      if person.need_to_go?
        restroom.enter person
      end
    end
    restroom.tick
  end
end

CSV.open('simulation1.csv', 'w') do |csv|
  lbl = []
  population_range.step(10).each {|population_size| lbl << population_size  }
  csv << lbl

  DURATION.times do |t|
    row = []
    population_range.step(10).each do |population_size|
      row << data[population_size][t]
```

```
    end
    csv << row
  end
end
```

We use the csv standard library to create the CSV files, so the first line includes this library, followed by the *restroom.rb* file we created earlier. Next, we create some variables we'll be using in the simulation:

`frequency`
: How many times a person visits the restroom during the simulation. As mentioned earlier in this chapter, we use three as the average number of visits per person.

`facilities_per_restroom`
: How many facilities the restroom has. In this simulation, we have three facilities per restroom and because we only have one restroom, this means there are three facilities altogether.

`use_duration`
: How long each person will use the facility during every visit. In this simulation, we assume that each person takes one tick to complete what he needs to do in the restroom.

`population_range`
: The range of populations we want to run simulations over. In this simulation, we use a range from 10 people up to 600 people in the office.

`data`
: A hash where we store the data generated temporarily.

The first part of the simulation focuses on generating the raw data. We do this by iterating through a list of populations we want to simulate, starting from 10 up to 600 people in the office. For each population, we loop tick by tick (representing minute by minute) through the 540 ticks that represent the 540 minutes (9 hours) of time spent in the office. Before we start the loop, however, we need to set up some of the objects we need:

1. First, we create the population by defining a `Person` object to represent each person in the population.
2. Next, we initialize the temporary data storage hash, `data`.
3. Finally, we create the `Restroom` object for `population` to use.

While we're in the loop, the only piece of information we really collect is just the restroom queue size. Once we have this, we look at the restroom queue and try to move the first person in line into the restroom. You might notice in the code that we have to clone the restroom queue first and work on the cloned queue instead of the original one. This is because we will move the people back into the restroom queue if the restroom is fully occupied. If we use the restroom queue itself, we'll end up in an infinite loop!

Once the queue is cleared (or at least everyone in the queue is requeued), we move on to the whole population. We check each person in the population and ask if he needs to use the restroom (using the calculation explained earlier) and if so, we move him to the restroom. We wrap up the loop by calling `tick` on the restroom and moving the whole simulation on in time.

The second part of the simulation is purely mechanical. We create a file named *simulation1.csv*, iterate through the temporary store, and copy all the data to the CSV file.

Simply run this simulation to generate the data. If you open up the file in any spreadsheet software, you should see something like Figure 3-1.

	A	B	C	D	E	F	G	H	I	J	K	L	M	N	O	P	Q	R	S	T	U	V	W	X
1	10	20	30	40	50	60	70	80	90	100	110	120	130	140	150	160	170	180	190	200	210	220	230	240
2	0	0	0	0	0	0	0	0	0	0	0	0	0	0	0	0	0	0	0	0	0	0	0	0
3	0	0	0	0	0	0	0	0	0	0	0	0	0	0	0	0	0	1	0	0	0	0	0	0
4	0	0	0	0	0	0	0	0	0	0	0	0	0	0	0	0	0	2	0	1	0	0	0	1
5	0	0	0	0	0	0	0	0	0	0	0	0	0	0	0	0	0	0	0	2	2	0	2	1
6	0	0	0	0	0	0	0	0	0	0	0	0	0	0	0	0	0	2	0	1	4	1	2	1
7	0	0	0	0	0	0	0	0	0	0	0	0	0	0	0	0	0	3	0	1	0	0	1	1
8	0	0	0	0	0	0	0	0	0	0	0	0	0	0	0	0	0	0	0	1	0	0	0	2
9	0	0	0	0	0	0	0	0	0	0	0	0	0	0	0	0	0	0	0	0	0	0	0	1
10	0	0	0	0	0	0	0	0	0	0	3	0	0	0	0	0	0	0	0	0	0	1	0	1
11	0	0	0	0	0	0	0	0	0	0	0	0	2	0	0	0	0	0	0	0	0	1	1	2
12	0	0	0	0	0	0	0	0	0	0	0	0	0	0	0	0	0	0	0	0	0	0	1	3
13	0	0	0	0	0	0	0	0	0	0	0	0	0	0	0	2	0	0	3	0	0	0	0	1
14	0	0	0	0	0	0	0	2	0	0	0	0	0	0	0	2	0	0	0	0	0	0	0	2
15	0	0	0	0	0	0	0	0	0	0	0	0	0	0	0	1	0	0	1	0	0	2	0	0
16	0	0	0	0	0	0	0	0	0	0	0	0	0	0	0	0	0	1	0	0	0	0	0	1
17	0	0	0	0	0	0	0	0	0	0	0	0	0	0	0	0	0	3	0	0	1	0	0	0
18	0	0	0	0	0	0	0	0	0	0	0	0	0	0	0	0	0	0	0	0	0	0	0	1
19	0	0	0	0	0	0	0	0	0	0	0	0	0	0	0	0	0	0	0	2	0	0	0	0
20	0	0	0	0	0	0	0	0	0	0	0	0	0	0	0	0	0	0	0	0	0	0	0	0
21	0	0	0	0	0	0	0	0	0	0	0	1	0	0	0	0	0	0	1	0	0	1	0	0
22	0	0	0	0	0	0	0	0	0	0	0	0	0	0	0	0	0	0	0	0	0	0	2	0
23	0	0	0	0	0	0	0	0	0	0	0	0	0	0	0	0	2	0	0	2	1	3	1	0
24	0	0	0	0	0	0	0	0	0	0	0	0	0	0	0	0	0	0	0	0	2	0	2	0
25	0	0	0	0	0	0	0	0	0	0	0	0	0	0	0	0	0	1	0	0	0	0	2	1
26	0	0	0	0	0	0	0	0	0	0	0	0	0	0	0	0	0	0	0	0	0	0	0	1
27	0	0	0	0	0	0	0	0	0	0	0	0	0	1	0	0	0	3	2	0	0	0	0	3
28	0	0	0	0	0	0	0	0	0	0	0	0	0	0	0	0	0	0	1	0	0	1	0	3

Figure 3-1. Simulation CSV raw data

That's it! We have successfully run a Monte Carlo simulation and gotten our raw observation data for the first simulation. But what does it say? That's where things become more interesting.

Interpreting the Data

We ran through a simple simulation of different populations of people in an office over a period of nine hours and captured the restroom queue size at various points in time. Armed with this data, we want to answer our first question: at what population does the queue size become unbearable with a restroom of three facilities?

One possible interpretation of this data is to look at the *maximum queue size* for each population. The maximum queue size is the longest queue that is formed for a given population. This also happens to be the longest time someone would have to wait for that particular population. For example, if the maximum queue size for a population of 100 people is 3, then the longest someone has to wait during that simulation is 3 ticks (3 minutes) before taking his turn at the restroom.

Another piece of information that can be extracted from the data is the average queue size, which we can describe using two statistical values: the *mean* and the *median.*

The mean is what we normally think of as the average. We add up all the queue sizes at every point in time, then divide the total by time (in this case, it's 540 ticks). We can do this because the use duration of the restroom is one tick, so the queue size is also one tick. However, this value normally ends up in decimal points, which produces the silly situation where we have an average queue size of 1.3 people. The median is a more sensible measurement and is the middle value of the list of all queue sizes.

To get the maximum queue size as well as the average queue size, we'll turn to an R script (Example 3-5) that crunches through our CSV file data and displays it in a nice maximum-queue-to-population line chart.

Example 3-5. Median, mean, and max queue sizes versus population

```
library(ggplot2)

data <- read.table("simulation1.csv", header=TRUE, sep=",")
mean <- mean(data)
median <- apply(data,2,median)
max  <- apply(data,2,max)
df <- data.frame(population=seq(from=10,to=600,by=10),mean=mean,
    median=median,max=max)

ggplot(data = df) + scale_shape_manual(name="Type", value=c(2,3,4)) +
  geom_smooth(aes(x = population, y = mean)) +
  geom_point(aes(x  = population, y = mean, shape = "mean")) +
  geom_smooth(aes(x = population, y = median)) +
  geom_point(aes(x  = population, y = median, shape = "median")) +
  geom_smooth(aes(x = population, y = max)) +
  geom_point(aes(x  = population, y = max, shape = "max")) +
  scale_y_continuous("queue size", breaks=0:35) +
  scale_x_continuous("population", breaks=seq(from=10,to=600,by=30))
```

Like the simulation, there are two parts to this script. First, we import the data and process it. Then we draw the chart using the processed data and try to make a conclusion based on that chart.

We will be using the `ggplot2` library in this script. For more information on the `ggplot2` library, please refer to Chapter 2. Although `ggplot2` code can be more concise, I chose to use relatively verbose code to help explain how the chart is created.

We start off by reading the data from the CSV file into an R data frame named `data` using the `read.table()` function. This is a very common function that we will be using often in this book, because we are going to load a lot of CSV fields into data frames.

Then, in rapid succession, we extract the mean, the median, and the max values from `data`. You might be puzzled as to why we can use the `mean()` function directly, but we have to get `median()` and `max()` indirectly through the `apply` method. This is because of the way these three functions have been defined. The `mean()` function is the only one that can take in a data frame directly; the `median()` and `max()` functions cannot. To get the data from the frame into the latter functions, we use the `apply()` function, which converts the data frame into an R matrix and then applies the given function accordingly. Here's a detailed look at how we're using the `apply()` function:

```
median <- apply(data,2,median)
```

The first parameter is the data, while the second indicates whether to apply the function by rows (`1`) or by columns (`2`). In our case, we are applying it by columns, so we use the parameter `2`. The last parameter is the name of the function to call. We use the `apply` function for both the median and max. Once we have the mean, median, and max, we create a data frame with columns made up of the mean, median, max, and population. This is the data frame we'll use to generate the chart, shown in Figure 3-2.

First, we create the plot with the new data frame as the input data. We add to that a manual shape scale with the following function:

```
scale_shape_manual(name="Type", value=c(2,3,4))
```

The `name` parameter will provide us with the name of the legend later. The value is a collection of numbers that determine the shape of the scatterplot markers we will be drawing. So why the numbers 2, 3, and 4? Figure 3-3 is the key to the answer.

The numbers represent *plot characters*, which are symbols used to represent values in R plot charts. The numbers 2, 3, and 4 refer to rows from the leftmost column of Figure 3-3, and they give us an unfilled triangle, a plus sign, and a multiplication sign, respectively. I chose this set of markers because they provided the cleanest differentiation, but you can play around with different types of markers.

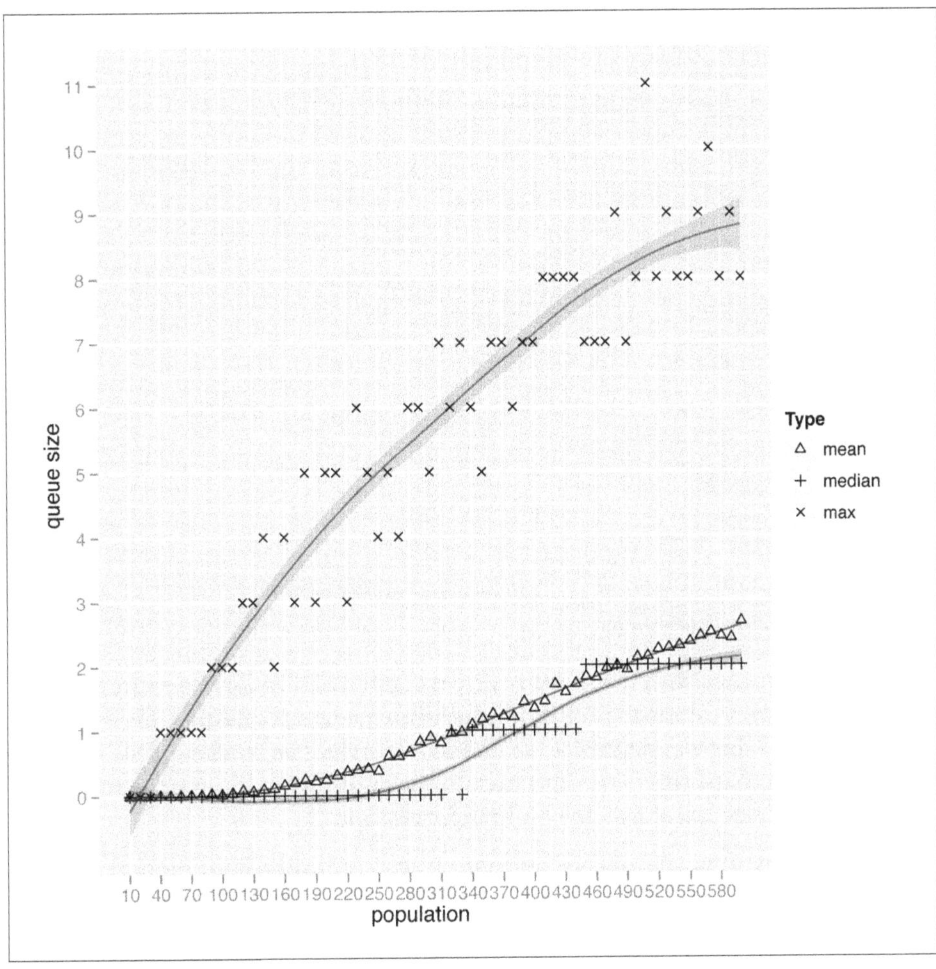

Figure 3-2. Max, median, and mean queue sizes for simulation 1

Next, we add on a scatterplot and a smoother for each set of values:

```
geom_smooth(aes(x = population, y = mean)) +
geom_point(aes(x  = population, y = mean, shape = "mean")) +
```

In each of the geom function calls, the only parameter is an aesthetic mapping that provides the necessary attributes and data. As discussed in Chapter 2, aesthetic mappings describe how variables in the data are mapped to visual properties. In this script, the aesthetic mappings simply tell the `geom_smooth()` function that there are two variables named `x` and `y`, and that they are assigned to the population and mean, respectively. In `geom_point()`, we add in the `shape` parameter to indicate which symbol we want. We do not actually specify which shape the point should take. Instead, we give it a label (in the preceding example, it's `mean`). This will then be mapped in

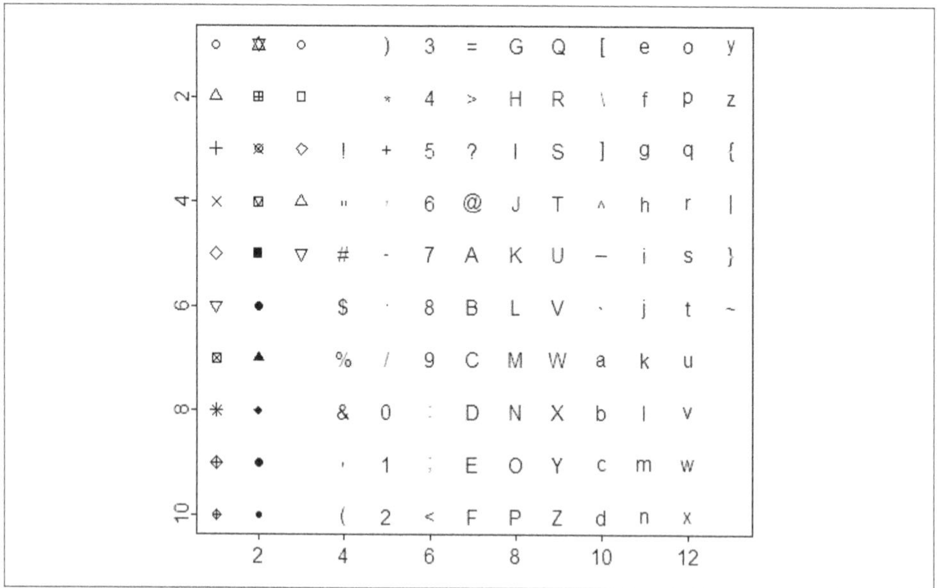

Figure 3-3. Plot characters in R

consecutive sequence with the shape scale we defined earlier for the entire chart. In the example code, we drew the points for the mean queue sizes first, so this is mapped to the first shape that was defined—the unfilled triangle. The median queue sizes will take the second shape (the plus sign) because it was drawn next, and the maximum queue sizes take the last shape, the multiplication sign.

While the points show discrete values that are widely scattered, as random samples tend to be, the smoother geom creates either a line or a shaded area that evens out the variations in each set of points (mean, median, and max) and helps us visualize the patterns in the data.

Finally, we wrap up with two continuous scales:

```
scale_y_continuous("queue size", breaks=0:35) +
scale_x_continuous("population", breaks=seq(from=10,to=600,by=30))
```

Scales control the mapping between variables and aesthetic properties, and we need one scale for each aesthetic property used. In our case, we have only two aesthetic properties, `x` and `y`, so we just need to add in the scales.

Let's zoom in further on the population with 70 people in the queue and see how often a queue forms. Again, we run another short R script to process the data and generate a chart, as shown in Example 3-6.

Example 3-6. Frequency of restroom queues

```
library(ggplot2)

data <- read.table("simulation1.csv", header=TRUE, sep=",")
df <- data.frame(table(data$X70))
colnames(df) <- c("queue_size", "frequency")
percent_labels <- paste(df$frequency, '(', round(df$frequency*100/540, 2), '%)')

ggplot(data=df) + opts(legend.position = "none") +
  scale_fill_grey(start = 0.6, end = 0.8) +
  geom_bar(aes(x = queue_size, y = frequency, fill = factor(queue_size))) +
  geom_text(aes(x = queue_size, y = frequency, label = percent_labels, size=1)) +
  scale_y_continuous("frequency") +
  scale_x_discrete("queue size")
```

Running this script creates the chart shown in Figure 3-4.

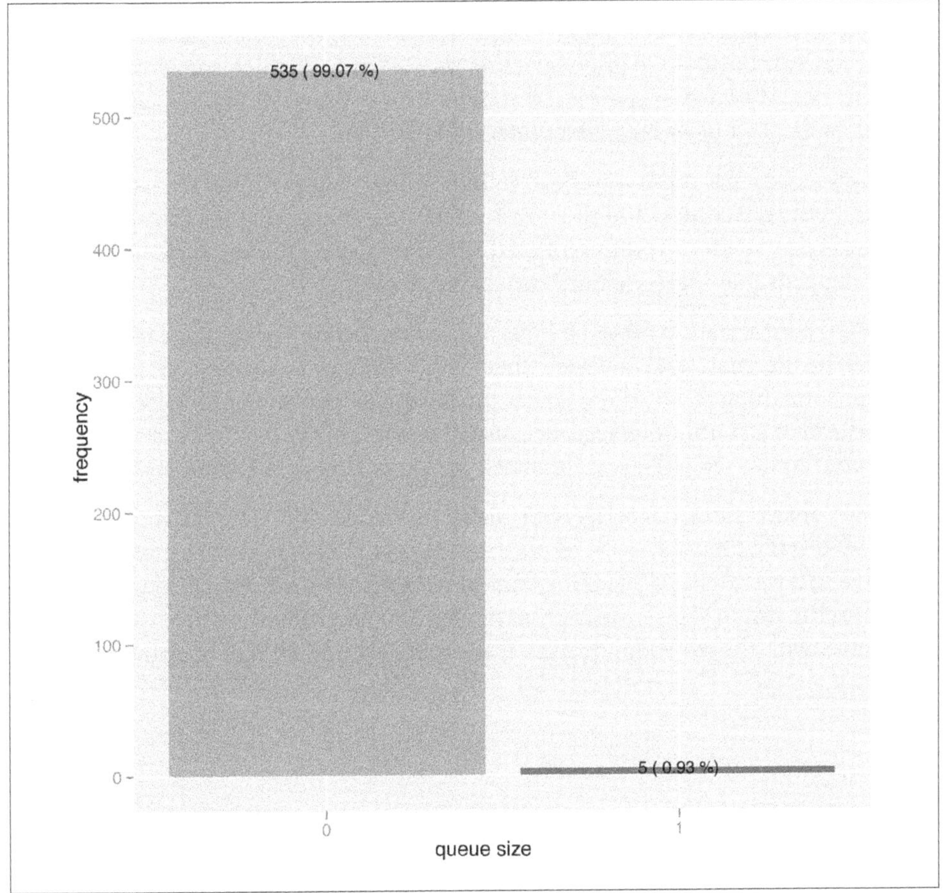

Figure 3-4. Frequency of restroom queues for a population size of 70 people

The code is similar to that of the previous script that created the chart in Figure 3-2. Instead of viewing all the data, however, I focused on using the data with the population of 70 people in the office (that is, the column named `X70`). The `table()` function counts the number of times a particular queue size appears, and the program converts the resulting table into a data frame. This method creates rather cryptic column names, so to make it more understandable, we convert the two column names into `queue_size` and `frequency`. At this point in time, the data frame looks something like this:

```
  queue_size frequency
1          0       535
2          1         5
```

This tells us that the restroom queue was empty 535 out of 540 times, while there was a queue of 1 person only 5 times. The rest of the script continues to generate the chart with the `ggplot2` library.

The code is straightforward. First, I created a plot with the data frame without the legend. To draw the chart in grayscale, I set the fill to `grey`, which runs from 0 (white) to 1.0 (black). My starting color is 0.6 and my final color is 0.8. If I had left the colors at the defaults, I would have had a pretty dark first bar.

Next, I attached a bar lot to the chart. In its aesthetic mapping, the x-axis attribute is mapped to the queue size, and the y-axis attribute is mapped to the frequency. I also threw in a fill attribute, and differentiated it by finding the different scales of the queue size (it happens that there are only two queue sizes).

To make the information more obvious, I also attached the percentage text labels on each bar in the chart and rounded them out with some cosmetic alterations and cleanup. Something to note here is that for the queue size attribute, I used a discrete scale instead of a continuous scale because there are only two queue sizes, either 1 or 0. The continuous scale is, as you'd guess, for a continuous set of values.

The chart answers our concerns over restroom congestion. The restroom queue is empty 99% of the time, while 1% of the time there is one person in the queue. So there you have it: a restroom of 3 facilities for 70 people in the office is absolutely OK. In fact, from the simulation, we learn that having 200 people in the office would still be acceptable, with the restroom queue being empty around 80% of the time.

The Second Simulation

The simulation we just ran fixed the number of facilities for a restroom while changing the population of the office over a nine-hour duration. It answered the question of how many people a restroom of three facilities can serve. However, if we're the ones planning the office, we'll know roughly how many people we want to serve. So let's turn the question around and ask: how many restrooms should we build to support the number of people in the office?

To answer this question, we will turn the previous simulation on its head, using a fixed population size while changing the number of facilities per restroom, as shown in Example 3-7.

Example 3-7. Simulation script 2 (varying number of facilities per restroom)

```
require 'csv'
require './restroom'

frequency = 3
use_duration = 1
population_size = 1000
facilities_per_restroom_range = 1..30
data = {}
facilities_per_restroom_range.each do |facilities_per_restroom|
  Person.population.clear
  population_size.times { Person.population << Person.new(frequency, use_duration) }
  data[facilities_per_restroom] = []
  restroom = Restroom.new facilities_per_restroom

DURATION.times do |t|
    queue = restroom.queue.clone
    restroom.queue.clear
    data[facilities_per_restroom] << queue.size

    unless queue.empty?
      restroom.enter queue.shift
    end

    Person.population.each do |person|
      if person.need_to_go?
        restroom.enter person
      end
    end
    restroom.tick
  end
end
```

```
CSV.open('simulation2.csv', 'w') do |csv|
  lbl = []
  facilities_per_restroom_range.each {|facilities_per_restroom|
                                  lbl << facilities_per_restroom  }
  csv << lbl

  DURATION.times do |t|
    row = []
    facilities_per_restroom_range.each do |facilities_per_restroom|
      row << data[facilities_per_restroom][t]
    end
    csv << row
  end
end
```

The code is almost the same as Example 3-4. The main difference is that we're no longer looping through a range of population sizes. Instead, we fixed the population size at 1,000 people and looped through the number of facilities per restroom. The reason why we're using a much larger population size is because if we used a smaller one, there might not be much data to process!

The data collected is also different. While we're still measuring the queue size, it's the queue size assuming different number of facilities per restroom instead of different population sizes.

As before, we're going to run the analysis through an R script (Example 3-8). This is very similar to the one we used in Example 3-5.

Example 3-8. Median, mean, and max queue sizes versus number of facilities in a restroom

```
library(ggplot2)

data <- read.table("simulation2.csv", header=TRUE, sep=",")
mean <- mean(data)
median <- apply(data,2,median)
max  <- apply(data,2,max)
df <- data.frame(population=seq(from=1,to=30),mean=mean, median=median,max=max)

ggplot(data = df) + scale_color_discrete(name="Type") +
  geom_smooth(aes(x=population,y=mean,color="mean")) +
  geom_point(aes(x=population,y=mean,color="mean")) +
  geom_smooth(aes(x=population,y=median,color="median")) +
  geom_point(aes(x=population,y=median,color="median")) +
  geom_smooth(aes(x=population,y=max,color="max")) +
  geom_point(aes(x=population,y=max,color="max")) +
  scale_y_continuous("queue size") +
  scale_x_continuous("number of facilities in a restroom")
```

The chart generated from this simulation is shown in Figure 3-5.

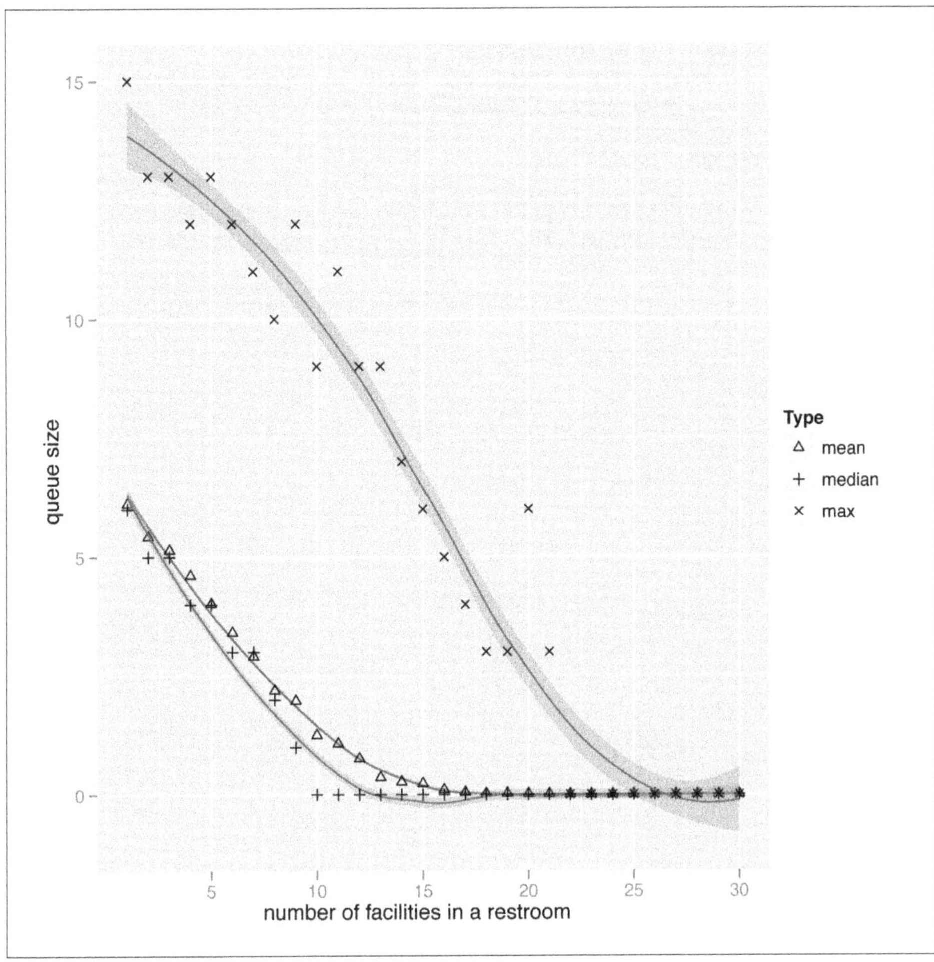

Figure 3-5. Median, mean, and max queue sizes for simulation 2

From the chart, we can easily tell that if we want to have 1,000 people in an office, we'd need restrooms with about 20 facilities. Now let's run the queue size frequency script again, but this time changing the data we want to chart. Instead of charting for a population size of 70 people, let's chart for 19 facilities per restroom (Example 3-9).

Example 3-9. Frequency of restroom queues

```
library(ggplot2)

data <- read.table("simulation2.csv", header=TRUE, sep=",")
df <- data.frame(table(data$X19))
colnames(df) <- c("queue_size", "frequency")
percent_labels <- paste(df$frequency, '(', round(df$frequency*100/540,2), '%)')
```

```
ggplot(data=df) + opts(legend.position = "none") +
  scale_fill_grey(start = 0.6, end = 0.8) +
  geom_bar(aes(x = queue_size, y = frequency, fill = factor(queue_size))) +
  geom_text(aes(x = queue_size, y = frequency, label = percent_labels, size=1)) +
  scale_y_continuous("frequency") +
  scale_x_discrete("queue size")
```

Figure 3-6 shows the chart that is generated when we run the script. As before, the restroom queue is empty almost 99% of the time.

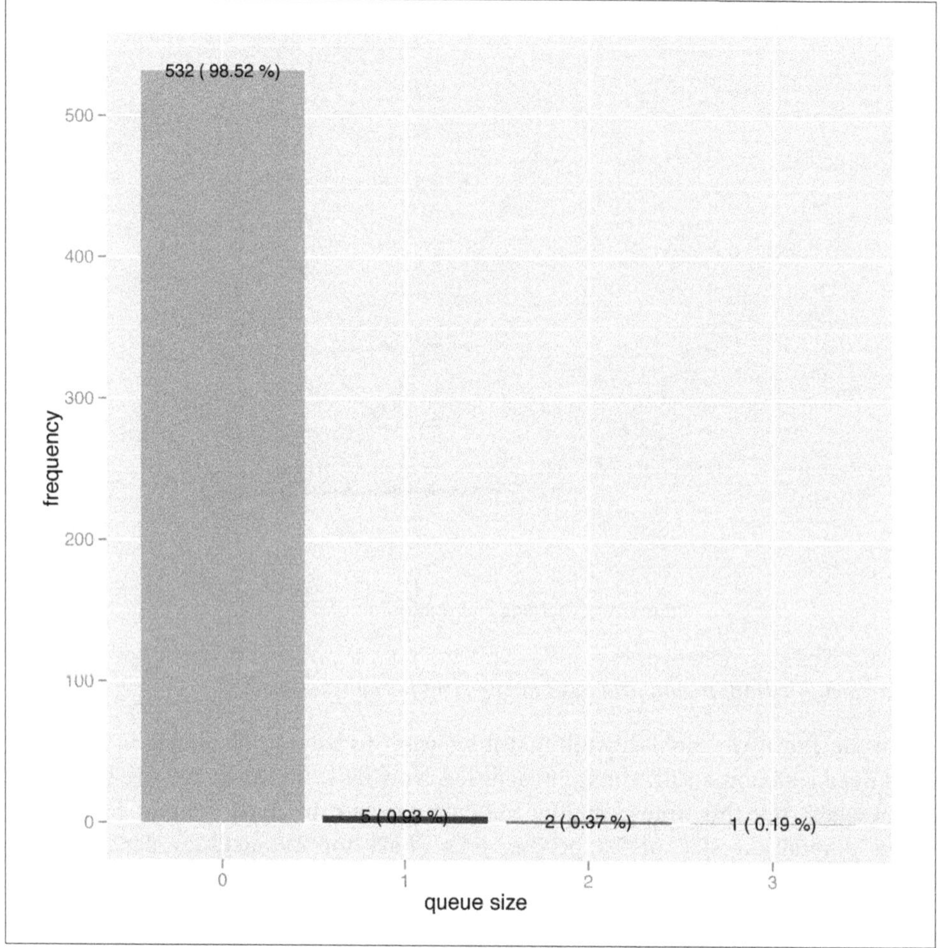

Figure 3-6. Frequency of restroom queues for a restroom with 19 facilities

You might notice a glaring lack of realism in both this simulation and the previous one (besides the people being blobs of software running around in a loop): we have only one restroom, which we scale from a tiny one with a single facility to a mega-restroom with 30 facilities. We'll look into injecting realism in the third simulation covered next.

The Third Simulation

Both of the previous simulations made a few assumptions:

- The probability of going to the restroom is the same for every person (three times within a period of nine hours).
- The probability of any person going to the restroom is the same throughout the whole nine hours of simulation.
- Everyone uses the restroom for exactly one tick (simulating one minute of real time).
- There is only one restroom in the whole office, with all the facilities we need.

This is obviously not realistic. In this third simulation, we are going to tweak our first simulation script to make it more realistic. The changes are:

- The probability of a person going to the restroom is randomly set to one to six times within a period of nine hours.
- The probability of any person going to the restroom during the half-hour before lunch until the half-hour after lunch (two hours in total) is higher than any other time over the period of nine hours.
- A person can use the restroom for a duration of either one or two ticks (any more than that wouldn't be realistic!).
- There are a few restrooms, each with a number of facilities (three in this simulation) and its own queue.

Let's look at the new script in Example 3-10.

Example 3-10. Simulation script 3 (tweaking simulation 1 for realism)

```
require 'rubygems'
require 'csv'
require 'restroom'

max_frequency = 5
max_num_of_restrooms = 1..4
facilities_per_restroom = 3
max_use_duration = 1
population_range = 10..600
```

```
max_num_of_restrooms.each do |num_of_restrooms|
  data = {}
  population_range.step(10).each do |population_size|
    Person.population.clear
    population_size.times { Person.population << Person.new(rand(max_frequency)+1,
                                                     rand(max_use_duration)+1) }
    data[population_size] = []
    restrooms = []
    num_of_restrooms.times {restrooms << Restroom.new(facilities_per_restroom)}

    DURATION.times do |t|
      data[population_size] << restrooms.inject(0) {|n,m| n + m.queue.size }
      restrooms.each {|restroom|
        queue = restroom.queue.clone
        restroom.queue.clear

        unless queue.empty?
          restroom.enter queue.shift
        end
      }

      Person.population.each do |person|
        person.frequency = (t > 270 and t < 390) ? 12 : rand(max_frequency)+1
        if person.need_to_go?
          restroom = restrooms.min {|a,b| a.queue.size <=> b.queue.size}
          restroom.enter person
        end
      end
      restrooms.each {|restroom| restroom.tick }
    end

  end

  CSV.open("simulation3-#{num_of_restrooms}.csv", 'w') do |csv|
    lbl = []
    population_range.step(10).each {|population_size| lbl << population_size }
    csv << lbl

    DURATION.times do |t|
      row = []
      population_range.step(10).each do |population_size|
        row << data[population_size][t]
      end
      csv << row
    end
  end
end
```

Instead of a single frequency, we now have a max_frequency; and instead of use_duration, we now have max_use_duration. We also have a new variable, max_num_of_restrooms, which, of course, describes the maximum number of restrooms.

The simulation runs through four scenarios, each with one, two, three, or four restrooms. Each restroom will have three facilities each. The first change is the way we create `Person` objects to populate the population. Instead of having every `Person` object have the same `frequency` and `use_duration`, we create a population of `Person` objects that have a random `frequency` from 1 to 6 and a random `use_duration` of either 1 or 2.

Next, we have a list of restrooms instead of a single restroom. This means the data collection will also change. Instead of using the queue size of the single restroom, we will look at all the restrooms, find the one with the shortest queue, and use that as the data point. (This is the purpose of the `restrooms.min` call.) Also, instead of clearing a single restroom queue, now we go through all the restrooms and clear each and every queue.

Another change is that the frequency of the `Person` objects will change between the 270th and the 390th ticks. For a period of 120 ticks (2 hours), we increase the frequency of the `Person` object to 12. Also, instead of automatically entering a person into the restroom, we look for the restroom with the shortest queue and move him into that queue.

Finally, since we have four scenarios, we'll be generating four CSV files labeled *simulation3-1.csv* through *simulation3-4.csv*.

After running the simulation, we turn to analyzing the data. Running the simulation script will produce four CSV files. We can't use the same set of R scripts as before because they are for one restroom only. What we want to do is to compare the queue size changes between the scenarios with different numbers of restrooms. However, if we did so, we'd end up with too many variables (the 3 `median`, `mean`, and `max` values × 4 scenarios would produce a chart with 12 lines). Instead, we'll just use the maximum queue size for all four scenarios, as shown in Example 3-11.

Example 3-11. Maximum queue size script for four scenarios

```
library(ggplot2)

df <- function(sim) {
  data <- read.table(paste(sim,".csv",sep=""), header=TRUE, sep=",")
  max  <- apply(data,2,max)
  return(data.frame(population=seq(from=10,to=600,by=10),max=max))
}

ggplot() + scale_shape_manual(name="Type", value=c(2,3,4,22)) +
  geom_smooth(data = df("simulation3-1"), aes(x=population,y=max)) +
  geom_point(data  = df("simulation3-1"), aes(x=population,y=max,shape="max1")) +
  geom_smooth(data = df("simulation3-2"), aes(x=population,y=max)) +
  geom_point(data  = df("simulation3-2"), aes(x=population,y=max,shape="max2")) +
  geom_smooth(data = df("simulation3-3"), aes(x=population,y=max)) +
  geom_point(data  = df("simulation3-3"), aes(x=population,y=max,shape="max3")) +
```

```
geom_smooth(data = df("simulation3-4"), aes(x=population,y=max)) +
geom_point(data  = df("simulation3-4"), aes(x=population,y=max,shape="max4")) +
scale_y_continuous("queue size", breaks=0:35) +
scale_x_continuous("population", breaks=seq(from=10,to=600,by=30))
```

The script is not much different from the ones we used earlier, except that this time, instead of reading the data from a single file and producing a single data frame, we read from four files and produce four different data frames. We also define a function called `df()` to read in a file and return a data frame with the `max` and `population` attributes.

Now that we have four data frames and not just one, we can't put our data points into the `ggplot()` function anymore. Instead, we place them in the geometry functions. Running the script in Example 3-11 will produce Figure 3-7.

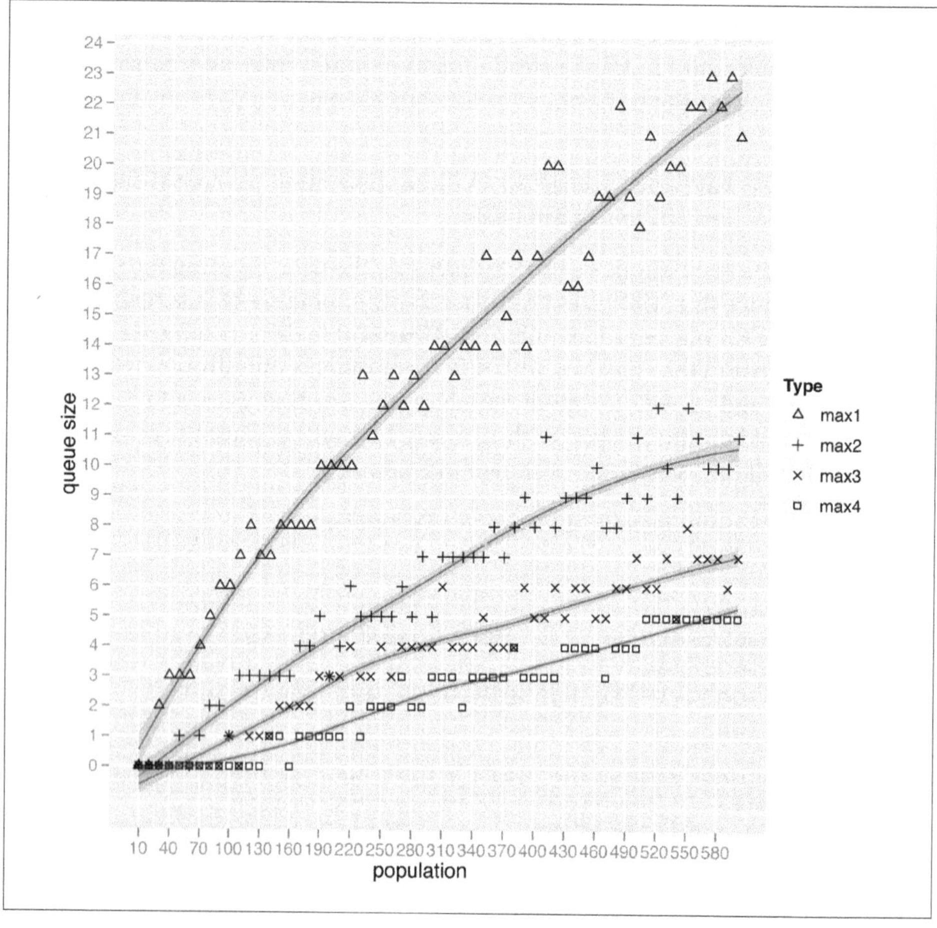

Figure 3-7. Maximum queue sizes for four scenarios in simulation 3

Let's look at the max1 line. This line represents one restroom and three facilities, which is the same as the first simulation but more realistic. So how does injecting more realism into the simulation affect the queue sizes? To find out, we need to compare this with the analysis of the first simulation, specifically Figure 3-2. We run the same script in Example 3-6 but change the filename from *simulation1.csv* to *simulation4-1.csv* to generate the chart in Figure 3-8.

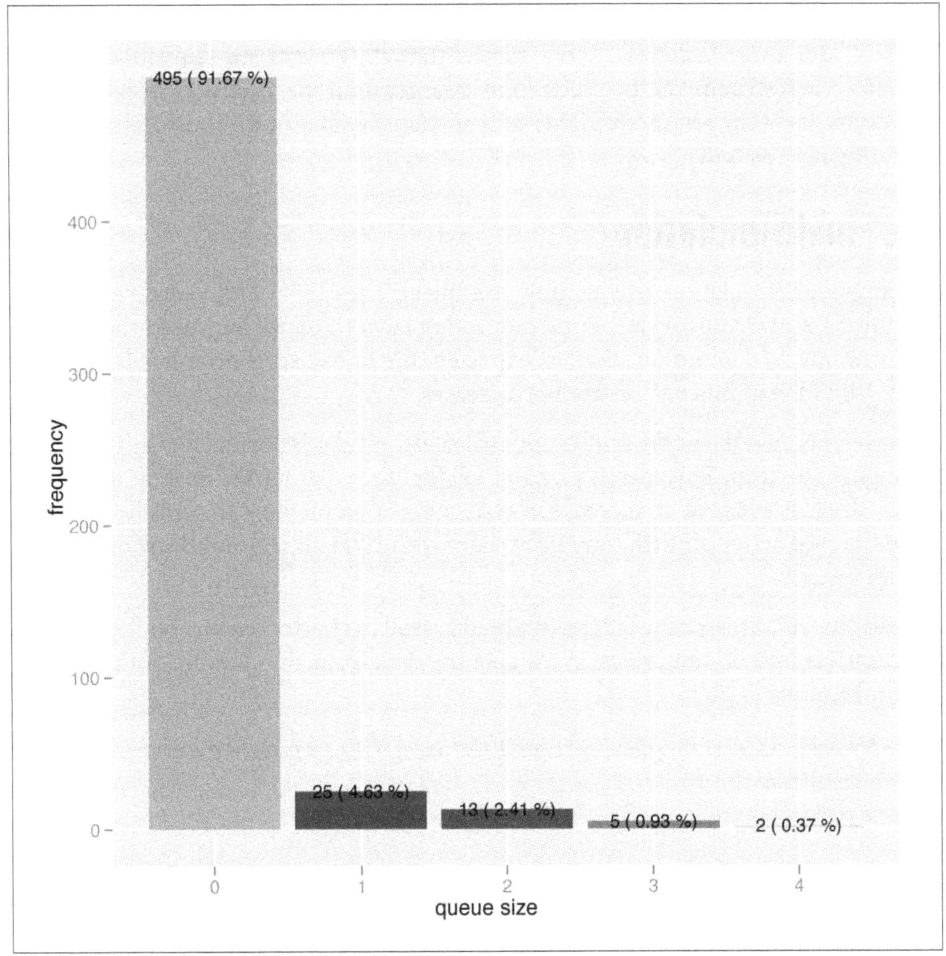

Figure 3-8. Realistic frequency of restroom queues for a population size of 70 people

If we compare Figures 3-8 and 3-4, we can immediately tell that the first simulation was too optimistic. We can see that with more realism in the simulation, the restroom will be empty 92% of the time instead of 99% of the time. We can also see that the maximum queue size is 4 instead of 1. What we can take comfort in, however, is that 92% is still pretty good, and we're in no real danger of bladder apocalypse.

From Figure 3-7, we can also tell that if we have more restrooms, we will have shorter maximum queue sizes given the same population. This is, of course, to be expected because the number of facilities also increases (remember that adding one restroom actually adds three facilities). More subtly, though, we can see that the difference between one restroom and two restrooms is larger than the difference between three restrooms and four restrooms. This tells us that the law of diminishing returns is operating here as well.

The Final Simulation

The previous simulation tells us how the queue sizes look with more realistic assumptions, and we uncovered some interesting facts when we increased the number of restrooms. We found out that, as expected, the queue sizes drop but the returns diminish as the number of restrooms increases.

However, because the number of facilities also increases, it's normal for the maximum queue sizes to drop. This means we can't tell for sure whether the drop in maximum queue size is because of an increase in restrooms or an increase in facilities. In other words, are we better off with, say, 1 restroom with 12 facilities, or 4 restrooms with 3 facilities each?

Intuitively, we'd assume the latter case should result in shorter queues, but let's crunch the numbers and do the charts. We'll take the data from simulation 3 and compare it with Example 3-12.

Example 3-12. Maximum queue size for 1 restroom with 12 facilities versus 4 restrooms with 3 facilities each

```
library(ggplot2)

df <- function(sim) {
  data <- read.table(paste(sim,".csv",sep=""), header=TRUE, sep=",")
  max  <- apply(data,2,max)
  return(data.frame(population=seq(from=10,to=600,by=10),max=max))
}

ggplot() + scale_shape_manual(name="Type", value=c(2,3,4,22)) +
  geom_smooth(data = df("simulation3"), aes(x=population,y=max)) +
  geom_point(data  = df("simulation3"), aes(x=population,y=max,shape="max-1x12")) +
```

```
geom_smooth(data = df("simulation4-4"), aes(x=population,y=max)) +
geom_point(data  = df("simulation4-4"), aes(x=population,y=max,shape="max-4x3")) +
scale_y_continuous("queue size", breaks=0:35) +
scale_x_continuous("population", breaks=seq(from=10,to=600,by=30))
```

If we plot the maximum queue size chart again with these two scenarios side by side, we get Figure 3-9.

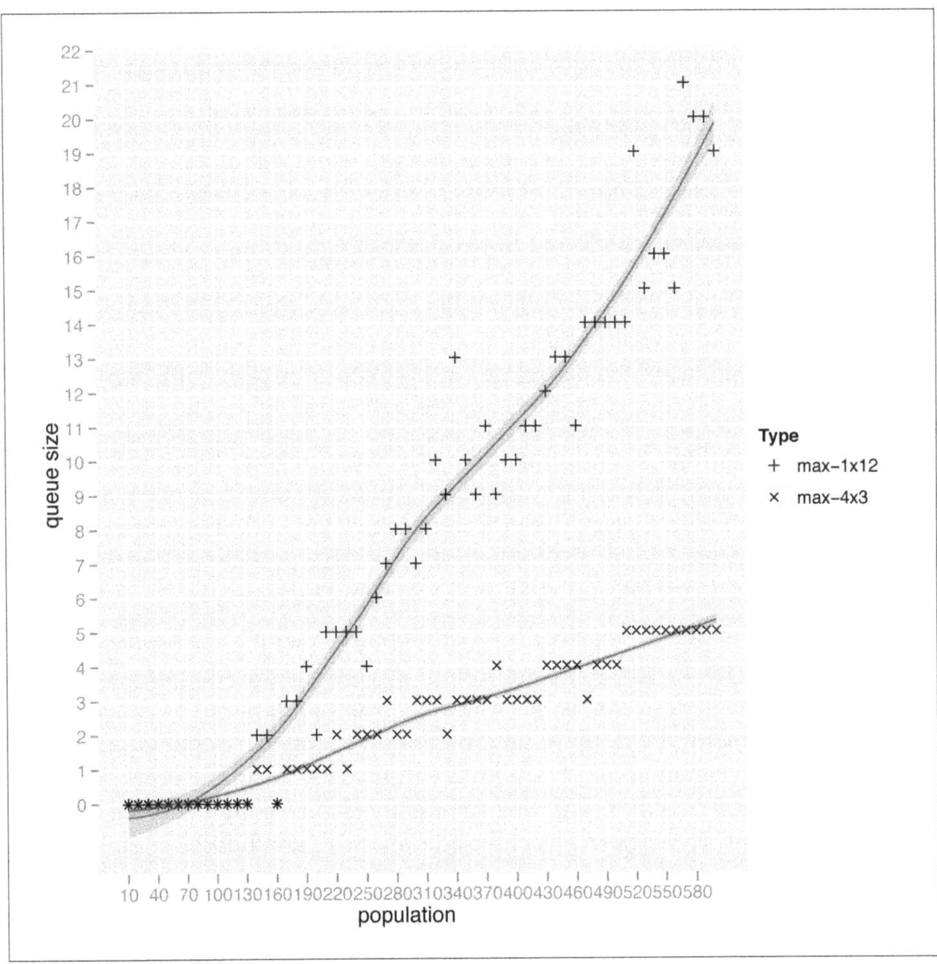

Figure 3-9. Frequency of restroom queues with the two scenarios side by side

You will notice that the maximum queue sizes increase gradually in the scenario with four restrooms, as compared with the scenario with one restroom. Our intuition seems validated, but wait—this is only the maximum queue size. We need one last check.

Let's take a look at the frequency of queue sizes by running Example 3-6 again. We need to run this for a population of 400 people, because smaller populations will not show many differences.

Example 3-13. Frequency of restroom queues for a population of 400 people

```
library(ggplot2)

data <- read.table("simulation3-4.csv", header=TRUE, sep=",")
df <- data.frame(table(data$X400))
colnames(df) <- c("queue_size", "frequency")
percent_labels <- paste(df$frequency, '\n', round(df$frequency*100/540, 2), '%')

ggplot(data=df) + opts(legend.position = "none") +
  geom_bar(aes(x = queue_size, y = frequency, fill = factor(queue_size))) +
  geom_text(aes(x = queue_size, y = frequency, label = percent_labels, size=1)) +
  scale_y_continuous("frequency") +
  scale_x_discrete("queue size")
```

For the scenario of four restrooms with three facilities each, the chart is shown in Figure 3-10.

Now compare this with the scenario of a single restroom with 12 facilities (Figure 3-11).

So what can we conclude by analyzing these two charts? If we're looking for the percentage of time that no restroom queues are formed, it doesn't matter whether we provide 1 restroom with 12 facilities or 4 restrooms with 3 facilities. However, with one restroom, if queues are actually formed, there is a high probability that the queues can get pretty long. With four restrooms, we can avoid long queues.

Having said that, though, it might be surprising to you that the last analysis doesn't really matter. Let's say there are 12 people waiting in the queues. For the first scenario, where there is a single restroom with 12 facilities, the wait time is 12 people divided by 12 facilities, which is 1 tick (or 1 minute). For the second scenario, given that the 12 people are distributed evenly among the 4 restrooms, this means each restroom would have a queue size of 3. The wait time is then three people divided by three facilities, which unsurprisingly turns out to be one tick also. In both scenarios, despite the length of the queue, the wait time remains the same!

The moral of the story here is that sometimes we tend to go overboard when we try too hard to analyze our data. It's always good to take a wider view or look at the data from a different perspective, and check whether the analysis is realistic.

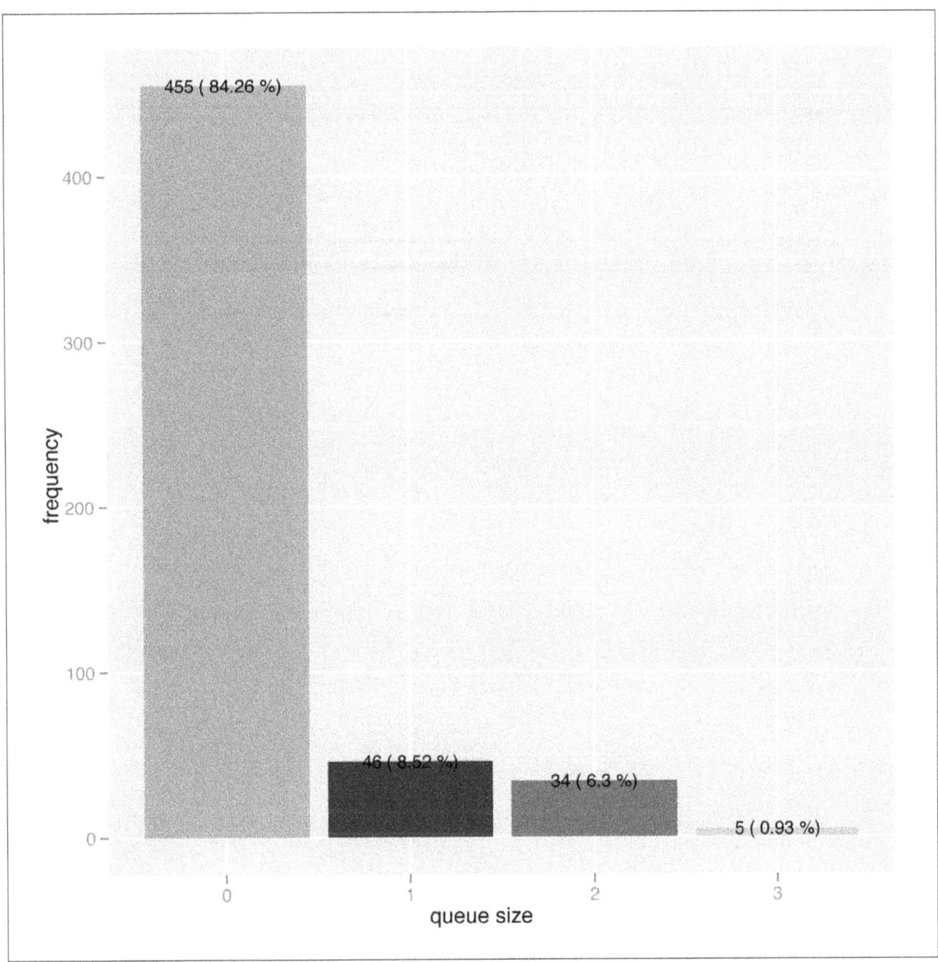

Figure 3-10. Frequency of restroom queues for the scenario of four restrooms with three facilities each

Wrap-up

Needless to say, it's a great relief to be proven wrong! The building people knew what they were doing and so did the HSE. An office of 70 male engineers can indeed be supported by a single restroom with 3 urinals.

We started with a simple simulation to make sure our models made sense. We built models that represented the restroom, the facilities, and the people using them, and then ran a simulated, simplified sequence of events. The end result was reasonable.

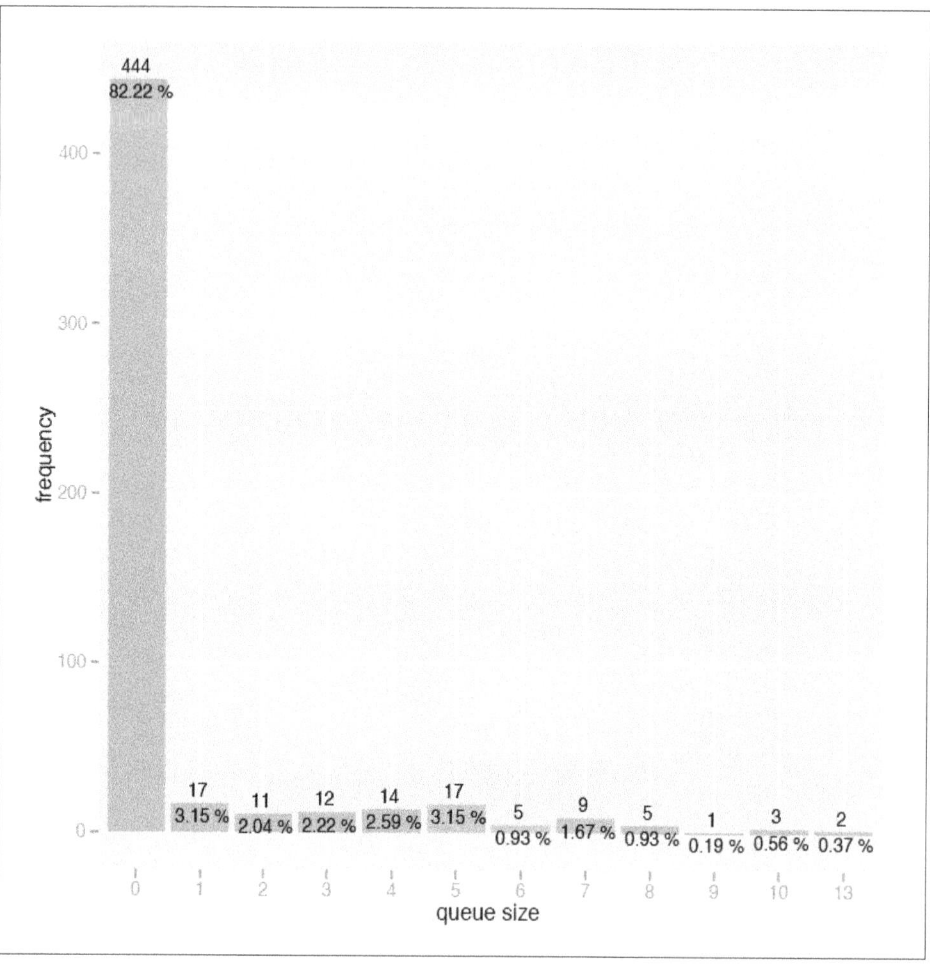

Figure 3-11. Frequency of restroom queues for the scenario of 1 restroom with 12 facilities

Next, we turned the simulation on its head and asked how many facilities a restroom should have to support 1,000 people in the office. With some tweaking of our simulation script, we managed to get a reasonable result again.

The third simulation attempted to inject more realism into the first simulation by changing a number of variables and including randomness in those variables. We also increased the number of restrooms in the simulations from one to four. This simulation made a lot more sense than the first one, as it mirrored reasonable behavior of people in the office. The results from this simulation were also more realistic.

Finally, we compared whether it was better to have a single restroom with 12 facilities, or 4 restrooms with 3 facilities each. The answer was surprisingly not as straightforward as expected. It turns out that the probability of having no restroom queues at all is the same for both scenarios, while the difference is that the maximum queue size for the former is much longer than that of the latter. However, we ended with a cautionary note not to overanalyze data, because taking a different perspective of the data sometimes reveals the foolishness of going overboard with our analysis.

This chapter described basic techniques that you can use in simulating everyday activities. You might want to do this for more serious work (the second simulation in this chapter, for example, would be useful if you want to determine the number of restrooms and facilities you need when you set up a large office), but it can also be used to simply explore the world around you. The techniques and the technologies are just tools to unlock your imagination.

CHAPTER 4

How to Be an Armchair Economist

I love reading popular science, a hobby that stems from a happy childhood encounter with Isaac Asimov's "science fact" books after I'd consumed all of his science fiction ones in the local library. I was a voracious reader, and soon my interests spilled over to other types of books, such as Martin Gardner's mathematics books and Stephen Jay Gould's biology books. While I didn't necessarily fully understand the science behind them all, the material was fascinating enough for me to develop a lifelong passion for such writing.

Nestled among my science books is a particular genre of popular writing that equally and frequently brought me wonder and amazement—popular economics books. No doubt the first book that probably flashed through your mind is the immensely popular and widely read *Freakonomics* (William Morrow). While that's a great book, the one book on popular economics that always tops my list (and I readily admit it might be entirely due to the mental image I get when I think of the title) is the *Armchair Economist* by Stephen E. Landsburg (Free Press).

Something from the *Armchair Economist* that stuck in my mind for a long time, eventually blossoming into this book, is how Landsburg described economics:

> Economics is...about observing the world with genuine curiosity and admitting that it is full of mysteries....Sometimes the mysteries themselves...are hard to solve, so we practice by trying to solve similar mysteries in fictional worlds that we invent and call models.

In this chapter, we explore how to model some very basic economic theories and then investigate how they work.

The Invisible Hand

Economists sometimes ask a rhetorical and seemingly silly question: "Who feeds Paris?"[1] The Parisians themselves, of course; who else? However, neither the question nor the answer is straightforward. There is a lot more to it than meets the eye.

During the days of the Soviet Union and the Cold War, the story goes, a Soviet official visited the United States and went into a supermarket. The brightly lit aisles were filled with all kinds of products from peanut butter to gardening tools. "Very impressive," said the official. "But how can you make sure that all the supermarkets have all these items?"

While we might laugh at the official's lack of understanding of market economy, you can probably find a parallel in the question of who feeds Paris. You've probably never heard of the Parisian sidewalk cafes running out of coffee, so how do they know what kind of coffee, and how much, to stock? How do the fashion boutiques know which clothes to stock and how much to sell them for? How does Darty (a French electronics chain) know which are the best mobile phones to sell?

These questions are answered succinctly by 18th-century Scottish economist and social philosopher Adam Smith. His book *An Inquiry into the Nature and Causes of the Wealth of Nations* (excerpted here) is considered the first modern work of economics, while he himself is often regarded as the father of economics:

> It is not from the benevolence of the butcher, the brewer or the baker, that we expect our dinner, but from their regard to their own interest. We address ourselves, not to their humanity but to their self-love, and never talk to them of our own necessities but of their advantages.

Smith coined the metaphor of the "invisible hand" to label this natural inclination, effectively describing what we know today as the market economy. In this chapter, we will simulate a market economy to see if we can observe the invisible hand in action.

A Simple Market Economy

First, let's take stock of the different roles and features of an ideal market economy (which are what we want to simulate).

Producers
: The people who produce the goods. Producers create the goods and sell them to the consumers at a price.

1. This question originated in economist Charles Wheelan's 2002 book *Naked Economics* (W. W. Norton & Company).

Consumers
: The people who consume the goods created by the producers. Consumers buy goods from producers at a price.

Price
: This is the value at which producers agree to exchange goods with consumers. The price is set by each producer.

Supply
: The amount of goods generated by the producers.

Demand
: The amount of goods that the consumers want to buy.

Market
: The overall ecosystem of buying and selling goods from and to producers and consumers.

In this idealized market economy, we will have the producers creating goods and selling them to consumers for a price. Each producer sets his own price.

The consumers, in turn, buy goods from the producer. However, this happens only if the consumer thinks the price is reasonable. Consumers have a certain amount of demand and will buy to fulfill that demand. In addition, consumers can buy from any producer, and will buy from the producer who sells at the cheapest price first.

The Producer

We start off our exercise with the producer. The `Producer` class is a rather simple one, as shown in Example 4-1.

Example 4-1. Producer class

```
class Producer
  attr_accessor :supply, :price
  def initialize
    @supply, @price = 0, 0
  end

  def generate_goods
   @supply += SUPPLY_INCREMENT if @price > COST
  end

  def produce
    if @supply > 0
      @price *= PRICE_DECREMENT unless @price < COST
```

```
    else
      @price *= PRICE_INCREMENT
      generate_goods
    end
  end
end
```

Producer has two variables: supply, which is the amount of unsold goods that the producer has at that moment, and price, which is the price she wants to sell the goods for. Both are initialized to 0 when the Producer class is first instantiated.

The Producer class also has a produce method that, well, produces the goods and sets the price:

```
def produce
  if @supply > 0
    @price *= PRICE_DECREMENT unless @price < COST
  else
    @price *= PRICE_INCREMENT
    generate_goods
  end
end
```

While the price is presumably set immediately after instantiation, we want to change the price accordingly to be more competitive with the other producers in the same market. To do this, we multiply the current price with either a PRICE_DECREMENT or PRICE_INCREMENT multiplier. Whether to increase or reduce the price depends on how well the goods have sold in the past.

If all the goods have been sold, this means they were well received, so the producer will want to make more—by calling the generate_goods method—and also increase the price slightly, to generate more profit.

If that's not the case, and there are still unsold goods, the producer will want to make them more attractive by dropping the price a little. Naturally, she will not decrease the price if it's below the cost of generating the goods, indicated by the constant COST.

The Producer class also has an instance method, generate_goods, which will create the goods. As mentioned earlier, this is called only if the producer's supply runs out:

```
def generate_goods
 @supply += SUPPLY_INCREMENT if Market.average_price > COST
end
```

The generate_goods method increases the amount of goods by adding on to its current supply a SUPPLY_INCREMENT amount. Of course, this happens only if the price is more than the cost of generating the goods.

The Consumer

Next is the consumer. The `Consumer` class, shown in Example 4-2, is an even simpler beast. It has only one purpose: to consume the goods up to the level of its demand.

Example 4-2. Consumer class

```
class Consumer
  attr_accessor :demands

  def initialize
    @demands = 0
  end

  def buy
    until @demands <= 0 or Market.supply <= 0
      cheapest_producer = Market.cheapest_producer
      if cheapest_producer
        @demands *= 0.5 if cheapest_producer.price > MAX_ACCEPTABLE_PRICE
        cheapest_supply = cheapest_producer.supply
        if @demands > cheapest_supply
          @demands -= cheapest_supply
          cheapest_producer.supply = 0
        else
          cheapest_producer.supply -= @demands
          @demands = 0
        end
      end
    end
  end
end
```

The `Consumer` class has a single variable, `demands`, which indicates the amount of goods it requires to fulfill its needs. The main method for the `Consumer` class is `buy`. When the `buy` method is called, the consumer will continue to buy goods until his demand is met or the supply in the whole market runs out.

Each consumer first looks for the cheapest producer and buys as much as it can from her. When the consumer buys from the producer, the producer's supply decreases and the demand also decreases accordingly. If the supplies run out first, the consumer buys from the next producer until his demand is satiated.

However, the consumer is not a buying machine. If the cheapest price is higher than the maximum acceptable price set by the constant `MAX_ACCEPTABLE_PRICE`, the consumer's demand is reduced by half.

Some Convenience Methods

Before we get into the simulation script, we're going to create some convenience methods. We'll define all of these convenience methods as static methods in a Market class, as shown in Example 4-3.

Example 4-3. Market class

```
class Market
  def self.average_price
    ($producers.inject(0.0) { |memo, producer| memo + producer.price}/
                                 $producers.size).round(2)
  end

  def self.supply
    $producers.inject(0) { |memo, producer| memo + producer.supply }
  end

  def self.demand
    $consumers.inject(0) { |memo, consumer| memo + consumer.demands }
  end

  def self.cheapest_producer
    producers = $producers.find_all {|f| f.supply > 0}
    producers.min_by{|f| f.price}
  end
end
```

The first of these convenience methods is `average_price`. We will be using this method to get the average price of the goods based on the prices from all the producers. Next are the `supply` and `demand` methods, which return the collective amounts of goods and demands of all the producers and all the consumers, respectively. Finally, we have a `cheapest_producer` method, which returns the cheapest producer. We determine this by finding all the producers who still have goods, comparing them by price, and returning the one with the cheapest price.

The Simulation

Now that we have all the pieces in place, let's get to the simulation. To prepare for it, we need to first create the population of producers and consumers, as shown in Example 4-4.

Example 4-4. Populating the simulation

```
$producers = []
NUM_OF_PRODUCERS.times do
  producer = Producer.new
  producer.price = COST + rand(MAX_STARTING_PROFIT)
  producer.supply = rand(MAX_STARTING_SUPPLY)
  $producers << producer
end
```

```
$consumers = []
NUM_OF_CONSUMERS.times do
  $consumers << Consumer.new
end

$generated_demand  = []
SIMULATION_DURATION.times {|n| $generated_demand << ((Math.sin(n)+2)*20).round  }
```

We store the producers in the global array `$producers` and the consumers in the global array `$consumers`. Each producer is created with a randomly generated price that is higher than the cost of producing the goods (`COST`), as well as a randomly generated amount of goods. We don't do anything to the consumers that are created at this point; we'll get to them in the simulation loop later.

We'll also create a fluctuating generated demand and store that in the `$generated_demand` variable. This will be used during the simulation to represent the fluctuation of demand over a period of time. This generated demand roughly follows a sine wave.

The simulation loop is shown in Example 4-5. Before we actually go into the loop, we prepare two empty arrays: `demand_supply` and `price_demand`. These are used to store the values generated from the simulation. The names of each array indicate what it contains; the `demand_supply` array stores the changes of demand versus supply of goods over the simulation period, while the `price_demand` array stores the changes of price versus demand over the same period.

Example 4-5. Simulation loop

```
SIMULATION_DURATION.times do |t|
  $consumers.each do |consumer|
    consumer.demands = $generated_demand[t]
  end
  demand_supply << [t, Market.demand, Market.supply]

  $producers.each do |producer|
    producer.produce
  end

  price_demand << [t, Market.average_price, Market.demand]

  until Market.demand == 0 or Market.supply == 0 do
    $consumers.each do |consumer|
      consumer.buy
    end
  end
end

write("demand_supply", demand_supply)
write("price_demand", price_demand)
```

The simulation is a loop that runs SIMULATION_DURATION times and executes a series of producer and consumer actions.

At the start of the loop, we set every consumer's demand to be a point in the demand curve in $generated_demand. Before we start with the producer, we populate the demand_supply array with the current market demand and supply. Then we loop through each producer and get her to create and set the price of goods by calling the produce method. This randomly generates the price of goods for each producer.

After that and before looping through each consumer, we populate the price_demand array with the average price of goods and the market demand. Finally, we loop through each consumer and get him to buy. We add in an extra loop to make sure all the demands are met unless the supply of goods runs out first. With this, we end a single simulation loop.

At the end of SIMULATION_DURATION loops, we use the write method to write the data to a CSV file, which we will use to analyze our simulation next (see Example 4-6).

Example 4-6. The write method

```
def write(name,data)
  CSV.open("#{name}.csv", 'w') do |csv|
    data.each do |row|
      csv << row
    end
  end
end
```

The write method simply uses the CSV library built into Ruby 1.9 and creates a file for writing, then loops through the given data array, writing each item of the array as a line in the CSV file.

Last, before we run the simulation to generate the files, let's look at the constants that we referred to in the simulation but whose values we never really examined (Example 4-7). This is not exactly exciting new stuff, but it will help us understand the values of the analysis later on.

Example 4-7. Constants used in the simulation

```
SIMULATION_DURATION = 150
NUM_OF_PRODUCERS = 10
NUM_OF_CONSUMERS = 10

MAX_STARTING_SUPPLY = 20
SUPPLY_INCREMENT = 80

COST = 5
MAX_ACCEPTABLE_PRICE = COST * 10
MAX_STARTING_PROFIT = 5
PRICE_INCREMENT = 1.1
PRICE_DECREMENT = 0.9
```

In Example 4-7, you can see that we will be running the simulation for 150 ticks with 10 producers and 10 consumers. The starting supply for the producers is somewhere between 0 and 20, while at each tick, depending on whether the supply runs out in the previous tick or not, each producer creates 80 units of goods at a cost of $5 each.

For the consumer, the maximum acceptable price of the goods is a multiple of the cost of the goods; for the producer, the starting profits are not more than $5 above the cost. Finally, the price of the goods increases or decreases by 10% each tick.

Now we can finally run the simulation, which should finish quite quickly. You should end up with two files, *demand_supply.csv* and *price_demand.csv*. We'll be using these two files in the next section when we inspect the results of our simulation.

Analyzing the Simulation

As in Chapter 3, we'll be using R scripts to chart and analyze the patterns of the data we've just generated from our simulation. However, our approaches will differ slightly. In Chapter 3, we were investigating the results of a simulation, while here we are trying to simulate and re-enact an existing effect. In other words, we didn't know the actual answers to the questions we were asking when we ran the Monte Carlo simulations in Chapter 3, but we *do* know what the results should be here.

Let's take a look at the first data file we generated, *demand_supply.csv*. It has three columns; the first is a point in time, the second is the demand of the goods at that point in time, and the third is the supply of the goods at that time. We'll grab this file, parse it, and generate two line charts—one superimposed on the other (see Example 4-8).

Example 4-8. Analyzing the demand and supply

```
library(ggplot2)
data <- read.table("demand_supply.csv", header=F, sep=",")

pdf("demand_supply.pdf")
ggplot(data = data) + scale_color_grey(name="Legend") +
  geom_line(aes(x  = V1, y = V2, color = "demand")) +
  geom_line(aes(x  = V1, y = V3, color = "supply")) +
  scale_y_continuous("amount") +
  scale_x_continuous("time")

dev.off()
```

As in Chapter 3, we use the `ggplot2` library first, then read in the data from the CSV file. The three columns—time, demand, and supply—are automatically labeled V1, V2, and V3. We use `ggplot` to create the base data plot, then set the scale color to `grayscale`. Next, we attach two `geom_lines` that set the necessary x- and y-axes with the correct data column. Finally, we add in the x- and y-axis labels.

We predetermined the demand pattern, which should be almost a sine wave, though sharper since we rounded off the numbers (see Figure 4-1). What interests us is the supply pattern. If the basic theories of economics are right and we've coded the simulation correctly, then the supply of the goods should fall when the demand increases, and vice versa. If you look at Figure 4-1, you will see this same pattern, so it's relief all around.

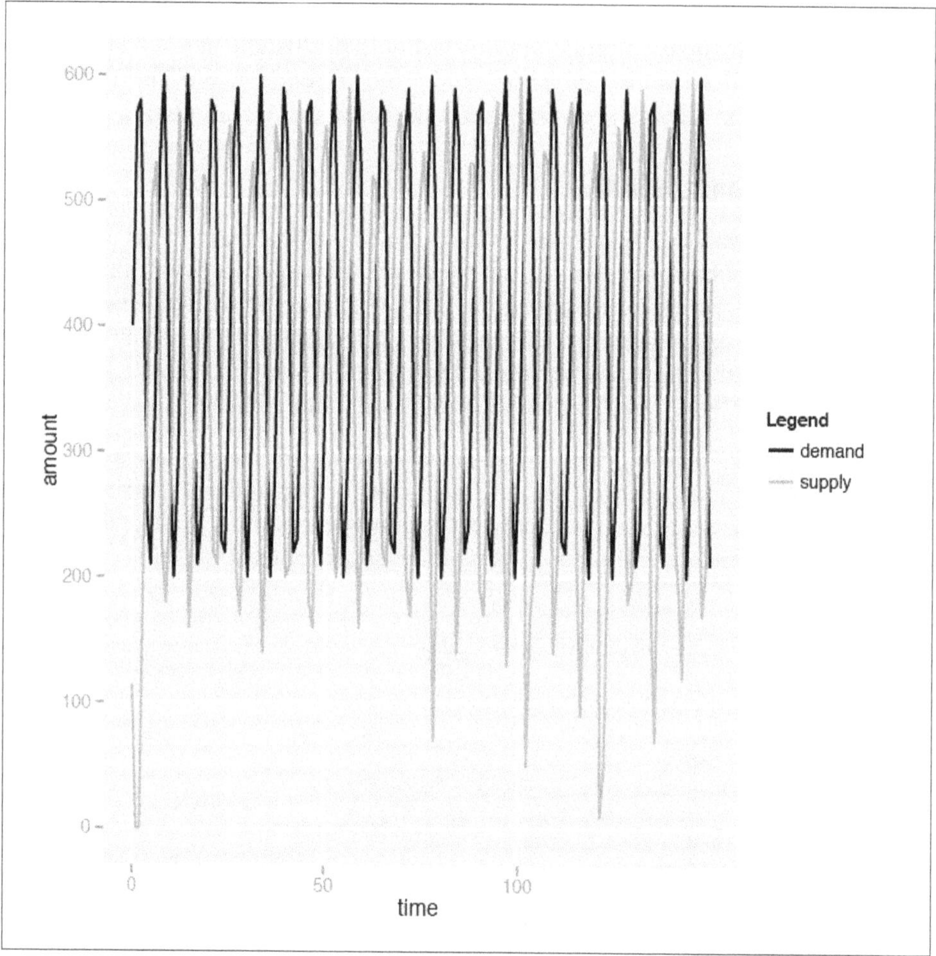

Figure 4-1. Demand and supply

This might seem obvious, but if you take a second look at the `Producer` and `Consumer` classes, you'll see that neither the produce nor the buy logic hinge on each other. The produce logic generates more goods only if the supplies are all sold out. The producer doesn't produce to meet the demands of the consumer; she produces when her own supplies run out.

Similarly, the buy logic chooses the cheapest goods and consumes until the demand is satiated (we added in the mechanism to stop when the supply in the market runs out, to prevent an infinite loop). The consumer doesn't care about the supply of the goods; he cares only about the price of the goods and will consume until his demands are satisfied or the goods become too expensive.

Let's take a look at the second data file, *price_demand.csv*. It has three columns again—the first is a point in time, the second is the average price of goods from all producers, and the third is the overall market demand. In Example 4-9, we do pretty much the same thing as in Example 4-8.

Example 4-9. Analyzing the price and demand

```
library(ggplot2)
data <- read.table("price_demand.csv", header=F, sep=",")

pdf("price_demand.pdf")
ggplot(data = data) + scale_color_grey(name="Legend") +
  geom_line(aes(x  = V1, y = V2, color = "price")) +
  geom_line(aes(x  = V1, y = log2(V3)-3, color = "demand")) +
    scale_y_continuous("amount") +
    scale_x_continuous("time")

dev.off()
```

There is a difference in charting the price, though. We take the logarithm of the demand to base 2 and chart that instead of the actual demand. Why do we do that? It's because if we charted the actual demand value, we would not be able to see how the price relates to the demand, and vice versa, as the scale of the demand is much higher than that of the price.

We can make a couple of quick observations from the chart in Figure 4-2. First, we can see that the peak price of goods follows after the peak demand. Similarly, the price is lowest after the demand has fallen to its lowest.

Second, while the price fluctuates with the demand, it actually decreases over time until it stabilizes at a price between $5 and $5.50. Notice this corresponds with the cost of creating goods, which we set at $5 at the beginning of the simulation. The logic in the `Producer` class's `produce` method prevents the price from ever dropping below the cost. This is the reason why the price stabilizes at around $5. But why does the price drop at all?

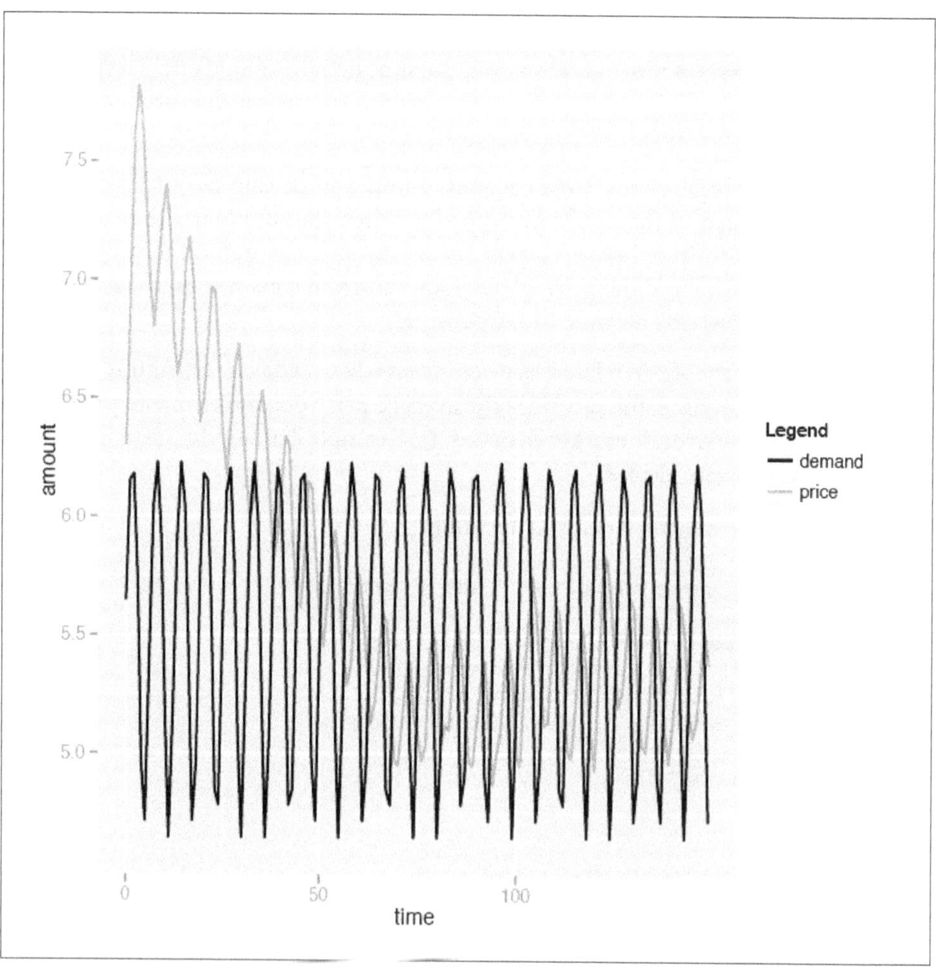

Figure 4-2. Price and demand

This is due to the market economy again. Remember that the consumer always buys the cheapest goods first. This means the producer with the higher prices will have unsold goods, which in turn forces the prices to go down. The end results are that the average price goes down until it nears the cost of producing the goods. Finally, we see the invisible hand! The invisible hand of Adam Smith has weighed in on our simulation and pushed the prices down.

Now that we have witnessed the invisible hand and charted its effects, let's get slightly more complicated.

Resource Allocation by Price

In the previous simulation, every producer creates only one type of goods, which we imaginatively called goods. This, of course, is not realistic (nothing modeled in economics is realistic, but that's a different point). In our next simulation, we will have producers creating two types of goods. These producers are farmers who can rear chickens or ducks on their farms. These farmers will rear either animal depending on the profits they can get in return for it. There is no cost to switching animals, and the farmers will remorselessly switch at a slightest hint of a profit to be earned.

What we want to investigate is the relationship between the prices of ducks and chickens, as well as the relationship between the supply of ducks and chickens over time. Let's look at changes we'll need to make to our simulation.

The Producer

We start off with the Producer class, which as you might have guessed, has the most changes, as shown in Example 4-10.

Example 4-10. Producer class for second simulation

```
class Producer
  attr_accessor :supply, :price
  def initialize
    @supply, @supply[:chickens], @supply[:ducks] = {}, 0, 0
    @price, @price[:chickens], @price[:ducks] = {}, 0, 0
  end

  def change_pricing
    @price.each do |type, price|
      if @supply[type] > 0
        @price[type] *= PRICE_DECREMENT unless @price[type] < COST[type]
      else
        @price[type] *= PRICE_INCREMENT
      end
    end
  end

  def generate_goods
    to_produce = Market.average_price(:chickens) > Market.average_price(:ducks) ?
        :chickens : :ducks
    @supply[to_produce] += (SUPPLY_INCREMENT) if @price[to_produce] > COST[to_produce]
  end

  def produce
    change_pricing
    generate_goods
  end
end
```

The first change you'll observe is that while we still have the supply and price variables, they are no longer integers but are in fact hashes, with the key being either chickens or ducks. Next, the generate_goods method is slightly different. The farmer will only produce either chickens or ducks depending on the prices. If the average market price of duck is higher, she'll produce more ducks, and if the average market price of chicken is higher, she'll produce more chickens.

Notice that in Example 4-1 in the previous simulation, the produce method changes the pricing, then calls the generate_goods method to generate the goods. In this simulation, the Producer class has a separate method named changed_pricing that will iterate through the prices of both chickens and ducks and check if there is any unsold poultry left. If there is, the farmer will lower the price in the hope that it can get sold more easily.

Finally, the produce method in this simulation is a simple one that just calls change_pricing and then generates the goods.

The Consumer

The changes to the Consumer class, as shown in Example 4-11, are done in the same way as the Producer class.

Example 4-11. Consumer class for the second simulation

```
class Consumer
  attr_accessor :demands

  def initialize
    @demands = 0
  end

  def buy(type)
    until @demands <= 0 or Market.supply(type) <= 0
      cheapest_producer = Market.cheapest_producer(type)
      if cheapest_producer
        @demands *= 0.5 if cheapest_producer.price[type] > MAX_ACCEPTABLE_PRICE[type]
        cheapest_supply = cheapest_producer.supply[type]
        if @demands > cheapest_supply then
          @demands -= cheapest_supply
          cheapest_producer.supply[type] = 0
        else
          cheapest_producer.supply[type] -= @demands
          @demands = 0
        end
      end
    end
  end
end
```

The main difference is in the buy method, which now takes in a parameter. This parameter is the type of poultry the consumer wants to buy—either chickens or ducks. Notice that the demands variable is not a hash, unlike in the Producer class. This is because the demands of the consumer can be met by either chickens or ducks. In fact, as you will see in a while, the consumer will choose the cheaper of the two to buy since either one of them can satisfy his needs.

Market

As in Example 4-3 in the previous simulation, we have a number of convenience methods that we place as static methods in the Market class in Example 4-12.

Example 4-12. Market class for the second simulation

```
class Market
  def self.average_price(type)
    ($producers.inject(0.0) { |memo, producer| memo + producer.price[type]}/
                             $producers.size).round(2)
  end

  def self.supply(type)
    $producers.inject(0) { |memo, producer| memo + producer.supply[type] }
  end

  def self.demands
    $consumers.inject(0) { |memo, consumer| memo + consumer.demands }
  end

  def self.cheaper(a,b)
    cheapest_a_price = $producers.min_by {|f| f.price[a]}.price[a]
    cheapest_b_price = $producers.min_by {|f| f.price[b]}.price[b]
    cheapest_a_price < cheapest_b_price ? a : b
  end

  def self.cheapest_producer(type)
    producers = $producers.find_all {|producer| producer.supply[type] > 0}
    producers.min_by{|producer| producer.price[type]}
  end
end
```

Except for the cheaper method, other methods are simply variants of the previous simulation that take in the type of poultry as the input parameter. The cheaper method performs a simple comparison by taking the cheapest chicken from the producer with the lowest price and comparing it with the cheapest duck, after which it returns either chickens or ducks.

The Simulation

This second simulation is only slighly more complex than the previous one. As in Example 4-4 in the previous simulation, we need to set up the population of producers and consumers before we start the simulation (Example 4-13).

Example 4-13. Populating the second simulation

```
$producers = []
NUM_OF_PRODUCERS.times do
  producer = Producer.new
  producer.price[:chickens] = COST[:chickens] + rand(MAX_STARTING_PROFIT[:chickens])
  producer.price[:ducks]    = COST[:ducks] + rand(MAX_STARTING_PROFIT[:ducks])
  producer.supply[:chickens] = rand(MAX_STARTING_SUPPLY[:chickens])
  producer.supply[:ducks]    = rand(MAX_STARTING_SUPPLY[:ducks])
  $producers << producer
end

$consumers = []
NUM_OF_CONSUMERS.times do
  $consumers << Consumer.new
end

$generated_demand  = []
SIMULATION_DURATION.times {|n| $generated_demand << ((Math.sin(n)+2)*20).round }
```

This is not much different from the previous setup, except now we need to set the price and initial starting supply of both chickens and ducks for every producer. When that's done, we're ready to start the simulation, as shown in Example 4-14.

Example 4-14. The second simulation loop

```
price_data, supply_data = [], []
SIMULATION_DURATION.times do |t|
  $consumers.each do |consumer|
    consumer.demands = $generated_demand[t]
  end
  supply_data << [t, Market.supply(:chickens), Market.supply(:ducks)]
  $producers.each do |producer|
    producer.produce
  end
  cheaper_type = Market.cheaper(:chickens, :ducks)
  until Market.demands == 0 or Market.supply(cheaper_type) == 0  do
    $consumers.each do |consumer|
      consumer.buy cheaper_type
    end
  end
  price_data << [t, Market.average_price(:chickens), Market.average_price(:ducks)]
end

write("price_data", price_data)
write("supply_data", supply_data)
```

As in Example 4-5, we start off the loop by setting the demands of the consumers according to the generated demand curve we created during the setup. Then we iterate through each producer to get her to produce.

Here's where this simulation differs from the previous one. While Example 4-5 simply iterates through each consumer and calls on the buy method, in Example 4-14 we need to first find out which is cheaper — chickens or ducks. Then, we iterate through each consumer and get the consumer to buy the cheaper goods.

Before we run the second simulation, let's look at the parameters we will be running it with (Example 4-15).

Example 4-15. Parameters for the second simulation

```
SIMULATION_DURATION = 150
NUM_OF_PRODUCERS = 10
NUM_OF_CONSUMERS = 10

MAX_STARTING_SUPPLY = Hash.new
MAX_STARTING_SUPPLY[:ducks] = 20
MAX_STARTING_SUPPLY[:chickens] = 20
SUPPLY_INCREMENT = 60

COST = Hash.new
COST[:ducks] = 12
COST[:chickens] = 12

MAX_ACCEPTABLE_PRICE = Hash.new
MAX_ACCEPTABLE_PRICE[:ducks] = COST[:ducks] * 10
MAX_ACCEPTABLE_PRICE[:chickens] = COST[:chickens] * 10

MAX_STARTING_PROFIT = Hash.new
MAX_STARTING_PROFIT[:ducks] = 15
MAX_STARTING_PROFIT[:chickens] = 15
PRICE_INCREMENT = 1.1
PRICE_DECREMENT = 0.9
```

Most of these parameters should be familiar to you by now, except that instead of using integers, we have a hash of values with the poultry type being the key. We will run the simulation with the values of cost, maximum acceptable price, and starting profit the same for both chickens and ducks.

Finally, as before, we write the data collected during the simulation loop to CSV files. In this simulation, we collect both the prices as well as the market supply of chickens and ducks. At the end of the simulation, we should have two files: *price_data.csv* and *supply_data.csv*.

Analyzing the Second Simulation

We want to investigate the relationship between chickens and ducks in terms of the price and the amount of goods in this analysis. Let's start with the amount first. Logically speaking, since the two types of poultry are in competition with each other, the two amounts of goods should be at opposite ends of the spectrum. In other words, when the supply of chickens is increasing, the supply of ducks should be decreasing. This is because as more consumers buy chickens, more duck farmers switch to chicken farming since it's more lucrative. As the consumer demand we specified in the model fluctuates, there is a corresponding supply fluctuation in our simulation—that is, when the supply of chickens is high, the supply of ducks will be low.

Let's look at the R script that we will run to analyze the data, shown in Example 4-16.

Example 4-16. Comparing the supply of chickens against the supply of ducks

```
library(ggplot2)
data <- read.table("supply_data.csv", header=F, sep=",")

ggplot(data = data) + scale_color_grey(name="Supply") +
  geom_line(aes(x  = V1, y = V2, color = "chickens")) +
  geom_line(aes(x  = V1, y = V3, color = "ducks")) +
  scale_y_continuous("amount") +
  scale_x_continuous("time")
```

This should be familiar now since it's almost exactly the same as the previous scripts. See the chart in Figure 4-3 for a closer look.

No surprises here. We can see that the supply of chickens and ducks alternates in highs and lows, confirming our earlier analysis. Next, we look at the comparison between the price of chickens and ducks. Just as with supply, we can guess that the prices will also alternate between chickens and ducks. This is because when the price of chickens goes up, more consumers will start buying ducks instead of chickens in the next turn. This will cause the duck supply to run low and the producers to increase their prices to maximize profit. In that same turn, though, because consumers are now buying ducks, the producers have no choice but to decrease the price of chickens.

Let's look at the R script in Example 4-17.

Example 4-17. Comparing the prices of chickens and ducks

```
library(ggplot2)
data <- read.table("price_data.csv", header=F, sep=",")

ggplot(data = data) + scale_color_grey(name="Average price") +
  geom_line(aes(x  = V1, y = V2, color = "chickens")) +
  geom_line(aes(x  = V1, y = V3, color = "ducks")) +
  scale_y_continuous("price") +
  scale_x_continuous("time")
```

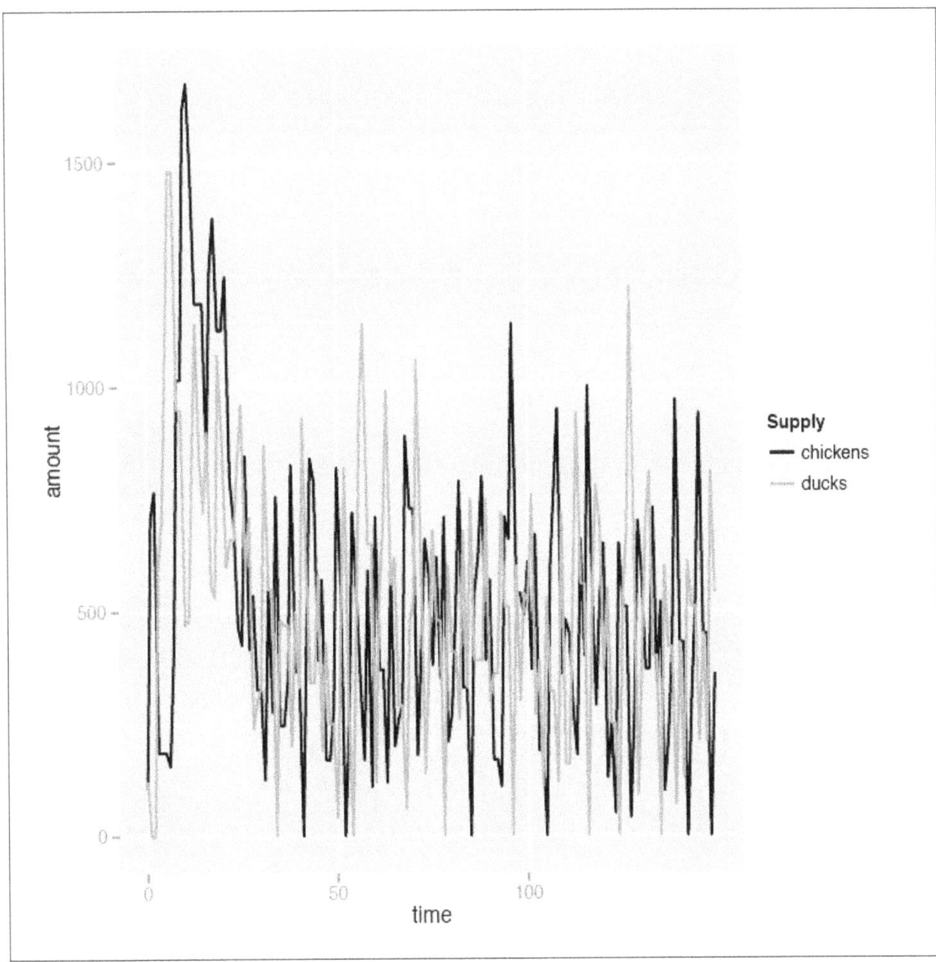

Figure 4-3. Comparing supply for chickens and ducks

Again, this is very familiar territory, so we'll just jump right ahead to the chart in Figure 4-4.

Again, we see the pattern of fluctuating prices for chickens and ducks. All pretty boring stuff by now. But wait—notice that the starting price of both chickens and ducks is quite high, but not long into the simulation, the prices competed with each other and dropped drastically until they both hit their costs, which is $12. This looks a lot like Figure 4-2. That's still not very interesting, though; in fact, this seems very much like Example 4-9 in our first simulation where the price dropped to around cost.

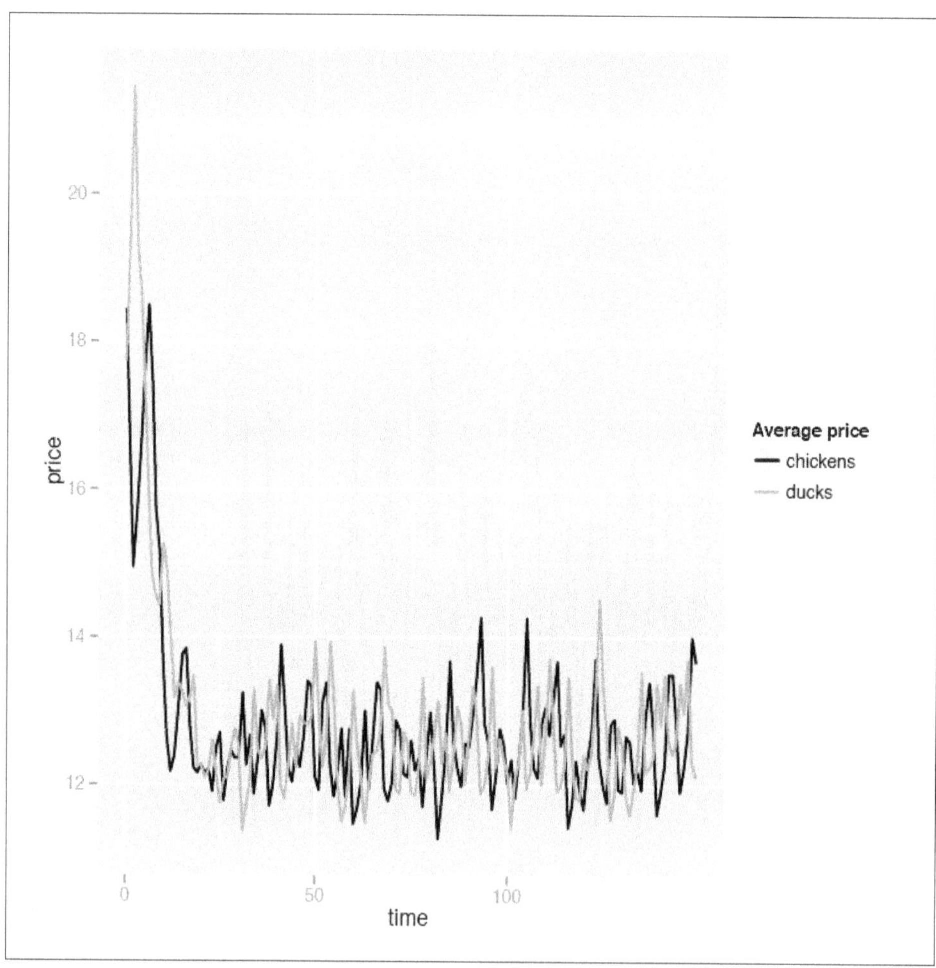

Figure 4-4. Comparing price for chickens and ducks

You're missing a very important point if you think that the results are boring. The fact that prices tend to drop to near cost shows that producers cannot set their prices arbitrarily. Very often, producers and merchants are accused of profiteering and arbitrarily setting up high prices in order to get as much profit as possible. While producers' main motivation is primarily profit, in a free market economy it is usually difficult for them to set arbitrary prices that are overly high.

Of course, there are circumstances that do cause this—for example, if all the producers collude (a cartel), if a single producer has a monopoly, or if the market is a large geographically isolated location—which really only means that it's not a free market economy. Given that the only difference between the two goods is the price, there is no choice but for the producers to drop their prices to stay competitive.

Having said that, remember that in our simulation the cost of producing chickens and ducks is the same. What if we increase the cost of producing ducks, meaning the difference is now not only the price?

```
COST[:ducks] = 24
COST[:chickens] = 12
```

Let's see how doubling the cost of producing ducks affects the prices (Figure 4-5).

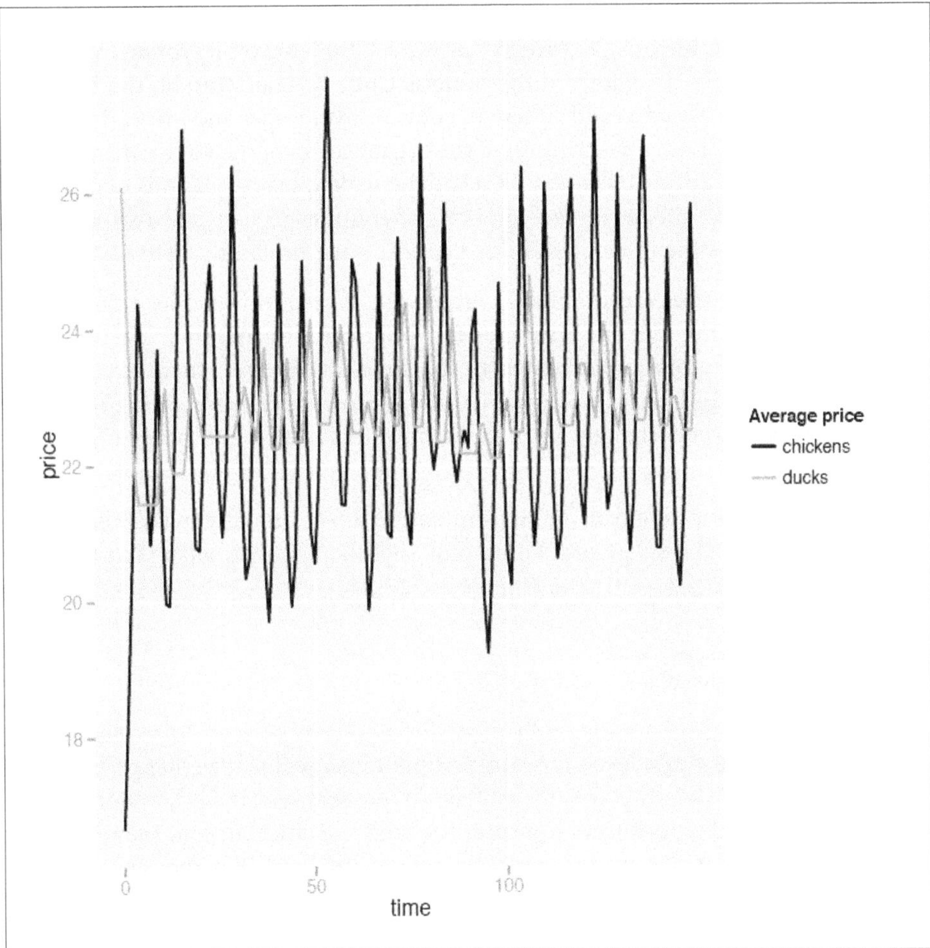

Figure 4-5. Effect of doubling the cost of producing ducks

The basic patterns remain the same: the prices of chickens and ducks still alternate in highs and lows. However, notice that the stable price is now between $22 and $26—that is, centering the cost of ducks. This means that while ducks are being sold with marginal profit, chickens are sold with high profits! In that case, why don't the farmers all sell chickens only? That doesn't work, of course, since if everyone produces and sells chickens only, the stable price will be back at the level of our first simulation, which hovers around the cost of producing the chickens.

Price Controls

Price controls are not a new phenomenon. The idea that there is a "fair" price for certain goods, which can be determined by governments or rulers, has been around since early recorded history. As early as 2800 B.C., the ancient Egyptians strived to maintain grain prices. In Babylon, the famous Code of Hammurabi, the first ever written law code, imposed a rigid system of controls over wages and prices. In ancient China, the Rites of Zhou, a description of the organization of the government during the Western Zhou period (1046–256 B.C) laid down detailed regulations of commercial life and prices. In ancient Greece, an army of grain inspectors called Sitophylakes was appointed to set the price of grain to what the government thought just.

None of these structures was eventually successful, of course. In modern times, such price controls are often the promises made by politicians during their election campaigns, and just as often implemented to the short-lived joy of their electorate. A proven way to win the hearts of voters is to promise lower prices for goods. However, as we have seen earlier, changes in prices cannot be isolated and necessarily affect supply of the goods.

Let's look at how price controls in our simulation affect our tiny market economy. We will be modifying our last simulation only slightly. First, we will add in the price control parameters:

```
PRICE_CONTROL = Hash.new
PRICE_CONTROL[:ducks] = 28
PRICE_CONTROL[:chickens] = 16
```

Notice that price control doesn't really mean forcing the producers to produce below their cost. If that's the case, even the dumbest politician will realize that no producer will produce and the whole economy will fail. In our example, the price control gives a bit of leeway for the producers to profit; for both the chickens and the ducks, the maximum profit that the producer will be able to get is $4. For most people, that would seem reasonable.

Now let's modify a line in the `Producer` class `change_pricing` method, as shown in Example 4-18.

Example 4-18. Adding the price control logic

```
def change_pricing
  @price.each do |type, price|
    if @supply[type] > 0
      @price[type] *= PRICE_DECREMENT unless @price[type] < COST[type]
```

```
      else
        @price[type] *= PRICE_INCREMENT unless @price[type] > PRICE_CONTROL[type]
      end
    end
  end
```

In this code, we're disallowing price increments if the price is above the price control level. That's the only change there is. Now let's run the code and see what happens.

After running the code, we'll run the same analysis as in our previous simulation on *price_data.csv* and *supply_data.csv*. We don't need to change the script, so let's look at the chart for the price data (Figure 4-6).

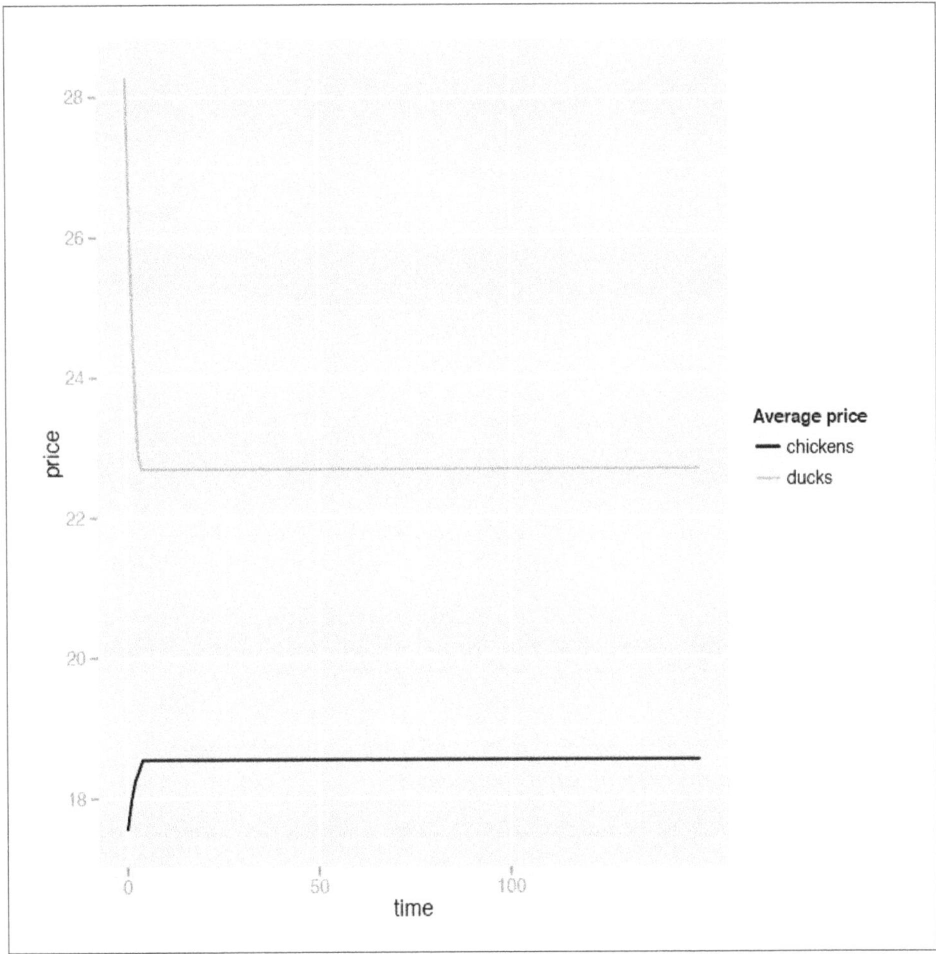

Figure 4-6. Price control effect on prices

Drastic change! As you can see, the price of chickens stabilizes and doesn't go beyond $20, and the price of ducks stabilizes and doesn't go beyond $23. This is well and good, since that's the intention of the price control. Now let's look at the chart for the supply data (Figure 4-7).

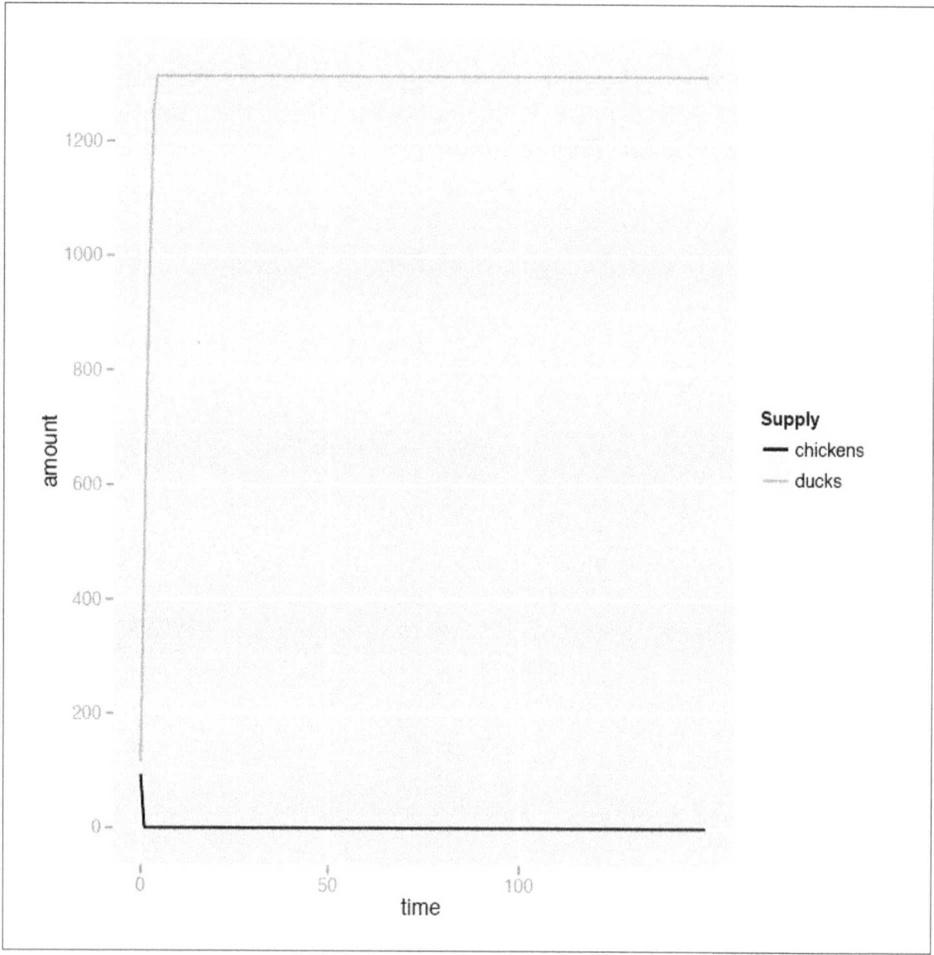

Figure 4-7. Price control effect on supply of goods

The devastation is obvious. After a turn or so, no farmers produce any chickens. Ducks can sell for more, so all farmers produce ducks. However, no consumer wants to buy ducks because chickens are cheaper, so the supply of ducks grows until it hits a ceiling, at which point both supplies stagnate until the end of the simulation. Our tiny chickens and ducks economy is broken.

Of course, our simulations are idealized, and as mentioned at the beginning of this chapter, simply models. However, they do give an indication of how price controls are fundamentally flawed. There are ways to get around the problems of our simulation (and in real life, no one is going to continually produce ducks if no one wants them, and neither will anyone give up eating because they can't get the cheapest food), but they involve increasingly complex solutions that necessarily take from one side of the equation to give to the other side. While they might work under certain specialized circumstances, in a larger context and in the longer term, price controls almost never work.

Wrap-up

This chapter provided only a brief glimpse into the world of economics modeling using software. We started with the most basic of economic theories and simulated a free market economy comprising a group of producers producing a single type of goods for a group of consumers.

The producers produce goods based on how well they sell. If the producers' supply runs out, they will start producing. The producers also change their pricing based on how well their goods sell. If their goods are sold out, they will try to maximize their profits by increasing the price of their goods. If there are unsold goods, the producers will try to sell them off more aggressively by reducing their price. Of course, the producers will not reduce the price below the cost of producing the goods. The consumers consume based on their own demand, which fluctuates over time. They will consume from the producers with the cheapest goods until their demands are met.

We analyzed this simple simulation, and discovered as expected, that the supply for goods goes up when the demand goes down, and vice versa. We also showed that the price of goods stabilizes near the cost of producing the goods over time.

Our second simulation took our first and modified it for an economy of two types of goods—chickens and ducks. The basic rules set down in our first simulation were applied, and we analyzed the results. As it turned out, when the supply of chickens increased, the supply of ducks went down, and vice versa, as expected. Also, the price of goods stabilizes again over time.

However, we made the interesting discovery that if the cost of producing one type of goods is different from the other (in our case, the cost of producing ducks is higher than the cost of producing chickens), the prices will stabilize near the higher cost.

Finally, we ended this brief investigation and simulation by analyzing how price control affects our tiny economy. We learned that controlling and fixing the prices for ducks and chickens, while allowing some profit for the producers, is disastrous for the economy. One type of goods simply vanishes from the market because no producer wants to produce it anymore, while the other type goes unsold even though the prices are more reasonable than when a free market economy existed.

Economics modeling is a huge field, and what we've gone through in this chapter is less than even a scratch on the surface. I invite you to apply the tools and techniques you've learned here to dive deeper into this fascinating subject.

CHAPTER 5

Discover Yourself Through Email

The Idea

Data mining is the current hot topic in high-tech industries, and you can hardly enter a tech conference or join a serious conversation about software without hearing that term—or its partner, data analytics—all around you. The ability to discover new and meaningful information from data seems to have taken over the enterprise mindset, as companies stumble over each other in their rush to offer their customers data analytics and mining.

One of the most common uses of enterprise-related data mining is for retail companies to find out more about you, the consumer. Companies want to learn as much as they can about you to sell more things to you. They want to find out what you like, what you are most likely to buy, who else is like you, when you buy things, and what payment methods you use to buy things. It's pretty scary stuff at times.

But why let the retail companies have all the fun and advantage? Wouldn't you want to know the same things about yourself? If you're like me and have been using email for a number of years, you have probably accumulated thousands to tens of thousands of messages. That's quite a treasure trove of information about yourself, which, as you might have guessed by now (if you hadn't already done so just by reading the title of the chapter) we're going to mine for precious, precious information about you and your emailing habits (Figure 5-1).

Figure 5-1. Gold miners (from http://www.flickr.com/photos/pingnews/424786913)

So how do we do it? Here's the plan, and it's quite straightforward:

1. We grab mails from your email account using Ruby.
2. We parse and store data in CSV files.
3. Using a set of R scripts, we try to discover patterns in the data that you didn't recognize before.
4. Profit (OK, maybe not this one).

Grab and Parse

Before we start with anything else, we need the data, of course. I'm assuming you have an email account with sufficient data to be mined and analyzed, and that you have it in Gmail. Other IMAP servers would work too with some minor tweaks.

The Ruby code is straightforward, and no fancy acrobatics are involved. The main effort really comes from determining what to discover and therefore what data to capture to enable the discovery. In this chapter, we will concentrate mostly on counting the number of email messages. Sound too easy?

As in the previous chapters, this code should be only the beginning of exploration for you. You should tweak it, extend it, and figure out what you want to find out about yourself from your email. For now, though, we'll be looking at only a few fields captured from the messages:

- Sender (from)
- Recipient (to)
- Date the message was sent

Example 5-1 demonstrates the code for the message-retrieving Ruby program, placed in a file unambiguously named *get_mails_gmail.rb*.

Example 5-1. Creating data source files with messages from Gmail

```
require 'csv'
require 'mail'

def write_row(mail, csv)
  data = []
  data << (mail.from ? mail.from.first : "")
  data << (mail.to ? mail.to.first : "")
  data << mail.date
  csv << data
end

EMAILS_TO_RETRIEVE = 10
USER = '<YOUR USERNAME>'
PASS = '<YOUR PASSWORD>'

Mail.defaults do
  retriever_method :imap, :address => "imap.gmail.com",
                          :port       => 993,
                          :user_name  => USER,
                          :password   => PASS,
                          :enable_ssl => true
end

{:inbox => 'INBOX', :sent => '[Gmail]/Sent Mail'}.each do |name, mailbox|
  emails = Mail.find(:mailbox => mailbox,
                     :what => :last,
                     :count => EMAILS_TO_RETRIEVE,
                     :order => :dsc)
```

```
  CSV.open("#{name}_data.csv", 'w') do |csv|
    csv << %w(from to date)
    emails.each do |mail|
      begin
        write_row mail, csv
      rescue
        puts "Cannot write this mail -> #{mail.from} to #{mail.to} with subject: \
            #{mail.subject}"
        puts $!
      end
    end
  end
end
```

All code examples may be downloaded from GitHub (*https://github.com/sausheong/everyday*).

We use two gem libraries in this email extraction script: `csv` and `mail`. The `csv` library is part of the Ruby standard library, which we have already encountered in Chapter 3. Just to recap, this is a library that comes bundled with Ruby 1.9. It's rather important that Ruby 1.9 is being used here, because the implementation in Ruby 1.8 and earlier is quite different. In fact, the current `csv` library used to exist as an optional library called FasterCSV outside the standard library. Version 1.9 absorbed FasterCSV as the main CSV package and delivered it as part of the standard library.

The `mail` gem is probably the most comprehensive email library in Ruby. Most email gems in Ruby are focused on sending messages. Only a few actually allow you to receive messages, and the `mail` library is one of them. We also set a constant, `EMAILS_TO_RETRIEVE`, that sets the number of email messages to grab from the account.

First, we need to set up the library with the correct credentials and parameters (Example 5-2).

Example 5-2. Email configuration

```
USER = '<YOUR USERNAME>'
PASS = '<YOUR PASSWORD>'
Mail.defaults do
  retriever_method :imap, :address => "imap.gmail.com",
                          :port       => 993,
                          :user_name  => USER,
                          :password   => PASS,
                          :enable_ssl => true
end
```

The `Mail.defaults` method takes in a block that sets up how we want to retrieve messages from the server. In this case, we're using IMAP to retrieve messages from the Gmail IMAP server. The default port for IMAP is 143, but Gmail uses IMAP over SSL, which uses port 993.

> **IMAP**
>
> The Internet Message Access Protocol (IMAP) is an Internet protocol that allows an email client to access messages on a remote mail server. The current version, IMAP version 4, is defined by RFC 3501. An IMAP server listens on the well-known port 143. Gmail uses IMAP over SSL, which uses the well-known port 993 instead. The other popular protocol for accessing messages on a remote mail server is POP, but POP removes email messages from the server by default once it reads them, and we don't want that to happen.

Now that we have connected to the IMAP server, we want to retrieve email messages from it. IMAP organizes messages in mailboxes, and it's important to know which mailboxes we want to retrieve. For this chapter, we are going to retrieve messages from your Gmail inbox as well as your sent mail folder. The name of the inbox in Gmail is `INBOX` (all caps), and the sent mail folder is `[Gmail]/Sent Mail`. Make sure you use this exact spelling and capitalization; it's important to get this part right because if it's not exactly the same, Gmail will simply say it can't find your mailboxes.

```
{:inbox => 'INBOX', :sent => '[Gmail]/Sent Mail'}.each do |name, mailbox|
  emails = Mail.find(:mailbox => mailbox,
                     :what => :last,
                     :count => EMAILS_TO_RETRIEVE,
                     :order => :dsc)
...
end
```

This code goes through the two mailboxes and uses the `mail` library to retrieve a number of messages. The `Mail.find` method shown here retrieves the last `EMAILS_TO_RETRIEVE` number of messages, sorted in descending order. Once we have the messages, we will invoke the `csv` library to write them into a CSV file, as shown in Example 5-3.

Example 5-3. Creating the data CSVs

```
CSV.open("#{name}_data_g.csv", 'w') do |csv|
  csv << %w(from to date)
  emails.each do |mail|
    begin
      write_row mail, csv
    rescue
```

```
        puts "Cannot write this mail -> #{mail.from} to #{mail.to} with subject: \
          #{mail.subject}"
        puts $!
      end
    end
  end
```

We start off by opening a new file for writing and passing it into the block. We then write the column headers to the file by appending an array that corresponds to the three fields we want to extract (`from`, `to`, and `date`). To extract these fields and write them into `csv`, we create a separate method named `write_row`, as shown in Example 5-4.

Example 5-4. write_row method

```
def write_row(mail, csv)
  data = []
  data << (mail.from ? mail.from.first : "")
  data << (mail.to ? mail.to.first : "")
  data << mail.date
  csv << data
end
```

In this method, we try to extract the first sender's email address as well as the first recipient's email address. You might notice that we are careful to make sure that the sender or the recipient exist; if not, we mark it with an empty string.

This gives us two files to start our discovery journey, *inbox_data.csv* and *sent_data.csv*, which both look like Example 5-5.

Example 5-5. Data CSV file contents

```
from,to,date
noreply@youtube.com,sausheong@gmail.com,2011-09-17T02:45:24-07:00
store-news@amazon.com,sausheong@gmail.com,2011-09-17T09:33:27+00:00
noreply@foursquare.com,sausheong@gmail.com,2011-09-17T04:17:28-05:00
noreply@quora.com,sausheong@gmail.com,2011-09-17T03:41:43-05:00
```

The Emailing Habits of Enron Executives

My assumption is that you're going to use these techniques on your own mailbox to find out more about your own emailing habits. For this chapter, though, it's obviously not a great idea for me to use my personal mailbox to explain how you can do this.

An alternative is to use a widely available email dataset and run through it for the examples in this chapter. In this case, there is no better choice (or any other choice, really, since publicly available, non-privacy-infringing email datasets are unsurprisingly rare) than the Enron email dataset (see the sidebar "The Enron Scandal").

The Enron Scandal

Enron Corporation was an American energy company, one of the largest in the world, with claimed revenues of nearly $101 billion in 2000. *Fortune* named Enron "America's Most Innovative Company" for six consecutive years. In October 2001, it was revealed that Enron's reported financial condition was fraudulent, cooked up by its executives. Shareholders lost nearly $11 billion when Enron's stock price, which hit a high of $90USD per share in mid-2000, plummeted to less than $1 by the end of November 2001. This eventually led to its bankruptcy in December 2001, which in turned dragged along to its grave the audit and accountancy firm Arthur Andersen (one of the top five in the world then). Enron's $63.4 billion in assets made it the largest corporate bankruptcy in US history until WorldCom's bankruptcy the following year. Besides being the largest corporate bankruptcy, Enron was also marked as the biggest audit failure.

The Enron email dataset contains 517,431 messages from 151 Enron executives and senior managers sent between 1998 and 2002. The original archive was made public and posted to the Web by the Federal Energy Regulatory Commission (FERC) in May 2002 during its investigations, and consisted of a bunch of Outlook PST files, each belonging to an Enron executive.

However, we're not using the PST files directly, but rather a dataset derived from these original archives. This dataset was collected and prepared by the CALO Project (a Cognitive Assistant that Learns and Organizes; see the sidebar "The CALO Project"). This dataset contains data from the original PST files, organized into folders. The corpus contains a total of about 500,000 messages.

The CALO Project

CALO was an artificial intelligence project funded by the Defense Advanced Research Projects Agency (DARPA) from 2003 to 2008. It brought together more than 300 researchers from 25 of the top university and commercial research institutions, with the aim of integrating numerous AI technologies into a cognitive assistant that could be told what to do and respond accordingly. (CALO's name was inspired by the Latin word calonis, which means "soldier's servant.") SRI International was the lead integrator responsible for coordinating the effort to produce an assistant that could live with and learn from its users. The most popularly known product spun out of SRI International is Siri, originally an independent piece of software running on iOS but later acquired by Apple. Siri is now an integrated and prominent part of iOS 5.

The email dataset was cleaned up and does not contain attachments. In addition, some messages have been deleted in response to requests from affected Enron employees. Invalid email addresses were converted to something of the form *user@enron.com* and to *no_address@enron.com* when no recipient was specified.

You can download the files from *http://www.cs.cmu.edu/~enron/* if you want to use this dataset to try out this chapter's code. After you unzip the file, you will see a directory structure that looks something like this:

```
enron_mail_20110402
|
- maildir
  |
  - allen-p
  |
  - arnold-k
  |
  - arora-h
    |
    - all_documents
    - deleted_items
    - ...
    - inbox
    - ...
    - sent
    - sent_items
      |
      - 1.
      - 2.
      - 3.
      - ...
```

Each original Outlook PST file has been converted into a directory. Within that directory, each mailbox is a subdirectory where each message is an individual text file, named sequentially with numbers. These files contain the email messages that comply with the Internet Message Format (described in RFC 2822; *http://www.rfc-editor.org/info/rfc2822*).

I will be using the mailbox of one of the Enron executives in this dataset and analyze his emailing habits. But wait. In the previous section, we used a Ruby script to extract messages from a Gmail account using SMTP. How do we extract email messages from a bunch of text files?

The answer is that email messages are really just a bunch of text files. In the case of the Gmail account, when we get a message from the mail server, what we're really getting is a text document (with communication protocol wrappers) that follows the

Internet Message Format in RFC 2822. The `mail` library we used before was used to communicate with the server and to parse the email document. To parse the Enron messages, we'll be using the same library to extract the data accordingly. Let's look at the script now in Example 5-6, which we store in a file named *get_mails_enron.rb*.

Example 5-6. Creating data source files from email files

```
require 'csv'
require 'mail'

def write_row(mail, csv)
  data = []
  data << (mail.from ? mail.from.first : "")
  data << (mail.to ? mail.to.first : "")
  data << mail.date
  csv << data
end

DIR_PATH = "/Users/sausheong/Downloads/enron_mail_20110402/maildir/kean-s"
EXCLUDED_DIRS = %w(. .. deleted_items all_documents)
SENT_DIRS = %w(sent sent_items)

sent = CSV.open("sent_data.csv", 'w')
sent << %w(from to date)
inbox = CSV.open("inbox_data.csv", 'w')
inbox << %w(from to date)

Dir.foreach(DIR_PATH) do |file_name|
  file = File.absolute_path(file_name, DIR_PATH)
  if File.directory?(file) and !EXCLUDED_DIRS.include?(file_name)
    Dir.foreach(file) do |mail_file|
      eml = File.absolute_path(mail_file, file)
      if File.file?(eml)
        mail = Mail.read eml
        begin
          if SENT_DIRS.include?(file_name)
            write_row mail, sent
          else
            write_row mail, inbox
          end
        rescue
          puts "Cannot write this mail -> #{mail.from} to #{mail.to} with subject: \
              #{mail.subject}"
          puts $!
        end
      end
    end
  end
end
```

```
inbox.close
sent.close

exit
```

This script looks a lot like the one in Example 5-1. The parsing of the messages in `write_row` is actually almost exactly the same. We start off by determining which mailbox we want to investigate and set a constant `DIR_PATH` to specify that. Next, we set up the `EXCLUDED_DIRS` array with a list of directories—including the deleted items in the mailbox—that we don't want to check.

Next, we set up both CSV files and open them up for writing, then insert the column headings as the first line in the CSV files. Once we have the files, we iterate through each item in the given directory `DIR_PATH`. Note that the *maildir* directory contains only a list of directories, each of them representing a mailbox. So if the item we've retrieved is a directory and it's not in the `EXCLUDED_DIRS` array, we will treat it as a mailbox, go into it, and iterate through each item in that subdirectory.

At this level, we should have a list of messages, each a numbered file. Here we use the `mail` library, read each mail file, and then parse the files accordingly using `write_row`, the same way we did in Example 5-1. The difference here is that if the mailboxes are named `sent` or `sent_items`, we will save the data to the *sent_data.csv* file, while all other messages are parsed and stored in *inbox_data.csv*.

With all that preparation work, we finally have the data in the format that we want, so it's time to take the next step: uncovering the patterns in the email data.

Discover Yourself

In this chapter, I will introduce a number of R scripts that will ferret out things about you that you didn't know before. Although I will mostly talk about the Enron email dataset here, in particular the messages of Steve Kean (who was the executive vice president and chief of staff at Enron), you can use the same scripts on your own email data.

Let's start with a simple script first—one that maps the number of email messages received by the day of the month.

Number of Messages by Day of the Month

Here's the plan of attack. We want to count the number of messages according to the day of the month. An obvious method is to use the `table()` function. In this case, we will need to pass in to `table()` a vector that looks something like this:

```
"01" "01" "01" "02" "02" "03" "03" "03" "03" "04" "04" "05" "05"  ...
```

This means that there are three messages on the 1st of the month (01), two messages on the 2nd of the month (02), four messages on the 3rd of the month (03), and so on until the 31st of the month. We already have this structure in our data file, where each line represents an email message and has a date when it was received. The data we need is in the date column only, so we're really looking at only one of the three columns in the data file. Let's see how we can access it. First, we need to load the data:

```
inbox_data <- read.table("inbox_data.csv", header=TRUE, sep=",")
sent_data <- read.table("sent_data.csv", header=TRUE, sep=",")
```

This gives us two data frames, all loaded up with our data. To select only the date column, we will use `inbox_data['date']` or `sent_data['date']`.

However, these are still data frames with a single column containing a string in each row. The string shows the message date, but nonetheless it's still a string. We want a vector of dates in order to extract just the day of the month, and it will take some effort to tease that out.

So, to retrieve the day of the month, first we need a vector of dates. The date column contains the dates we want, so we use `$` on both the inbox and the sender data to reference this column. While the values in the column look like dates, they are actually characters, so we need to convert them into actual `date` objects, using the `as.Date` function:

```
dates <- as.Date(inbox_date$date,"%Y-%m-%dT%H:%M:%S")
```

Note that when we're converting from characters to a date, we need to provide the desired format (or the *conversion specification*) for the date. Of course, we don't really want the whole date, just the day of the month, `%d`, so we use the `format` function on our vector of dates:

```
elements <- format(dates, '%d')
```

This gives us a vector of day of the month, each item representing a message in a day of the month. We pass `elements` into the `table()` function to get a table (of course), which looks something like this:

```
01  02  03  04  05  06  07  08  09  10  11  12  13  14  15  ...
390 340 413 351 396 421 340 393 309 343 295 331 330 369 306 ...
```

This is the count of the messages in the inbox by day of the month. We need to generate this for the sent mail folder as well.

Using the aforementioned method, we create two variables, `inbox_count` and `sent_count`, which represent the frequency of messages by day of the month. What we want to do next is plot these two sets of data in a chart. For convenience, we create a third data frame that wraps around `inbox_count` and `sent_count`, and also the x-axis scale we want to use for the chart.

The x-axis in the chart is the day of the month and is a discrete scale, as compared to the y-axis, which is a continuous scale. To create this discrete x-axis scale, we create a vector of characters, not too subtly named `days_of_month`, representing the days of the month. Then, we use the factors of `days_of_month` as x-axis input in the chart plotting functions later. We set the optional `levels` parameter to be `days_of_month` in order to set our preferred order of elements.

Let's look at the whole script now in Example 5-7.

Example 5-7. Number of messages by day of the month

```
library(ggplot2)

inbox_data <- read.table("inbox_data.csv", header=TRUE, sep=",")
sent_data <- read.table("sent_data.csv", header=TRUE, sep=",")

dates <- as.Date(inbox_data$date,"%Y-%m-%dT%H:%M:%S")
elements <- format(dates, '%d')
inbox_count <- data.frame(table(elements))$Freq ❶

dates <- as.Date(sent_data$date,"%Y-%m-%dT%H:%M:%S")
elements <- format(dates, '%d')
sent_count <- data.frame(table(elements))$Freq ❷

days_of_month <- c("01","02","03","04","05","06","07","08","09","10",
                   "11","12","13","14","15","16","17","18","19","20",
                   "21","22","23","24","25","26","27","28","29","30","31")
df <- data.frame(days=factor(days_of_month, levels=days_of_month),
                              inbox=inbox_count,sent=sent_count) ❸

ggplot(data=df) + scale_shape_manual(name="Mailbox", values=c(2,3)) +
  geom_point(aes(x=days,y=inbox, shape='inbox')) +
  geom_smooth(aes(x=days,y=inbox, shape='inbox', group=1)) +
  geom_point(aes(x=days,y=sent, shape='sent')) +
  geom_smooth(aes(x=days,y=sent, shape='sent', group=2)) +
  scale_y_continuous('number of emails') +
  scale_x_discrete('day of month')
```

❶ A data frame with a single column; the frequency count of messages by day of the month for the inbox

❷ Another data frame, this time for the sent mails

❸ The data frame used in plotting the chart, consisting of the frequency count columns of the inbox and the sent mail folder as well as the days of the month

Running this script will create the chart in Figure 5-2.

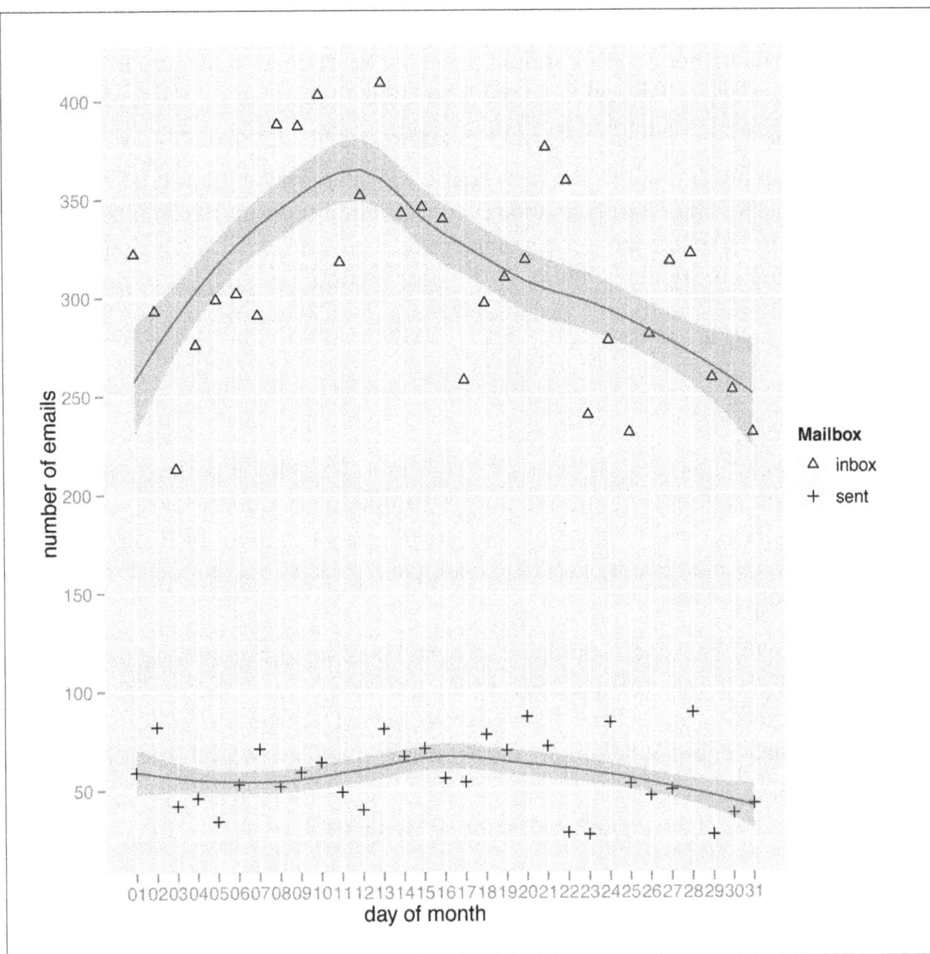

Figure 5-2. Message count by day of the month

Now we're talking! A few immediate observations:

- The sent mail folder has fewer messages than the inbox. This is quite normal in most cases. We often get more messages than we send, because we get messages from a lot of sources—people we know, people we don't, and machines (as in alerts and mailing lists we subscribe to).
- There is an interesting climb to the peak around the 8th to 13th days of each month, topping 350 messages received, at which point it goes into steady decline until the end of the month.
- The amount of messages sent out, however, is pretty consistent throughout the month.

In this chapter, I won't be doing any analysis deeper than making observational notes on the patterns. Further analysis should probably be done with the whole dataset in view, as well as deeper research into the whole Enron saga. In other words, we will just observe the patterns here, not try to interpret them.

Before we jump headlong into the next script, let's step back a bit and take a second look at Example 5-7. It certainly includes variables and functions that will be repeated in the other scripts, so like any good programmer would do, we'll single them out and make a common library out of them. In the next section, we will look at how we can abstract common elements and variables into an R package, and then we'll refactor Example 5-7 to use it.

MailMiner

The package we will be creating is called MailMiner. Creating R packages is not very difficult, despite sounding quite daunting. Admittedly, it's not as easy as defining Ruby libraries. It's actually somewhat like creating a Ruby gem. In this section, we will go through the basic steps of creating a simple R package that rounds up common functions we will be using.

Before creating the package, though, let's figure out what common elements we want to extract and place into this package. From Example 5-7, it's obvious that we can substitute a function for the three lines of code that extract the date column from the data and produce a single data frame containing the mailbox count. In other words, we can replace:

```
dates <- as.Date(inbox_data$date,"%Y-%m-%dT%H:%M:%S")
elements <- format(dates, '%d')
inbox_count <- data.frame(table(elements))$Freq
```

with this:

```
inbox_count <- dates_count(dates=inbox_data$date, element='%d')
```

by creating a function called `dates_count()`:

```
dates_count <- function(dates,element) {
  dates <- as.Date(dates,"%Y-%m-%dT%H:%M:%S")
  elements <- format(dates, element)
  data.frame(table(elements))$Freq
}
```

As you can see, the `dates_count()` function essentially repackages the three lines of code into a single, reusable function. To reuse code (and often also data) in R, we need to bundle this function into an R package, which is what will we do next.

Let's go through the steps of creating a basic R package:

1. Use the `package.skeleton()` function to create the file structure and stubs needed for the package.

2. Modify various files in the stub, mostly providing information on the package you're writing.
3. Build the package using the `build` command.
4. Check the package using the `check` command, to make sure that the package can be installed.

Let's start with creating the skeleton file structure. First, we need to create the library file that we want to include in the package. We create a file named *mailminer.r* that contains the code in Example 5-8.

Example 5-8. The mailminer.r file

```
dates_count <- function(dates,element) {
  dates <- as.Date(dates,"%Y-%m-%dT%H:%M:%S")
  elements <- format(dates, element)
  data.frame(table(elements))$Freq
}
```

Then we run this command in the R environment:

```
> package.skeleton(name = "mailminer", code_files = "mailminer.r")
```

The `code_files` parameter should point to the *mailminer.r* file we just created. This will generate a bunch of files with the following structure:

```
mailminer
|
- DESCRIPTION
- man
  |
  - mailminer-package.Rd
- R
  |
  - mailminer.r
- Read-and-delete-me
```

Besides the *mailminer.r* file, which was copied from the file we pointed to, all other files need to be populated with the correct information. Edit the *DESCRIPTION* file and change the values for the various fields accordingly. The version number in this file will be used later in generating the filename of the R package. There is also one (or possibly more) *.Rd* file in the *man* directory. These are the manual files, described in a TeX-like format. We should also modify these accordingly. The *Read-and-delete-me* file can be removed after you've read it (it doesn't really say much more than what you'll read here).

Next we'll need to build the package. We need to do this outside of the R environment and at the console terminal, at the same level as the *mailminer* directory:

```
$ R CMD build mailminer
```

This will create a package named *mailminer_1.0.tar.gz* (if the version number is 1.0). After building the package, you should test it and check whether there are any errors:

```
$  R CMD check mailminer_1.0.tar.gz
```

This should give us a long output listing that ideally ends in everything being OK. Sometimes we might end up with errors involving creating the manuals or generating the PDF versions of the manual. In such cases, we can try to avoid generating the manual by using the `--no-manual` option:

```
$ R CMD check --no-manual mailminer_1.0.tar.gz
```

Finally, once it's tested, we can install the package:

```
$ R CMD install mailminer_1.0.tar.gz
```

To check whether we've successfully installed the package, just go into the R environment again and type:

```
> library(mailminer)
```

You'll get an error if the package wasn't installed properly. Otherwise, we're all set! Next stop is to modify our existing script to use this brand-new package, as shown in Example 5-9.

Example 5-9. Modified script to use a common library package

```
library(ggplot2)
library(mailminer)

inbox_data <- read.table("inbox_data.csv", header=TRUE, sep=",")
sent_data <- read.table("sent_data.csv", header=TRUE, sep=",")

inbox_count <- dates_count(dates=inbox_data$date, element='%d')
sent_count <- dates_count(dates=sent_data$date, element='%d')

days_of_month <- c("01","02","03","04","05","06","07","08","09","10",
                   "11","12","13","14","15","16","17","18","19","20",
                   "21","22","23","24","25","26","27","28","29","30","31")
df <- data.frame(days=factor(days_of_month, levels=days_of_month),
                             inbox=inbox_count,sent=sent_count)

ggplot(data=df) + scale_shape_manual(name="Mailbox", values=c(2,3)) +
  geom_point(aes(x=days,y=inbox, shape='inbox')) +
  geom_smooth(aes(x=days,y=inbox, group=1)) +
  geom_point(aes(x=days,y=sent, shape='sent')) +
  geom_smooth(aes(x=days,y=sent, group=2)) +
  scale_y_continuous('number of emails') +
  scale_x_discrete('day of month')
```

We need to include the `mailminer` package in the library before we start using the `dates_count()` function. We use it twice for the inbox as well as the sent mailbox. There are no other changes to the code.

Now that we have the MailMiner package, let's get back to our scripts.

Number of Messages by Day of Week

Before being sidetracked to create the MailMiner package, we were investigating Steve Kean's email frequency patterns by day of the month. Moving on, we can extend this to investigate his email frequency pattern by day of the week. Intuitively, the count of messages received and sent would be different on different days of the week, as shown in Example 5-10. For example, I should expect the volume of messages to drop over the weekend since this is a business email account. Let's see whether this is true.

Example 5-10. Number of messages by day of the week

```
library(ggplot2)
library(mailminer)

inbox_data <- read.table("inbox_data.csv", header=TRUE, sep=",")
sent_data <- read.table("sent_data.csv", header=TRUE, sep=",")

inbox_count <- dates_count(dates=inbox_data$date, element='%a')
sent_count <- dates_count(dates=sent_data$date, element='%a')

days_of_week <- c("Mon","Tue","Wed","Thu","Fri","Sat","Sun")
df <- data.frame(days=factor(days_of_week, levels=days_of_week),inbox=inbox_count,
                             sent=sent_count)

ggplot(data=df) + scale_shape_manual(name="Mailbox", values=c(2,3)) +
  geom_point(aes(x=days,y=inbox, shape='inbox')) +
  geom_smooth(aes(x=days,y=inbox, group=1)) +
  geom_point(aes(x=days,y=sent, shape='sent')) +
  geom_smooth(aes(x=days,y=sent, group=2)) +
  scale_y_continuous('number of emails') +
  scale_x_discrete('day of week')
```

The script is mostly similar to the one in Example 5-7, except that we use the days of the week instead of days of the month. To do this, we need to extract the count of messages by the day of the month. In this case, we use the datetime conversion specification of `%a` instead of `%d` to create `inbox_count` and `sent_count`. The `%a` specification extracts the short form of the day name (for example, Mon instead of Monday, and Tue instead of Tuesday). Next, we create a vector of the short day names, then use the `factor()` function to convert it into a factor just as we did before. With these changes, we run the script, which will generate the chart in Figure 5-3.

Interestingly, the volume of messages is the highest during the weekends—the opposite of our expectations! Also, there is a big dip to minimal emailing activity midweek, which is surprising. It almost seems that the workweek started on Friday and ended on Tuesday, and that Wednesdays and Thursdays are the "weekends."

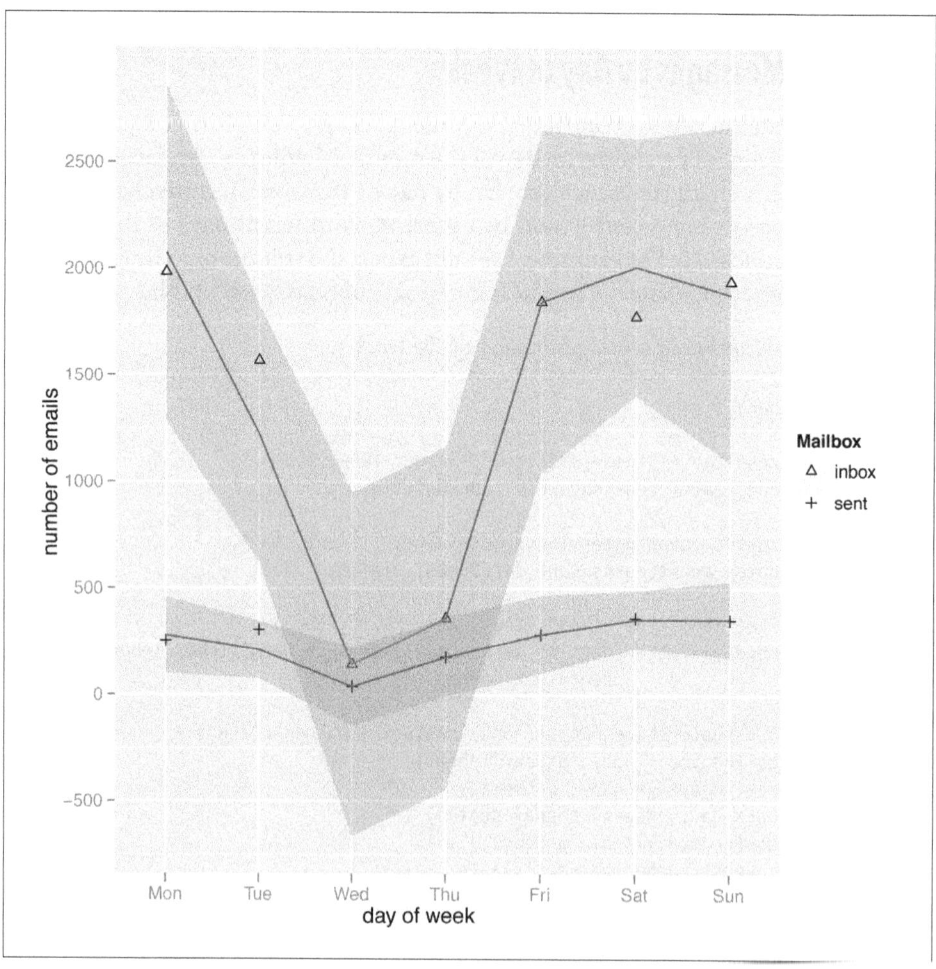

Figure 5-3. Message count by day of week

Number of Messages by Month

Let's move on to a larger scale now and investigate the email frequency pattern for each month (Example 5-11). The exercise remains the same, and the code similar to that in the previous section.

Example 5-11. Number of messages by month

```
library(ggplot2)
library(mailminer)

inbox_data <- read.table("inbox_data.csv", header=TRUE, sep=",")
inbox_data['date']
sent_data <- read.table("sent_data.csv", header=TRUE, sep=",")
```

```
inbox_count <- dates_count(dates=inbox_data$date, element='%b')
sent_count <- dates_count(dates=sent_data$date, element='%b')

month_names <- c("Jan","Feb","Mar","Apr","May","Jun","Jul","Aug","Sep","Oct","Nov",
                 "Dec")
df <- data.frame(mths=factor(month_names, levels=month_names),inbox=inbox_count,
                            sent=sent_count)

ggplot(data=df) + scale_shape_manual(name="Mailbox", values=c(2,3)) +
  geom_point(aes(x=mths,y=inbox, shape='inbox')) +
  geom_smooth(aes(x=mths,y=inbox, group=1)) +
  geom_point(aes(x=mths,y=sent, shape='sent')) +
  geom_smooth(aes(x=mths,y=sent, group=2)) +
  scale_y_continuous('number of emails') +
  scale_x_discrete('month')
```

This almost looks familiar now. Instead of `%d` or `%a`, we use `%b` to get the months as abbreviated names. Running through this script creates the chart in Figure 5-4.

From the chart, we can observe that Steve received more messages in the earlier parts of the year and that there is a dip in the middle of the year, around the month of July. The volume of messages received also drops at the end of the year. In contrast, the number of messages Steve sent was constant throughout the year, rising slowly toward the end of the year.

Number of Messages by Hour of the Day

Having investigated the larger scale of message count by month, let's look at the other end of the spectrum by investigating the number of messages received and sent by the hour of the day. The analysis should be a no-brainer here, since the message count should be low during the early hours of the morning, progressively increase during the day, then taper off during the night.

Example 5-12. Number of messages by hour of the day

```
library(ggplot2)
library(mailminer)

inbox_data <- read.table("inbox_data.csv", header=TRUE, sep=",")
sent_data <- read.table("sent_data.csv", header=TRUE, sep=",")

inbox_count <- times_count(times=inbox_data$date, element="%H")
sent_count <- times_count(times=sent_data$date, element='%H')

hours_of_day <- c("00","01","02","03","04","05","06","07","08","09",
                  "10","11","12","13","14","15","16","17","18","19",
                  "20","21","22","23")
df <- data.frame(hours=factor(hours_of_day, levels=hours_of_day),
                 inbox=inbox_count,sent=sent_count)
```

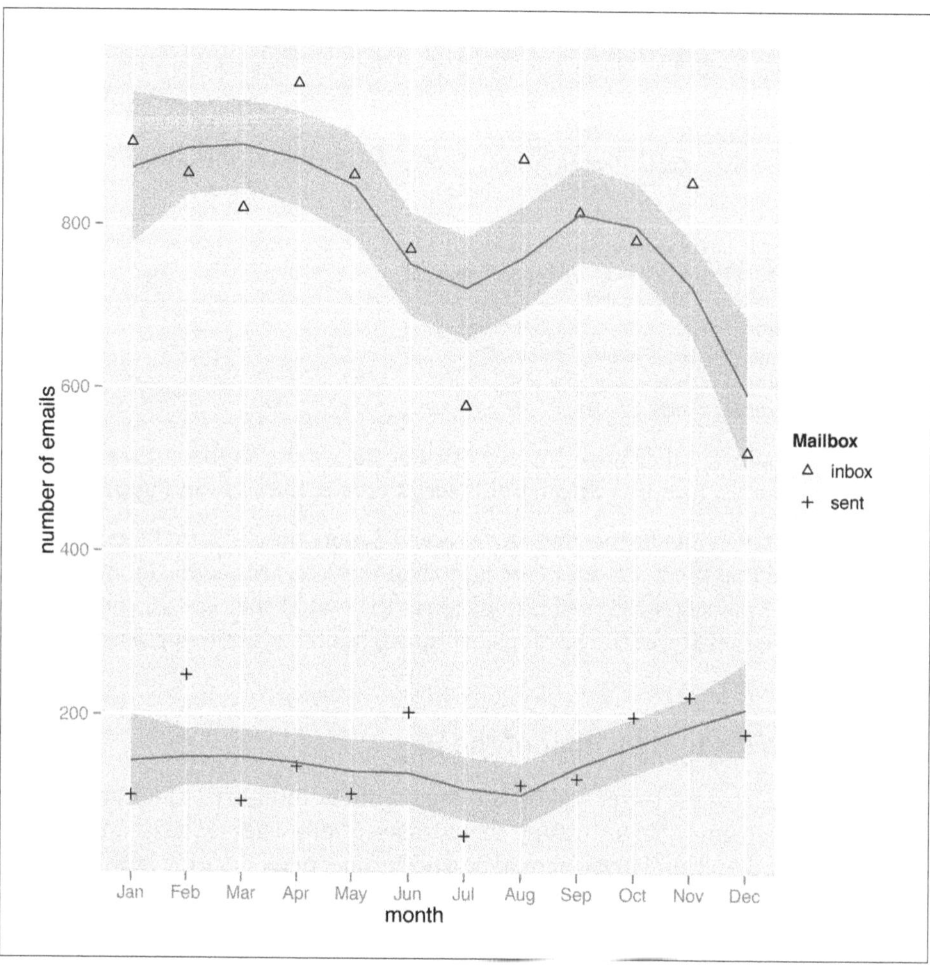

Figure 5-4. Message count by month

```
ggplot(data=df) + scale_shape_manual(name="Mailbox", values=c(2,3)) +
  geom_point(aes(x=hours,y=inbox, shape='inbox')) +
  geom_smooth(aes(x=hours,y=inbox, group=1)) +
  geom_point(aes(x=hours,y=sent, shape='sent')) +
  geom_smooth(aes(x=hours,y=sent, group=2)) +
  scale_y_continuous('number of emails') +
  scale_x_discrete('hour of day')
```

You might notice something different this time around. Instead of `dates_count()`, there's a new function called `times_count()`. Where did this come from? As it turns out, to extract the hour of the day, we cannot use the same mechanism as we did with `dates_count()`. Here's `times_count()`:

```
times_count <- function(times,element) {
  elements <- strftime(strptime(times, format="%Y-%m-%dT%H:%M:%S"), element)
  data.frame(table(elements))$Freq
}
```

As before, we need to convert the datetime string into a vector. However, instead of using `as.Date`, we use `strptime` to convert it into a time format, then use `strftime` to extract just that single element (in this case, using the conversion specification `%H`). To use this function, we add it to the *mailminer.r* file in the MailMiner package and repackage it.

Let's get back to the script. Running Example 5-12 will create the chart in Figure 5-5.

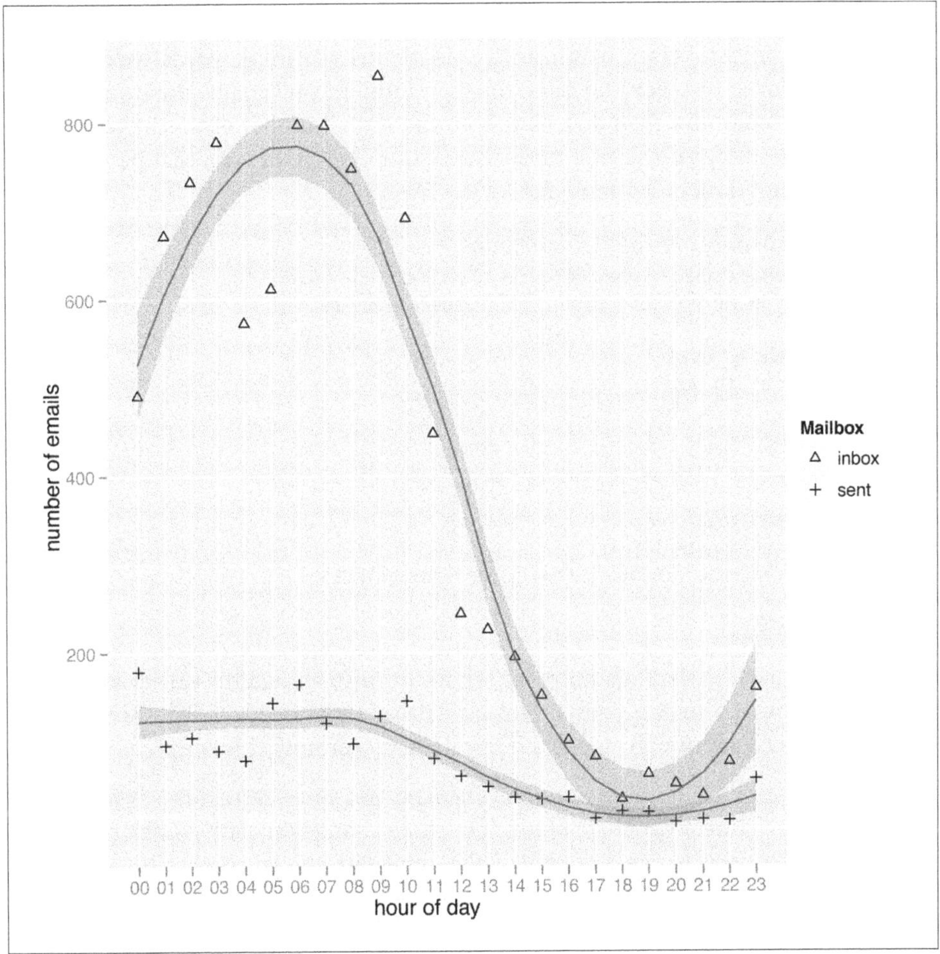

Figure 5-5. Message count by hour of day

From the chart, it's obvious that Steve follows a different email activity cycle, because the volume of messages received peaks at around 4 or 5 a.m.! At the height of activity, the number of messages topped 800. This is followed by a rapid decline throughout the day, and the messages received declined drastically such that by early afternoon, it dropped below 200. The number of messages sent is also correspondingly higher in the early hours of the morning as compared to the afternoon and evening.

Interactions

We've investigated the anonymous count of messages for long enough. It's time to dive deeper and look at the patterns that are formed from the list of people Steve received messages from and sent messages to. To start off simply, we take the list of all people (uniquely identified by their email addresses) that Steve sent to, and the list of people who sent messages to him, and combine them. In other words, we're looking at the `from` column in `inbox_data` and the `to` column in `sent_data`. We want to combine these two columns, then do a simple count of the number of times they appear. The more times they appear, the more interaction Steve had with that person. Let's look at the script now in Example 5-13.

Example 5-13. Number of email interactions

```
inbox_data <- read.table("inbox_data.csv", header=TRUE, sep=",")
sent_data <- read.table("sent_data.csv", header=TRUE, sep=",")

from <- inbox_data['from']
colnames(from)[1] <- 'mail'

to <- sent_data['to']
colnames(to)[1] <- 'mail'

all <- rbind(from,to)
counted <- data.frame(table(all))
sorted <- counted[order(counted['Freq'],decreasing=TRUE),]

print(sorted[0:20,])
```

You probably noticed that this script is a whole lot simpler than the earlier ones. Also, it doesn't seem to plot any charts. Not all data analysis needs to be charted if the information is clear enough, as are the results from running this script.

The first two lines are familiar enough. The next two lines extract the `from` column from `inbox_data` into a variable named `from`, then change the name of the column to `mail`. The subsequent two lines do exactly the same with the `to` column in `sent_data`. We change the names of the columns because we want to use the `rbind` function to combine these two columns together, and they need to have the same name.

The combined data is placed into an `all` variable, on which we run the `table()` function and then convert it into a data frame. Using `table()` on `all` will give us a count of the number of times each row appears. Unfortunately, the result, stored in the `counted` variable, is unsorted. This makes it difficult for us to extract any information, so we have to sort the data next.

Sorting the data is not difficult, but it requires some explanation. We want to sort the data by the number of messages that Steve sent to or received from a particular email address, in descending order. This will tell us who Steve interacted with the most.

To sort the data, first we use the `order()` function on the `Freq` column in `counted`, also setting `decreasing` to be `TRUE`:

```
order(counted['Freq'],decreasing=TRUE)
```

This will give us a vector of row numbers, sorted by `Freq` in descending order:

```
 [1] 1512 1424   23 1555 1320 1900  708  580  889 1511  606  207  909  103
[15] 1708 1131  205  577 1378  965 1086  718 1574 1697 1591  983  832  819
[29]  750 1386  157 1085  553 1668  842  986  821 1222  252 1543  415 1432
[43]  696 1323  340  826  914 1151  161   95  605  735 1351  905  466 ...
```

Unfortunately, this tells us almost nothing. What we need is the email address and the corresponding count for the number of messages. To get this, we use the square brackets notation `list['value']` on `counted`. This notation is much more powerful than the similar-looking method in Ruby. Besides referencing a single element or a range of elements, we can use the same notation to search for a list of elements to return. If we pass the preceding code into `counted` with the bracket notation, we will get the list of corresponding elements that we want:

```
counted[order(counted['Freq'],decreasing=TRUE),]
```

Notice that there aren't any expressions after the comma. This is not a typo. If we leave the expression, it will return all the elements. In the previous code, what we're telling R to do is to return all rows that match the values in the first expression, and all columns in those rows.

Finally, say we're interested only in the top 20 people we interacted with, so we simply print out the data, and filter off just the top 20 rows:

```
print(sorted[0:20,])
```

This is the result of running the script:

```
                           all Freq
610        steven.kean@enron.com 1422
268      jeff.dasovich@enron.com  691
419 maureen.mcvicker@enron.com  421
528   richard.shapiro@enron.com  330
250      james.steffes@enron.com  261
614          susan.mara@enron.com  201
407     mark.schroeder@enron.com  198
```

```
101   christi.nicolay@enron.com  187
448     miyung.buster@enron.com  166
313       karen.denne@enron.com  162
576         sgovenar@govadv.com  158
560     sarah.novosel@enron.com  153
208    ginger.dernehl@enron.com  132
117 cynthia.sandherr@enron.com  124
40        ann.schmidt@enron.com  118
589       sherri.sera@enron.com  113
366   linda.robertson@enron.com  103
405       mark.palmer@enron.com  103
271    jeffrey.keeler@enron.com   91
197 gavin.dillingham@enron.com   89
```

The first column contains the row numbers. If we ignore the first line (the fact that Steve cc'd himself on a lot of messages tells us a bit about his emailing habits), we find that the person Steve interacted with the most was Jeff Dasovich, followed by Maureen McVicker and Richard Shapiro.

Comparative Interactions

In the previous section, we assumed that the more messages either being sent to or received from a person, the higher the level of interaction between the sender and recipient. This is a simplistic assumption because there are always cases where we keep getting messages from someone but we never respond to him or her. This is generally the case with mailing lists, newsletters, or notification messages from automated services. There are also cases where we send messages to someone and he or she seldom replies. An example of this scenario is when someone sends regular reports or updates to his management or instructions to a group of subordinates.

In this section, we use a different view of email interactions. We calculate the amount of interaction someone has as the ratio between the number of messages he sends to a person over the number of messages he receives from that person. In this chapter, we're referring, of course, to Steve. So a high value means Steve sends more messages to that person than he receives from him or her, while a low value means Steve receives more messages from that person than he sends to him or her.

Let's look at some code. First, we want to get a list of email addresses and their count. To do this, we apply the `table()` function on the `from` column in `inbox_data` and the to column in `sent_data`, and create a data frame for each of them:

```
from <- data.frame(table(inbox_data['from']))
to <- data.frame(table(sent_data['to']))
```

The resulting data frames both look like this:

```
                                           Var1 Freq
...
12                       alan.comnes@enron.com   43
13                      alberto.gude@enron.com    3
```

```
14                          aleck.dadson@enron.com    3
15                   alejandro.hernandez@enron.com    3
16                      alex.goldberg@williams.com    2
...
```

The first column (Var1) is the email address, and the second column (Freq) is the number of times this address appeared. However, what we want is a single list of addresses, not two lists, so we combine these two data frames with the union() function. Also, because we just want a list of email addresses, we combine the email addresses only, not the count of the messages:

```
mails <- union(from$Var1, to$Var1)
```

Next, we will iterate through this list of email addresses. For each, we will find the count of messages sent to it and the count of messages received from it, then find the ratio between them. In the end, of course, we want a data frame that has a column of email addresses and a corresponding column of ratios. To get this data frame, we first create an empty one, then populate it by iterating through the list of addresses:

```
df <- data.frame(email=NA,ratio=0)
for (mail in mails) {
  to_count <- to[to$Var1 == mail,]$Freq
  from_count <- from[from$Var1 == mail,]$Freq
  ratio <- to_count/from_count
  if (length(ratio) == 0) {ratio <- 0}
  row <- c(mail, ratio)
  df <- rbind(df, row)
}
```

To get the to_count value, we take the to variable and use the square brackets notation discussed earlier, with the first parameter being an expression that filters the rows we want. This returns a row with both email as well as Freq, but we just want the count, so we extract the value of Freq only. After repeating this with from_count, we calculate the ratio. If either the to_count or from_count is 0, the ratio is numeric(0) or a zero-length vector of floating-point numbers. We can't have numeric(0) as the ratio, so we need to take care of this by testing its length (it will return 0 if it's numeric(0) since it is zero length) and set ratio to be 0 accordingly.

Finally, we create a vector with the address as the first element and the ratio as the second, then add this row to the empty data frame we created earlier.

Are we done yet? Wait, what we are left with is a data frame with a column consisting of email addresses and another column with the corresponding count of messages. Unfortunately, it's not sorted, and the floating-point division really makes some numbers quite unwieldy to display, so let's clean things up a bit.

First, we shorten the number of digits to show in the ratio column to three. To do this, we use the transform function df() and apply the round() function on the ratio:

```
df <- transform(df, ratio = round(as.numeric(ratio),digits=3))
```

Then we sort the data frame according to the ratio column:

```
df[order(df['ratio'],decreasing=TRUE),]
```

This is similar to what we did earlier in Example 5-13. With this done, let's look at the entire script in Example 5-14.

Example 5-14. Comparative interactions

```
in_data <- read.table("inbox_data.csv", header=TRUE, sep=",")
sent_data <- read.table("sent_data.csv", header=TRUE, sep=",")

from <- data.frame(table(in_data['from']))
to <- data.frame(table(sent_data['to']))

mails <- union(from$Var1, to$Var1)
df <- data.frame(email=NA,ratio=0)
for (mail in mails) {
  to_count <- to[to$Var1 == mail,]$Freq
  from_count <- from[from$Var1 == mail,]$Freq
  ratio <- to_count/from_count
  if (length(ratio) == 0) {ratio <- 0}
  row <- c(mail, ratio)
  df <- rbind(df, row)
}
df <- transform(df, ratio = round(as.numeric(ratio),digits=3))
df <- df[df$ratio!=0,]
data <- df[order(df['ratio'],decreasing=TRUE),]
print(data)
```

Running this script on our data will provide the following output:

```
                              email  ratio
332           kenneth.lay@enron.com 16.500
631          terrie.james@enron.com  5.500
291         john.brindle@enron.com  3.500
296        john.sherriff@enron.com  3.000
372           liz.taylor@enron.com  3.000
555     sandra.lighthill@enron.com  3.000
219              grwhit@rice.edu  2.500
489          paula.rieker@enron.com  2.500
108           cindy.olson@enron.com  2.250
59     bernadette.hawkins@enron.com  2.062
6               a..hughes@enron.com  2.000
117        cynthia.barrow@enron.com  2.000
199           gay.mayeux@enron.com  2.000
273       jeffrey.mcmahon@enron.com  2.000
597       slipin@brunswickgroup.com  2.000
128        david.delainey@enron.com  1.667
171      elizabeth.tilney@enron.com  1.667
167       elaine.overturf@enron.com  1.500
407        mark.pickering@enron.com  1.500
417           mary.joyce@enron.com  1.500
436        michelle.cash@enron.com  1.500
```

```
604            stanley.horton@enron.com  1.333
7                aaron.brown@enron.com  1.000
...
420         maureen.mcvicker@enron.com  0.862
...
529          richard.shapiro@enron.com  0.182
...

269            jeff.dasovich@enron.com  0.082
```

As you can see, the output is quite different from the previous section! Right at the top of the list is Ken Lay, the CEO of Enron at that point in time. This means Steve sent Ken a lot more messages than Ken sent Steve. Maureen McVicker's ratio is close to 1, which means Steve and Maureen corresponded equally with each other. Richard Shapiro and Jeff Dasovich's ratios are pretty low. This means that both Richard and Jeff sent Steve lots of messages, but he rarely replied.

Text Mining

We've done quite a bit of email message counting in this chapter so far. It would be nice if we could go a bit further and get into the text of the message itself to explore it. There are a large number of ways this can be done, but for this chapter we'll go for a relatively simple technique (which unfortunately involves counting again, but not in a way you'd expect).

For this section, we'll need to get the text of the messages, so we'll jump back to the Ruby code once more and create a script that extracts the text body from the messages. The code (shown in Example 5-15) is very similar, except that instead of picking up the From and To email addresses, it pulls out only the date and the text body of the message.

Example 5-15. Creating a data source for text mining with messages from Gmail

```
require 'csv'
require 'mail'
require 'nokogiri'

def write_row(mail, csv)
  data = []
  data << mail.date
  text = ""
  if mail.text_part
    text = mail.text_part.to_s.force_encoding("utf-8")
  else
    html = Nokogiri::Slop(mail.body.to_s)
    text = html.text.force_encoding("utf-8")
  end
  data << cleanup(text)
  csv << data
end
```

```
def cleanup(text)
  text = text.gsub("/", " ")
  text = text.gsub(/[^a-zA-Z@\s]/u,'')
  text.gsub(/\b[a-zA-Z0-9._%+-]+@[a-zA-Z0-9.-]+\.[a-zA-Z]{2,4}\b/,'')
end

EMAILS_TO_RETRIEVE = 2000

USER = '<YOUR USERNAME>'
PASS = '<YOUR PASSWORD>'
Mail.defaults do
  retriever_method :imap, :address => "imap.gmail.com",
                          :port       => 993,
                          :user_name  => USER,
                          :password   => PASS,
                          :enable_ssl => true
end

{:inbox => 'INBOX', :sent => '[Gmail]/Sent Mail'}.each do |name, mailbox|
  emails = Mail.find(:mailbox => mailbox,
                     :what => :last,
                     :count => EMAILS_TO_RETRIEVE,
                     :order => :dsc)

  CSV.open("#{name}_txt_data_gmail.csv", 'w') do |csv|
    csv << %w(date body)
    emails.each do |mail|
      begin
        write_row mail, csv
      rescue
        puts "Cannot write this mail -> #{mail.from} to #{mail.to} with subject: \
            #{mail.subject}"
        puts $!
      end
    end
  end
end
```

The big difference here is in the implementation of `write_row`. Instead of the From and To email addresses, we get the body of the message as a string. We force the string to be encoded in UTF-8 in case it's not (this is required by Ruby 1.9), then clean it up with the `cleanup` method. We also use Nokogiri, the XML parsing library, to parse through the HTML part of the message if it exists.

The `cleanup` method runs through three sets of changes. The first removes the forward slash (/) and replaces it with an empty space. The second removes all other characters except the letters in the alphabet, both lower and uppercase, as well as the at sign (@). This will remove all dates and numbers but retain the email addresses. Finally, we remove the email addresses.

Running the Ruby script for the Gmail messages creates two files: *inbox_txt_data_gmail.csv* and *sent_txt_data_gmail.csv*. These files can be pretty big, depending on how many messages we take.

Getting the body of the Enron messages for text mining is very similar, as shown in Example 5-16.

Example 5-16. Creating a data source for text mining from Enron email files

```
require 'csv'
require 'mail'

def write_row(mail, csv)
  data = []
  data << mail.date
  text = mail.body ? mail.body.to_s.force_encoding("utf-8") : ""
  data << cleanup(text)
  csv << data
end

def cleanup(text)
  text = text.gsub("/", " ")
  text = text.gsub(/[^a-zA-Z@\s]/u,'')
  text.gsub(/\b[a-zA-Z0-9._%+-]+@[a-zA-Z0-9.-_]+\b/,'')
end

DIR_PATH = "/Users/sausheong/Downloads/enron_mail_20110402/maildir/kean-s"
EXCLUDED_DIRS = \
    %w(. .. deleted_items all_documents archiving calendar discussion_threads)
SENT_DIRS = %w(sent sent_items)

sent = CSV.open("sent_txt_data_enron.csv", 'w')
sent << %w(date body)
inbox = CSV.open("inbox_txt_data_enron.csv", 'w')
inbox << %w(date body)

Dir.foreach(DIR_PATH) do |file_name|
  file = File.absolute_path(file_name, DIR_PATH)
  if File.directory?(file) and !EXCLUDED_DIRS.include?(file_name)
    Dir.foreach(file) do |mail_file|
      eml = File.absolute_path(mail_file, file)
      if File.file?(eml)
        mail = Mail.read eml
        begin
          if SENT_DIRS.include?(file_name)
            write_row mail, sent
          else
            write_row mail, inbox
          end
```

```
          rescue
            puts "Cannot write this mail -> #{mail.from} to #{mail.to} with subject: \
                #{mail.subject}"
            puts $!
          end
        end
      end
    end
end

inbox.close
sent.close

exit
```

The code here is more or less a mix of the previous example and the code in Example 5-6. The implementation of `write_row` is different again, although with the same purpose. As before, instead of getting the From and To email address fields, we just extract the body of the message as text and clean up the data to prepare it for mining. Notice that this time around we didn't use the full set of regular expressions to remove email addresses. This is because the message format in the Enron email dataset is based on Outlook and thus is different from the standard format.

Running the Ruby script for the Enron messages creates two files: *inbox_txt_data_enron.csv* and *sent_txt_data_enron.csv*. These files are big. The *inbox_txt_data_enron.csv* file is about 40 MB, while the *sent_txt_data_enron.csv* is smaller, at around 5 MB.

Now that we have the data, we'll turn to the actual text mining in R. This script is different from the earlier ones. In the previous scripts, we used mainly the core packages and functions that R provides out of the box. We did most of the processing work.

In this script, we'll be taking out the big guns and using one of the more popular text mining packages around, aptly named `tm` (did you guess it stands for "text mining"? If so, you're right). What we want to do in this analysis is find out, for each month in the available data, the most frequently used words in the messages that were sent out or received.

Before we begin, there are a few terms you'll need to be familiar with. First, we'll be dealing with the message body as a *text document*. The `tm` library adds some metadata to this, but we can safely ignore it for the purpose of this analysis. Next, a *corpus* is a collection of text documents. Finally, a *term-document matrix* is a matrix (a table-like structure) that describes the frequency of terms that occur in a corpus.

In this script, we'll create, for each month in the dataset, a corpus out of the messages sent or received in that month. Then, using that corpus, we will create a term-document matrix, and find the terms most frequently used for that month. It sounds a bit complicated, but it's really quite straightforward, and it can literally be done in a few lines of code.

Let's look at it now, starting with the sent data (Example 5-17).

Example 5-17. Frequently used terms in every month

```
library(tm)

sent_data <- read.csv("sent_txt_data.csv", header=TRUE, sep=",")

alldates <- format(as.Date(sent_data$date), '%Y-%m')
for (date in levels(factor(alldates))) {
  data <- sent_data[format(as.Date(sent_data$date), "%Y-%m") == date, ]
  source <- VectorSource(data$body)
  corpus <- Corpus(source)
  matrix <- TermDocumentMatrix(corpus, control = list(stopwords = TRUE,
            removeNumbers = TRUE, removePunctuation = TRUE))
  frequent_terms <- findFreqTerms(matrix, 100)
  print(date)
  print(nrow(data))
  print(frequent_terms)
}
```

As before, the first thing we need to do is to read the generated data into a data frame. Then we convert the column with the date from characters to an actual date, but only taking into account the year and the month:

```
alldates <- format(as.Date(sent_data$date), '%Y-%m')
```

This gives us a list of year-months, but we need a unique list because we want to iterate through each month. To get this, we use the `factor()` function on `alldates` before iterating through it with the `for` loop:

```
for (date in levels(factor(alldates))) {
...
}
```

Now that we have `date` (which is really a string with a format like `'2001-03'`), we want to select all the rows for a given month. We use the square brackets notation here to filter out the rows we want:

```
data <- sent_data[format(as.Date(sent_data$date), "%Y-%m") == date, ]
```

With this, we have the data, so it's time to break out the `tm` library and create the corpus. To create a corpus, we need to give it a source. The easiest way to do this is probably to create a `VectorSource()` function from the data frame we've just created:

```
source <- VectorSource(data$body)
```

Next, we create a corpus with the source:

```
corpus <- Corpus(source)
```

After creating the corpus, we can use it to create the term-document matrix, like so:

```
matrix <- TermDocumentMatrix(corpus, control = list(stopwords = TRUE,
                                                     removeNumbers = TRUE,
                                                     removePunctuation = TRUE))
```

This looks a bit long, but it's relatively simple to understand. We've just created a term-document matrix from the corpus, applying certain processing before creating it. First, we remove all stopwords (words so common they're not worth counting, such as *a* and *the*) using the `tm` library's standard set of English stopwords. (`tm` works with other languages too, but the default is English.) Next, we remove all numbers from the corpus. For this exercise we just want words, and numbers aren't so relevant here. Finally, we remove all punctuation characters.

With the term-document matrix, we want to find out the frequently used words in the dataset. To do this, we use the `findFreqTerms()` function:

```
frequent_terms <- findFreqTerms(matrix, 100)
```

This function has two parameters. The first is the term-document matrix. The second parameter tells the function not to bother returning any words that appear fewer than a certain number of times in the corpus. In our case, we used 100, but this number can be tweaked for the best fit.

Finally, of course, we print out our findings. These are select results from running the script. From the sent data, we find the following frequently used words from February 2001 to October 2001:

```
[1] "2001-02"
[1] 123
 [1] "california"  "corp"         "davis"        "electricity"  "energy"
 [6] "enron"       "forwarded"    "hou"          "kean"         "plants"
[11] "power"       "steven"       "subject"      "transmission" "utilities"
[1] "2001-03"
[1] 113
 [1] "california" "company"     "corp"        "davis"     "dow"
 [6] "energy"     "enron"       "forwarded"   "gas"       "hou"
[11] "jones"      "kean"        "power"       "steven"    "subject"
[1] "2001-04"
[1] 88
 [1] "california" "corp"        "energy"      "enron"     "gas"
 [6] "hou"        "kean"        "power"       "steven"    "subject"
[1] "2001-05"
[1] 122
[1] "corp"    "enron"   "hou"     "kean"    "steven"  "subject"
[1] "2001-06"
[1] 52
character(0)
```

```
[1] "2001-07"
[1] 146
[1] "email"    "energy"  "enron"    "hou"       "kean"     "please"  "power"
[8] "steven"   "subject"
[1] "2001-08"
[1] 99
[1] "august"    "enron"     "kean"      "message"  "original" "sent"      "steven"
[8] "subject"
[1] "2001-09"
[1] 62
[1] "enron"
[1] "2001-10"
[1] 118
[1] "enron"     "kean"      "message"  "october"  "original" "security" "sent"
[8] "steven"   "subject"
```

For the inbox data for the same period, but with 300 words as the cut-off point (otherwise, there are too many words), we get another set of frequently used words:

```
[1] "2001-02"
[1] 422
 [1] "attached"    "california" "corp"         "email"       "energy"
 [6] "enron"       "generation" "hou"          "power"       "subject"
[11] "utilities"
[1] "2001-03"
[1] 382
 [1] "california"  "davis"        "electricity" "email"        "energy"
 [6] "enron"       "gas"          "hou"         "market"       "plants"
[11] "power"       "prices"       "subject"     "utilities"
[1] "2001-04"
[1] 340
 [1] "april"          "bankruptcy"  "bill"          "billion"       "california"
 [6] "californias"    "commission"  "companies"     "company"       "corp"
[11] "crisis"         "customers"   "davis"         "edison"        "electric"
[16] "electricity"    "email"       "energy"        "enron"         "federal"
[21] "ferc"           "gas"         "generators"    "governor"      "market"
[26] "million"        "pay"         "percent"       "pge"           "plan"
[31] "plants"         "power"       "price"         "prices"        "public"
[36] "rate"           "rates"       "san"           "summer"        "time"
[41] "transmission" "utilities"   "utility"       "week"
[1] "2001-05"
[1] 381
 [1] "billion"     "business"     "california"  "company"     "corp"
 [6] "davis"       "electricity" "email"        "energy"      "enron"
[11] "gas"         "government"  "market"       "meeting"     "plan"
[16] "power"       "price"
[1] "2001-06"
[1] 250
 [1] "california"  "companies"    "company"      "electricity" "email"
 [6] "energy"      "enron"        "gas"          "market"       "power"
[11] "price"       "prices"
[1] "2001-07"
[1] 283
```

```
[1] "california"  "davis"       "electricity" "energy"      "enron"
[6] "power"
[1] "2001-08"
[1] 100
[1] "enron" "power"
[1] "2001-09"
[1] 93
character(0)
[1] "2001-10"
[1] 175
[1] "company" "credit"  "enron"   "enrons"
```

The first line shows the month and year, the second line shows the number of messages in that month, and the third line shows the list of frequently used words in that month.

You might notice that in April 2001, some more prominent words are *bankruptcy*, *PG&E*, *crisis*, and *Edison*. The California electricity crisis happened in April 2001, causing the bankruptcy of Pacific Gas and Electric Company (PG&E) and the near-bankruptcy of Southern California Edison. Enron Corporation was one of the energy wholesalers that became notorious for "gaming the market" and reaping huge speculative profits.

Wrap-up

There you have it! We have just completed a simple exercise to help you mine your own email account to understand your emailing habits. Along the way, we looked at the publicly available Enron email dataset and focused on one of the executives in that dataset. The code we have written might be simple, but the insights could be significant. I have ventured a bit into the territory of text mining, but overall we've barely scraped the surface of what could be done. The `tm` library, for example, is extremely powerful for text mining, and various other text mining packages have been built on it as well.

A few things you should take note of (especially for text mining) before you wend your way to mining your mailbox:

- The Enron dataset was cleaned up before it was published, so it was a lot easier to mine. Your own mailbox, on the other hand, could be wild and unruly, so your mileage will definitely vary.
- The Enron dataset comprises office email accounts derived from Exchange and Outlook files. For the text mining section, you will definitely want to tweak the `write_row` method to give you better results. The message format in the Enron dataset follows that of Exchange (in the actual text). For example, Steve's email ID is "Steven J Kean/HOU/EES@EES" in the mailbox.

- Your Gmail mailbox would have a lot more HTML messages than the Enron dataset. We used a very simple method (with Nokogiri) to extract the text content from the message, but this might not work on all possible types of HTML formats.
- If you have a lot of spam in your mailbox, it will skew the results. Correspondingly, if you see weird results in your mailbox, this is probably an indication that you have a lot of spam there.

My final word of advice for this chapter, as with the other chapters, is to play around with the code and try out different combinations. For example, you might want to know how often you get attachments and at what time of day. If you get messages in different languages, you might want to find out how many messages you get for each language. You can investigate the length of the messages you get over a period of time. You can also limit your dataset to specific people or groups of people you send or receive from, and try to get similar information on the messages you send to or receive from them.

Happy spelunking!

CHAPTER 6

In a Heartbeat

Growing old sucks. True, you gain experience and knowledge, but in exchange you must give up a fully functional and effectively working body. Different parts of your body start to show signs of wear and tear. The most telling is the upward-creeping (or rocketing, depending on your lifestyle) numbers that show your blood pressure and cholesterol. Then goes the vision, as presbyopia sets in and you need reading glasses to make out those pesky words. And soon, the all-day, all-night hackathons you so eagerly jump into at every opportunity become a disaster of epic proportions, involving massive backaches and a creaky neck. Eventually the realization sets in that taking care of your own health is important, after all.

So what does taking care of yourself have to do with programming? There is no medicine for old age (at least not yet), and spending time programming is hardly the means to improve your health. Today's healthcare technologies, however, have vastly improved our chances of growing old with fewer health problems. Research into genetics, stem cell transplants, advanced drugs, and information technology has enabled us to live longer and healthier. Naturally, in this book the main thing we're interested in is the information technology bit.

We can't explore many of these advances in information technology (there are just too many), but we'll take a simple example and do some poking around.

My Beating Heart

What we'll be exploring in this chapter is your heart, including your heart rate and your heartbeat. The heart rate, or the rate at which your heart beats, is one of the measurements you've probably heard most about in relation to exercise. It's also often a good indication of your health, because a heart rate that is too high or low could indicate an underlying health issue. The heart rate is usually measured in beats per minute (bpm) and varies from 40 to 220 bpm. An average healthy person at rest has a heart rate of 60–90 bpm, while conditioned athletes have a resting heart rate of 40–60 bpm.

The maximum heart rate is the highest heart rate anyone can safely achieve through exercise, and this depends on the age of the individual. A common formula for calculating maximum heart rate is to subtract the person's age from 220. For example, if you're 30 years old, your maximum heart rate would be 190 bpm.

The heartbeat, or heart sounds, refers to the noises generated by the beating heart and the resultant flow of blood through it. In healthy adults, there are two normal heart sounds, often described as a *lub* (the first heart sound, S1) and a *dub* (the second heart sound, S2), which occur one after the other with each heartbeat. Heart sounds can also help diagnose certain types of problems, including heart murmurs.

We'll start with the heart sounds, which incidentally also give us the heart rate.

Auscultation

Auscultation (based on the Latin verb *auscultare*, "to listen") is the practice of listening to the internal sounds of the body, usually using a stethoscope. Auscultation is a skill that takes a lot of clinical experience and a good stethoscope and can include listening to the heart, lungs, and the gastrointestinal system. In this chapter, we'll attempt only heart auscultation using a stethoscope. Not to worry, though, I have no intention of asking you to get an actual stethoscope!

Homemade Digital Stethoscope

The stethoscope we'll use in this chapter is very simple and homemade. Just use any paper or plastic disposable cup, poke a small hole in the bottom, and then stick a microphone through it. You can use any kind of microphone (or even an earphone instead) because the cup will act as an amplifier, very much like a proper stethoscope or hearing tube.

For this chapter, I used my old iPhone earphones, which have an attached microphone. To prevent your microphone from dangling about, tape it to the inner sides of the cup. Finally, using a small piece of plastic (I just cut one out from a plastic bag), cover the mouth of the cup and secure it with a rubber band (Figure 6-1). Our digital stethoscope is done!

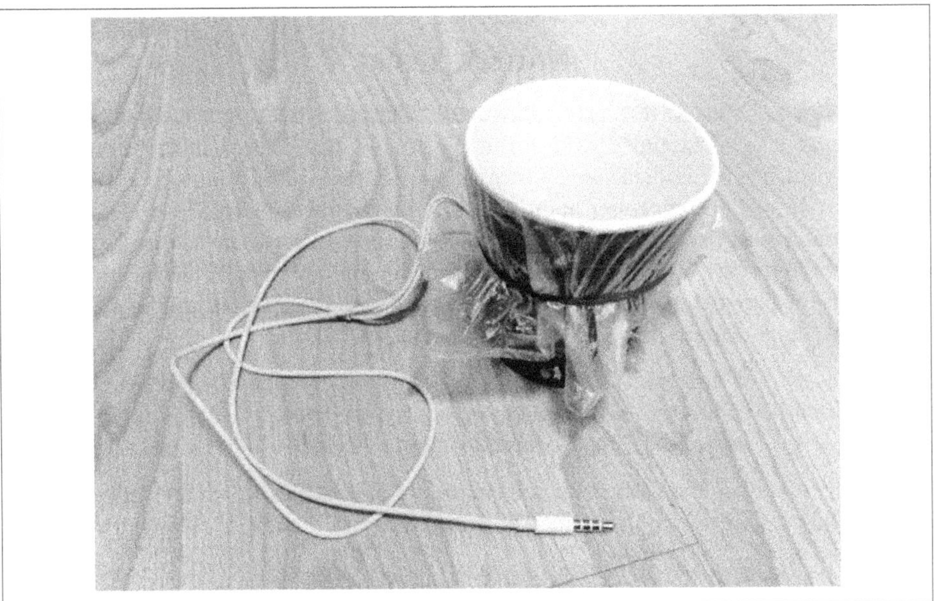

Figure 6-1. Homemade stethoscope

Make sure the plastic (which acts as a membrane or drumhead that vibrates and resonates the sounds to the cup) is pulled taut, then place your stethoscope against the left side of your chest, near your heart. Insert the other end of the microphone into your computer or any device that can record sound. In my case I ran Audacity, an open source audio editor, on my computer, then recorded my heartbeat through my homemade digital stethoscope. Once I had recorded enough, I exported the sound into a WAV file. You could use any other means to record your own heart sounds and export them into a WAV file. Have a bit of fun and be inventive!

Extracting Data from Sound

Now let's take a deeper look at the WAV file of your heartbeat, which we'll name *heartbeat.wav*. What we'll be doing is taking apart the WAV file and extracting the data out into a CSV data file. However, before we do that, we need to understand the WAV format a bit more; see the sidebar "WAV File Format" (page 160) for an in-depth explanation.

WAV File Format

WAV is an audio file format, originating from IBM and Microsoft, used to store audio bitstreams. It is an extended RIFF format, a little-endian version of the older AIFF format (which is big-endian). WAV is the main format used on Windows systems for raw and typically uncompressed audio. The usual bitstream encoding is the linear pulse-code modulation (linear PCM) format. In RIFF, data is stored in "chunks," and for WAV, there are basically two types of chunks: format and sound data. The format chunk contains the parameters describing the waveform—for example, its sample rate—and the data chunk contains the actual waveform data.

Figure 6-2 shows the format of a WAV file as a series of fields, listed from the top down. Some are little-endian and some are big-endian, as the leftmost column in the figure shows. A few contain fixed, invariable text values, as shown in the rightmost column.

There are other chunks, such as the cue chunk and playlist chunk, but for our purposes in this chapter, we need only the format and sound data chunks, so I'll skip the details about the rest.

The data chunk has a chunk ID, which is always "data," and a chunk size that is a long integer. Data in the data chunk is stored in *sample points*. A sample point is a value that represents a sample of a sound at a given moment in time. Each sample point is stored as a linear 2's-complement value from 9 to 32 bits wide, the exact number of bits being specified in the `BitsPerSample` field in the format chunk.

Sounds in a WAV file can also come in multiple channels (for instance, a stereo sound will come in two channels). For such multichannel sounds, the sample points are interleaved, one from each channel (Figure 6-3). A grouping of sample points for a single moment in time for all the channels is called a *sample frame*.

Our goal is clear: we want to extract the data out of the channels. Let's inspect our WAV file now using a hex editor. A hex editor, or binary file editor, allows us to view the actual bits and bytes of the file. There are quite a few such editors around, both open source and commercial. For this chapter, I used a hex editor named Hex Fiend.

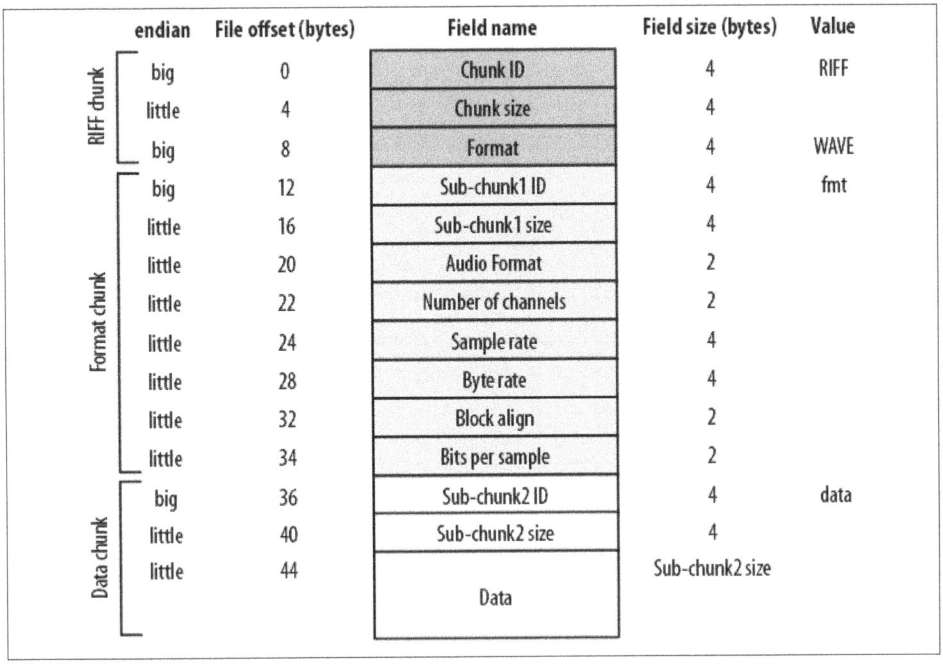

Chunk	endian	File offset (bytes)	Field name	Field size (bytes)	Value
RIFF chunk	big	0	Chunk ID	4	RIFF
	little	4	Chunk size	4	
	big	8	Format	4	WAVE
Format chunk	big	12	Sub-chunk1 ID	4	fmt
	little	16	Sub-chunk1 size	4	
	little	20	Audio Format	2	
	little	22	Number of channels	2	
	little	24	Sample rate	4	
	little	28	Byte rate	4	
	little	32	Block align	2	
	little	34	Bits per sample	2	
Data chunk	big	36	Sub-chunk2 ID	4	data
	little	40	Sub-chunk2 size	4	
	little	44	Data	Sub-chunk2 size	

Figure 6-2. WAV file format

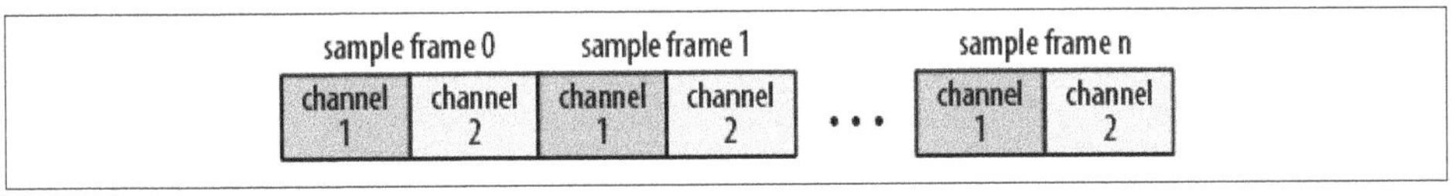

sample frame 0: channel 1 | channel 2
sample frame 1: channel 1 | channel 2
...
sample frame n: channel 1 | channel 2

Figure 6-3. Sample frames

Opening up the *heartbeat.wav* file shows us the actual bits and bytes that form it (Figure 6-4). This gives us visual confirmation of what we will do next in the Ruby code.

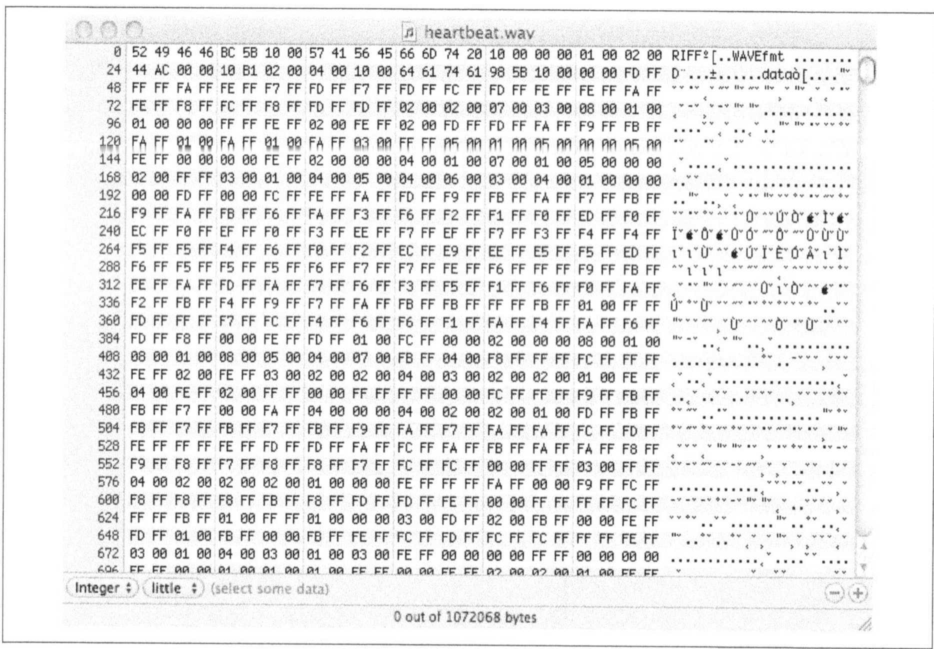

Figure 6-4. Opening the WAV file with a hex editor

Now let's jump into the code (Example 6-1).[1]

Example 6-1. Extracting data from the WAV file

```
require 'csv'

CSV.open('heartbeat.csv', 'w') do |csv|
  csv << %w(time ch1 ch2 combined)
  File.open('heartbeat.wav') do |file|
    file.seek(8)
    if file.read(4) == "WAVE"
      file.seek(36)
      if file.read(4) == 'data'
        file.seek(4, IO::SEEK_CUR)
        n = 1
        while !file.eof?
          ch1, ch2 = file.read(4).unpack('ss')
          csv << [n, ch1, ch2, ch1.to_i+ch2.to_i]
          n += 1
```

1. For this example I have not used any libraries, other than **CSV** to help us save the data into a CSV file, in order to show that it is possible to manipulate WAV files directly. If you're doing something more complex or actually reproducing WAV format files, you would want to use BinData (*http://bindata.rubyforge.org*), a Ruby library to parse and write binary data, or something equivalent.

```
          end
        end
      end
    end
  end
```

Before we actually get into the WAV file, we open a fresh *heartbeat.csv* data file to hold the data, then place a three-column header in it. One column represents the first channel, another the second channel, and the last a combination of the first and second channels. Note that we're assuming that this file is stereo and therefore has two channels and is running at 44,100 Hz.

Once we open the file, we skip the first 8 bytes and read bytes 9 through 12 to make sure that they are the string `"WAVE"`. If they're not, the file is not a WAV file and the rest is, of course, meaningless.

When we've confirmed the file format, we jump right in to read the data chunk. Our script ignores the format chunk, since we already know our file well enough.

Skipping to the 36th position, we grab the 4 bytes that make up the subchunk ID for the data chunk. Once we've confirmed that it is the data chunk, we move 4 bytes ahead and start reading data 4 bytes at a time. We skipped reading the size of the chunk because we're assuming that there aren't any other chunks in the file and we're simply reading the file until we run out of bytes to read.

To read the data to produce something meaningful, we use the `unpack` method in the `String` class. The `unpack` method is probably something most programmers never use unless they deal with binary data. To use `unpack`, we need to know the format of the data we're extracting, and that's where the WAV specifications come in handy. Return to Figure 6-2 and take a look at the endian, file offset, and field sizes. We also know that the WAV format stores its 16-bit data as signed, so we specify `'s'` when we want to extract each value as a short integer (2 bytes) and `'l'` when we want to extract it as a long integer (4 bytes).

Each sample has two channels and each sample point has 16 bits, so we need to retrieve 32 bits, or 4 bytes. Since each sample point has 16 bits, forming a short integer, we unpack the 4 bytes that are read into two short integers; this will give us the two sample points recording the two channels of that sample frame. After that, it's a simple matter of stuffing the sample points into a CSV file. When we're done, we'll have a file with three columns populated with data that we can now use to generate the heart sounds waveform.

Generating the Heart Sounds Waveform

As Example 6-2 demonstrates, it's quite simple to generate a waveform from the data we've extracted from the WAV file.

Example 6-2. Generating the heart sounds waveform

```
library(ggplot2)
png("heart_sounds.png")
data <- read.csv(file='heartbeat.csv', header=TRUE)
ggplot(data=data) + geom_point(aes(x=time, y=ch1), size = 0.8)
dev.off()
```

As in the previous chapters, we use the `ggplot2` library. We read in the CSV file into a data frame as usual, then create the waveform using the point geom, setting the size of each point to 0.8. For the amplitude, we can choose the left channel, the right channel, or the combined stereo channels. In this example, I chose the left (first) channel. My results are shown in Figure 6-5.

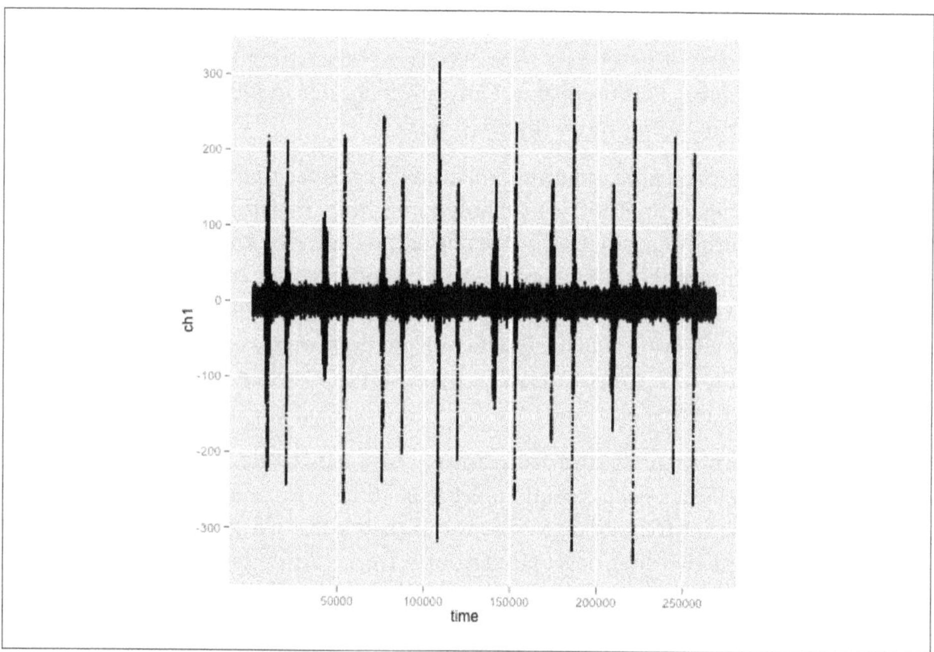

Figure 6-5. The heart sounds waveform

If you inspect the waveform, you'll notice a regular pattern: two spikes happening in rather close proximity at a regular interval. These are the two heart sounds, lub and dub, described further in the sidebar "Heart Sounds" (page 165).

> ### Heart Sounds
>
> S1 and S2 refer to sounds caused by the heart valves shutting when the heart contracts (ventricular systole). S1 (lub) is caused by the sudden blockage of reverse blood when the triscuspid and mitral valves shut at the beginning of the contraction. S2 (dub) is caused by the sudden blockage of reverse blood when the aortic and pulmonary valves shut at the end of the contraction. See Figure 6-6 for a picture of the human heart.

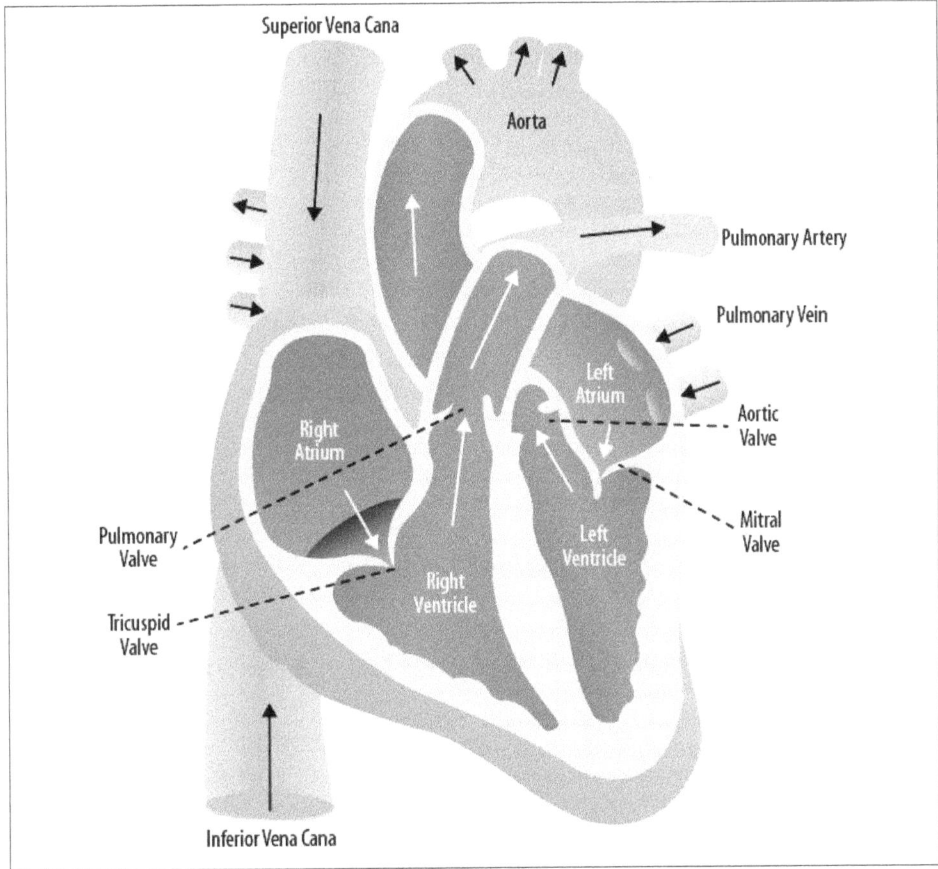

Figure 6-6. The human heart (adapted from Wikimedia Commons, licensed under the Creative Commons Attribution-Share Alike 3.0 Unported license)

The heart sounds waveform looks pretty good; I seem quite healthy. But what's my heart rate? How can we get the heart rate from the heart sounds?

Finding the Heart Rate

Finding the heart rate from the heart sounds turns out to be a bit trickier than we initially thought. Getting the heart rate seems obvious—each heartbeat is essentially the time taken from either one S1 to the next S1, or one S2 to the next S2. If we count the number of cycles or data points between these consecutive S1s or S2s, we'll be able to calculate the heart rate. Unfortunately, there is no good way to get the S1 or S2 because the sound that we recorded is inherently noisy. What we can do is simply to visually gauge the amplitude of the data and determine at which points we should consider S1 or S2 to have occurred.

A quick eyeballing of the waveform chart we created earlier in Figure 6-5 tells us that the amplitude 100 is a good level to start our calculations. Let's get down to an R script to calculate the heart rate (Example 6-3).

Example 6-3. Calculating the heart rate

```
data <- read.csv(file='heartbeat.csv', header=TRUE)
filtered_data <- data[data$ch1 > 95 & data$ch1 < 105,]
cycle <- as.numeric(rownames(filtered_data))

beats <- unique(round(cycle/1000))
intervals <- c()
count <- 1
while (count < length(beats)) {
  intervals <- append(intervals, beats[count+1] - beats[count])
  count <- count + 1
}

intervals <- intervals[!intervals<5]

steps = seq(from=1, to=length(intervals), by=2)
frequency <- c()
count <- 1
for (step in steps) {
  frequency <- append(frequency, intervals[step] + intervals[step+1])
  count <- count + 1
}

average_frequency <- mean(frequency, na.rm=T)
heart_rate <- round(60/(average_frequency/44.1))

print(paste("Interval between successive S1 + S2 sounds is",
    round(average_frequency*1000), "cycles"))
print(paste("Heart rate is ", heart_rate, "bpm"))
```

This script contains straightforward arithmetic. As usual, we read the CSV file into a data frame. As mentioned, we filter off all data that is not within the amplitude range of 100, give or take 5. This means any data value of less than 95 or more than 105 will be filtered away. This will give us the amplitude reading, but what we really want is the cycle the heart sounds are in, so we extract the `rownames` value (which is returned as a string) and convert row names into numeric values.

The values are large (44,100 Hz means there are 44,100 cycles in a second), and we're really not that interested in whether the cycle is at 8,010 or 8,500 or 8,324—we just need to know that it's approximately 8,000 (i.e., rounded to the nearest thousand). So we simply truncate each number at the thousand by dividing it by 1,000, then rounding it off. However, this can result in multiple identical values (for instance, 8,010, 8,500, and 8,324 all resolve to 8), so we use the `unique` function to remove duplicates. I call what is left `beats`, which is a vector of cycles in which a sound exists. Here's an example of two vectors:

```
 [1]   8   9  10  20  21  41  42  43  54  76  87 108 109 119 120 140 141 152 153
[20] 174 186 187 209 221 244 245 256
```

Although identifying a beat is a good indication that it represents a heart sound, there is still a chance that it's simply noise. For example, if we have levels 8,723, 8,954, and 9,045, they will resolve to two beats, 8 and 9. Obviously, there is only one heart sound, so we need to remove the beats that are close to each other.

To do this, we find the distance between consecutive elements in the `beats` vector by iterating through the vector and subtracting the current element from the next. The result is a vector of distances between consecutive beats, stored in another vector named `interval`:

```
[1]  1  1 10  1 20  1  1 11 22 11 21  1 10  1 20  1 11  1 21 12  1 22 12 23  1
[26] 11
```

Notice that many elements in the vector are 1, meaning the distance between the beats is just 1,000 or so cycles. They are simply too close to each other to be really different heart sounds, so we need to eliminate the 1s. We do this by filtering off any elements in the vector that are 5,000 or fewer cycles apart:

```
intervals <- intervals[!intervals<5]
```

This gives us a vector of actual heart sounds, and the intervals between them:

```
[1] 10 20 11 22 11 21 10 20 11 21 12 22 12 23 11
```

Notice that this produces a nice pattern of alternating 10,000–11,000 cycles between S1 and S2 and 20,000–22,000 cycles between S2 and the next S1. Since the heart rate is the cycle between consecutive S1s, we can guess that the heart rate is between 30,000 and 33,000 cycles. The bit rate is 44,100 Hz, so there are 44,100 cycles in a second, and therefore my heart rate is about three-quarters of a second per beat.

Let's go on, though—we want to calculate the heart rate in terms of beats per minute. To do this, we add up consecutive elements in the interval vector to come up with yet another vector, this time called `frequency`. The elements in this vector represent the number of cycles between consecutive S1s or S2s:

```
[1] 30 33 32 30 32 34 35 NA
```

We take the average of the elements in this vector to derive the average frequency. Note that we have to remove the `NA` (not available) element in this vector when calculating the average. We do this through a parameter in the `mean()` function. This is a common pattern you will see in many R scripts (`NA` is pretty common in raw data analysis):

```
average_frequency <- mean(frequency, na.rm=TRUE)
heart_rate <- round(60/(average_frequency/44.1))
```

Finally, to get the heart rate, we know that each beat takes about 32,300 cycles, which turns out to be around 0.73 seconds. To get the beats per minute, we divide 60 seconds by 0.73 seconds to get approximately 82 beats per minute.

Oximetry

Auscultation is, of course, not the only way to take the heart rate. A popular and fast way to effectively get the heart rate is pulse oximetry. A pulse oximeter is a device placed on a thin part of a person's body, often a fingertip or earlobe. Light of different wavelengths (usually red and infrared) is then passed through that part of the body to a photodetector. The oximeter works by measuring the amounts of red and infrared light absorbed by the hemoglobin and oxyhemoglobin in the blood to determine how oxygenated the blood is. Because this absorption happens in pulses as the heart pumps oxygenated blood throughout the body, the heart rate can also be determined.

We are not going to build an oximeter, but in this section we'll use the same concepts used in oximetry to determine the heart rate. We will record a video as we pass light through our finger for a short duration of time. With each beat of the heart, more or less blood flows through our body, including our finger. The blood flowing through our finger will block different amounts of the light accordingly. If we calculate the light intensity of each frame of the video we captured, we can chart the amount of blood flowing through our finger at different points in time, therefore getting the heart rate.

Homemade Pulse Oximeter

This process is really simple. You can use any of the following techniques, or even try your own methods. It doesn't really matter, as long as you can capture the video. Record for about 30 seconds. (Recording for a longer time can be more accurate, but not significantly so.)

Finger on a webcam
: Place your finger directly on your computer's webcam (I used the iSight on my Mac). Shine a small light (penlight or table lamp; it doesn't matter much) through your finger. Then use any video recording software to record what's on the webcam (I used QuickTime video recording).

Finger on the phone camera
: Place your finger directly on your phone camera. Turn on the flash or use a small light and shine it through your finger. Then use your phone's video recording software to record what's on the phone camera.

Finger on a digital video camera
: This is slightly harder because the camera lens is normally larger than your finger. The parts that aren't covered don't really matter, but you need to position your finger so that the image captured is consistent throughout your recording. A trick is to use a lamp as the background, so you can have the light shining through your finger and maintain a consistent background at the same time.

In the following example, I used the phone camera method with my iPhone. That's the easiest for me, because the flash on the phone is very effective. If you did things right, you'll end up with a video filled with a red blotch that's your finger.

Extracting Data from Video

Assuming that you have a nice video file now (it doesn't really matter what format it is in; you'll see why soon), let's dig in a bit deeper to see how we can extract information from it. For the sake of convenience, I'll assume the file is called *heart beat.mov*. Next we'll be using FFmpeg, a popular free video library and utility, to convert the video into a series of individual image files.

Let's take a look at the Ruby code in Example 6-4.

Example 6-4. Extracting data from video

```
require 'csv'
require 'rmagick'
require 'active_support/all'
require 'rvideo'

vid = RVideo::Inspector.new(:file => "heartbeat.mov")
width, height = vid.width, vid.height
fps = vid.fps.to_i
duration = vid.duration/1000

if system("/opt/local/bin/ffmpeg -i heartbeat.mov -f image2 'frames/frame%03d.png'")
  CSV.open("data.csv","w") do |file|
    file << %w(frame intensity)
    (fps*duration).times do |n|
      img = Magick::ImageList.new("frames/frame#{sprintf("%03d",n+1)}.png")
```

```
      ch = img.channel(Magick::RedChannel)
      i = 0
      ch.each_pixel {|pix| i += pix.intensity}
      file << [n+1, i/(height*width)]
    end
  end
end
```

It doesn't look complicated, does it? The most complex part you'll probably have to tackle is installing the necessary Ruby libraries. In the case of both RMagick and RVideo, described next, you need native developer tools support in order to compile the native components of the gem for your platform.

RMagick is a popular library for manipulating still images with Ruby. It's an interface between Ruby and the ImageMagick and GraphicsMagick image processing libraries, so you have to install at least ImageMagick as well (see "ImageMagick" for more details). There is lots of information on installing all the necessary libraries for your platform (Linux, Windows, OS X, etc.) on both the RMagick website (*http://rmagick.rubyforge.org*) and around the Internet. The code in this chapter uses RMagick 2.

ImageMagick

ImageMagick is an open source, Apache 2–licensed software project used to manipulate bitmap images. It supports a multitude of image formats and is available on several platforms, including Linux, Windows, and OS X. Although it has a command-line tool, ImageMagick's functions are often used through bindings created for many programming languages, including Ruby, Python, PHP, Java, .NET, and even Ada and Lisp. As we're using Ruby in this book, we'll be using the Ruby bindings—RMagick.

RVideo (*http://rvideo.rubyforge.org*) is a relatively new library for inspecting and manipulating video files. It is an interface between Ruby and FFmpeg, a popular video processing software project (described in more detail in the sidebar "FFmpeg" (page 171)). To install RVideo, you will need to install FFmpeg first, then a number of associated audio and video libraries.

In terms of importance, while it's necessary to install RMagick and ImageMagick, it's not entirely necessary to install RVideo (you will still need FFmpeg, though). This is because the extraction of still frames from the video is actually just a single command line issued to FFmpeg.

FFmpeg

FFmpeg is a free, GPL-based software project with a number of audio- and video-related libraries and programs. Among these are libavcodec, a popular audio/video codec; libacformat, an audio/video container library; ffserver, an HTTP and RTSP multimedia streaming server; and a command-line tool called ffmpeg. Although FFmpeg might not be as well known to actual end users as ImageMagick, it has been used by many other projects, including VLC, HandBrake, and MPlayer.

We start off the code by inspecting the video and getting some attributes from it. These will be useful later on in the code. Specifically, we will need the number of frames per second, the duration of the video, and the height and width of the video. You can obtain these through RVideo, but if you didn't succeed in getting it installed, you can still find the information by simply opening up the video with any player and viewing its properties.

Next, we use the `system` method to issue a command to the underlying shell, and return either true or false depending on whether it succeeds or not:

```
system("/opt/local/bin/ffmpeg -i heartbeat.mov -f image2 'frames/frame%03d.png'")
```

This runs ffmpeg, taking in the input file *heartbeat.mov* and converting it frame by frame into a set of images ordered by number. This is the reason why the video format is unimportant. As long as FFmpeg has the correct library to support the codecs, it will convert the video file to a series of PNG image files, numbered sequentially.

In this example, we specify that there are three digits to this series of numbers. How do we know this? In my case, I have a 30-second video with a frame rate of 30 frames per second, so the number of still frames that will be created by FFmpeg is 30×30, or 900 frames. Slightly more frames could be created—some video players round off the duration—but the total would not be more than 999 frames. If the command runs successfully, we will get a set of frames in the *frames* folder, each named *framennn.png*, where *nnn* runs from 001 to 900 or so.

Next, we create a CSV file to store the data and enter the column names, which are the frame number and the average frame intensity:

```
file << %w(frame intensity)
```

Then, for every frame image, we create the RMagick `Image` object that represents that frame and extract the red channel (the file uses the RGB colorspace):

```
i = 0
ch.each_pixel {|pix| i += pix.intensity}
file << [n+1, i/(height*width)]
```

We iterate through each pixel in the red channel and add up their intensities, then divide the sum of pixel intensities by the total number of pixels:

```
i = 0
ch.each_pixel {|pix| i += pix.intensity}
file << [n+1, i/(height*width)]
```

This is the value we consider to be the average frame intensity. Finally, we store the frame number and intensity in the CSV file.

Once we have done this, we will end up with a data file with two columns. The first is the frame number, and the second is the corresponding frame's average intensity.

Generating the Heartbeat Waveform and Calculating the Heart Rate

Generating the heartbeat waveform is trivial, so we'll combine both creating the waveform and calculating the heart rate into a single R script, shown in Example 6-5.

Example 6-5. Generating the heartbeat waveform and calculating the heart rate

```
library(PROcess)
library(ggplot2)

data <- read.csv(file='data.csv', header=T)

png("heartbeat.png")
qplot(data=data, frame, intensity, geom="line")
dev.off()

peaks <- peaks(data$intensity,span=10)
peak_times <- which(peaks==T, arr.in=T)
intervals <- c()
i <- 1
while (i < length(peak_times)) {
  intervals <- append(intervals, peak_times[i+1] - peak_times[i])
  i <- i + 1
}

average <- round(mean(intervals))
print(paste("Average interval between peak intensities is", average))
heartbeat_rate <- round(60 * (30/average))
print(paste("Heartbeat rate is",heartbeat_rate))
```

All it takes to generate the waveform (Figure 6-7) is a single line that calls `qplot` with the frame and the intensity and uses the `line` geom.

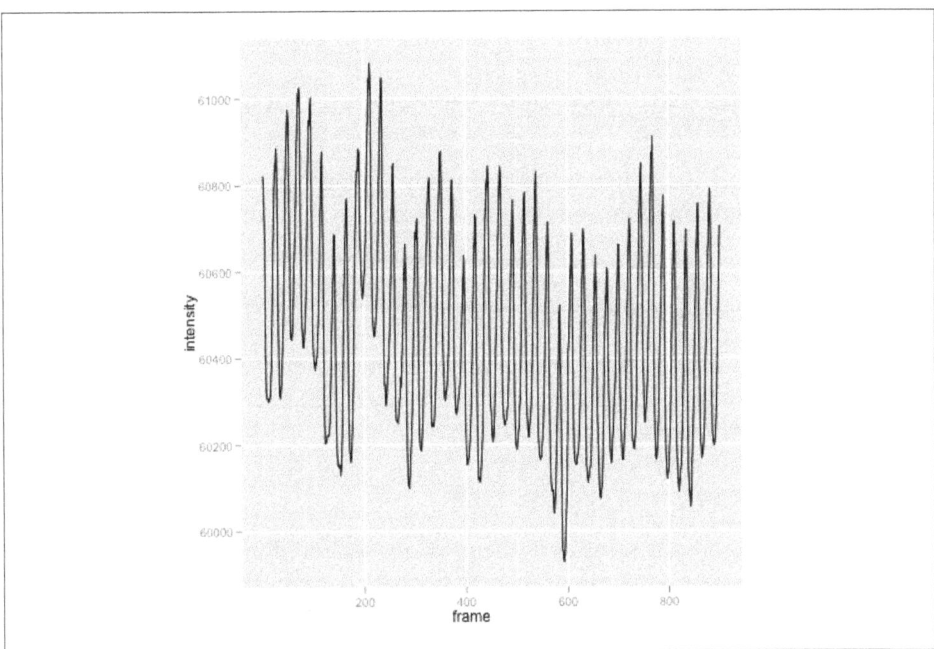

Figure 6-7. Heartbeat waveform

As you can see from the chart in Figure 6-7, the light intensity changes over time. Each pulse corresponds with a heartbeat. To find the heart rate, we need to find the number of frames between two peaks of the wave. We know that there are 30 frames in one second. Once we know the number of frames between the two peaks, we'll know how much time it takes to go from peak to peak, and therefore can calculate the number of beats per minute.

To calculate the distance from peak to peak, we need to first determine where the peaks are in the chart. For this, we will be using an R package that was originally designed to process protein mass spectrometry data, found in the Bioconductor library. The Bioconductor library is a free/open source project that provides tools for analyzing genomic data. It's based primarily on R, and most of the Bioconductor components are R packages. The package we will be using is called PROcess. Once we include the library in our script, we can start using the `peaks()` function, which, true to its name, determines which values are peaks in data.

The input parameter to the `peaks()` function is the intensity data and a span value. This span value determines how many of its neighboring values it must exceed before it can be considered a peak. This is useful to filter off noise, though not perfectly.

The returned result is a logical vector that is the same length as the data. This means we have a vector of TRUEs and FALSEs, where the TRUEs indicate a peak:

```
 [1] FALSE FALSE FALSE FALSE FALSE FALSE FALSE FALSE FALSE FALSE FALSE FALSE
[13] FALSE FALSE FALSE FALSE FALSE FALSE FALSE FALSE FALSE FALSE FALSE FALSE
[25] FALSE FALSE FALSE  TRUE FALSE FALSE FALSE FALSE FALSE FALSE FALSE FALSE
```

While this vector is informative, it's not really the answer we want, so we pass it through the `which()` function, and it returns a vector of the indices where the element is TRUE:

```
 [1]  28  50  73  96 119 142 167 190 213 236 259 282 306 330 353 374 397 420 445
[20] 469 494 517 540 563 586 610 632 656 678 701 723 746 769 791 812 836 859 882
```

As before, we want to find the distance between the two peaks, so we take two consecutive elements and subtract the first from the second. This gives us a new vector that contains the differences:

```
 [1] 22 23 23 23 23 25 23 23 23 23 23 24 24 23 21 23 23 25 24 25 23 23 23 23 24
[26] 22 24 22 23 22 23 23 22 21 24 23 23
```

The final two steps are the same as in the previous section. First, we find the average distance using the `mean()` function. Then, from that, we know that there are 23 frames between two peaks, meaning each heartbeat takes 23 frames or 23/30 seconds (since each second has 30 frames). From that, we calculate that the heart rate is 78 bpm.

If you're concerned about why the heart rate found with this pulse oximetry differs from the one we found with heart auscultation, you shouldn't be. I captured the data at different points in time, and in order to make the heartbeat stronger so it could be heard better in auscultation, I exerted myself a bit more before using the homemade stethoscope.

Wrap-up

Although it seems like we've covered quite a bit of ground, this is only the tip of the iceberg that is healthcare technology. In fact, we've talked only briefly about the heart, specifically the heart sounds and the heart rate. Healthcare technology is still a vast, uncharted territory and has plenty of potential to be explored yet.

For this chapter at least, we've gone through two specific techniques: heart auscultation with a homemade digital stethoscope, and pulse oximetry with a camera. With our homemade stethoscope, we first captured the sounds made by our heart and stored them as a WAV file. Then we extracted the raw data from this file and converted it into a CSV file. Using R scripts, we built a waveform chart and determined the first and second heart sounds, S1 and S2. Finally, we calculated the distance between consecutive S1 sounds and came up with the heart rate.

To build our makeshift pulse oximeter, we first captured a video of our finger on a digital camera, with light shining through it. Then, using this FFmpeg, we converted this video into a series of frames. We derived numeric data based on the average light intensity of each frame, and stored the data once again into a CSV file. Using this file, we first charted the heartbeat waveform, then determined the distance between consecutive peaks. Finally, we used this distance to calculate our heart rate.

CHAPTER 7
Schooling Fish and Flocking Birds

Part and parcel of using public transportation is walking home from the train station in the evening. It is also the most nerve-racking part of my weekday ritual, as the walk goes through a path lined gently with trees that occasionally bear purple berries. But neither the trees nor the berries are the problem—rather, it's the swarms of Javan mynahs that roost in them as the sun gradually sets. While I'm not describing Hitchcockian-level terror here, it is quite a gauntlet to run through, because Javan mynahs have some "restroom problems" that would make it quite complex to carry out for them the kind of analysis I presented in Chapter 3. As the swarm settles when the sky darkens, the birds generally let loose their daily intake indiscriminately over the pathway, and any unlucky souls who happen to be under them run the risk of zoonosis.

This naturally encourages me to walk hurriedly by before the sun sets, often in time to see the dramatic aerial acrobatics the mynahs perform before settling on their communal roosts in the trees. It can be startling to watch as the birds rise, twist, and turn as one, beautifully maneuvering in seeming exuberance. What is even more amazing is that the birds often number in the hundreds, so it can be both an astonishing and scary sight. While not as spectacular as the starling swarms in Europe, which often number in the hundreds of thousands and are sometimes referred to as the "Black Sun," the mynah swarms are interesting enough to start a train of thought that has eventually led me to this basic question: how and why do these birds flock the way they do?

As usual, I started off my quest with some searches on trusty old Google, which brought up a number of intriguing results. As it turns out, there is a whole bunch of existing research on flocking birds and swarming insects, dating back to more than 30 years ago. One popular and well-known product of this research is the Boids algorithm created by Craig Reynolds in 1986.

Figure 7-1. Flocking birds, adapted from a photo taken by Eugene Zemlyanskiy (http://www.flickr.com/photos/pictureperfectpose/81938785/)

The Origin of Boids

Boids is an artificial life program developed by Craig Reynolds to simulate the behavior of flocking birds. The name refers to the birdlike objects that populate the simulation. Instead of programming complex behavior for the boids, Reynolds provided three simple rules:

Separation
: Each boid should stay away from its flockmates to avoid overcrowding.

Alignment
: Each boid should move toward the average direction and with the average speed of its flockmates.

Cohesion
: Each boid should move toward the average position of its flockmates.

Much to Reynolds's astonishment, these three rules produced a surprisingly lifelike simulation of bird flocking behavior. His research made its way into a paper in ACM SIGGRAPH 1987, an annual conference on computer graphics, and has since been one of the most cited examples of the principles of artificial life.

Reynolds's work on Boids also made a lot of headway into, unsurprisingly, a number of Hollywood movies. One of the first movies that made use of his research was

Batman Returns, in which swarms of bats were created as computer simulations. Other famous movies that used similar technologies to create lifelike simulations include *The Lion King*, *Avatar*, and the *Lord of the Rings* trilogy. In the *Lord of the Rings*, Massive Software used these simulations to enact the colossal battles between hordes of orcs and the forces of good. Massive Software even received an Academy Award for Scientific and Engineering Achievement for its work on the trilogy.

The Boids program demonstrates what is now commonly called *emergent behavior*—that is, complex and global behavior arising from simple and local rules. By following a simple set of rules (three, in this case) that relate only to its immediate environment, a flock of boids can behave in unpredictable and unanticipated ways. For example, when an obstacle is placed in front of a flock, the boids swerve around it and regroup after passing it, even though this behavior is not programmed.

In this chapter, we'll use Reynolds's Boids technology to attempt to simulate the behavior of the flock of Javan mynahs. The Boids simulation has been recreated in many programming languages, and here we'll step through simulating a flock of boids with Ruby.

Simulation

Our simulation is quite a straightforward implementation of the Boids algorithm in Ruby. We'll be implementing the simulation with the Shoes GUI toolkit. Shoes was described in detail in Chapter 1, but this is our first chance to use this minimalist GUI toolkit.

I called the objects in this simulation `roids`, which is short for "Ruby boids." The whole simulation is written in a single file named *roids.rb*. Let's look at each step of the simulation. Before we start on the simulation proper, we need to set up some constants to configure the simulation:

```
FPS = 24
ROID_SIZE = 10
WORLD = {:xmax => ROID_SIZE * 100, :ymax => ROID_SIZE * 100}
POPULATION_SIZE = 50
```

`FPS` (frames per second) is the *frame rate*, or the speed at which the animation runs. `ROID_SIZE` is the size of the individual roid, while `POPULATION_SIZE` is the number of roids created for the simulation. The `WORLD` constant is a hash with two keys, where the first is `xmax`, the maximum width of the animation window, and the second is `ymax`, the maximum height of the animation window.

All code examples may be downloaded from GitHub (*https://github.com/sausheong/everyday*).

With that, let's get into the main Shoes application, as shown in Example 7-1.

Example 7-1. Main simulation loop

```
Shoes.app(:title => 'Roids', :width => WORLD[:xmax], :height => WORLD[:ymax]) do
  stroke slategray
  fill gainsboro
  $roids = []
  POPULATION_SIZE.times do
    random_location = Vector[rand(WORLD[:xmax]),rand(WORLD[:ymax])]
    random_velocity = Vector[rand(11)-5,rand(11)-5]
    $roids << Roid.new(self, random_location, random_velocity)
  end

  animate(FPS) do
   clear do
     background ghostwhite
     $roids.each do |roid| roid.move; end
   end
  end
end
```

You might notice that the entire simulation is wrapped within the app class method, which happens to be the main application window. The first line creates the Shoes application window with the appropriate width and height.

Next, we set up the line color and the fill colors for all subsequent shapes created in this application. Shoes uses the standard W3C-defined CSS level 3 color names, all predefined and ready to be used. We set the colors here because every roid will have the same line color and fill, and we don't want to set them individually.

The `$roids` global variable is an array that contains all the roids in the simulation. We will be accessing this variable from a number of places, and in order to avoid passing it around as an argument to many methods, we set it up as a global variable. The next few lines populate `$roids` with a population of roids, randomly scattered all over the simulation window, with randomly set velocities.

Now that we've prepared the simulation, the rest of the code goes through an animation loop. The `animate` method is a method in the Shoes app that loops continuously at a given frame rate. The animation loop in our case is the actual simulation, which goes through every roid in the population at each frame and moves it. Note that we clear the screen at the start of each iteration of the animation loop. This is because we are actually redrawing the roids at every frame instead of moving them. Shoes provides the facility to move the sprites we draw on the application window, so why are we going the heavyweight route of completely redrawing the elements? Because redrawing gives us a capability that moving the sprite doesn't: it allows us to draw a "tail" on each roid that indicates its velocity and direction of movement. If we move the roid sprite instead of redrawing it, we would need a more complicated algorithm to display the "tail."

The preceding code shows how we can add a background color to the application window. Shoes allows you to paint the background with a color, add a gradient, or simply use an image as the background. This is mainly cosmetic.

Roids

Now that we have the simulation loop, let's step back a bit and look at the `Roid` class itself, shown in Example 7-2.

Example 7-2. Roid class

```
class Roid
  attr_reader :velocity, :position

  def initialize(slot, p, v)
    @velocity = v
    @position = p
    @slot = slot
  end

  def distance_from(roid)
    distance_from_point(roid.position)
  end

  def distance_from_point(vector)
    x = self.position[0] - vector[0]
    y = self.position[1] - vector[1]
    Math.sqrt(x*x + y*y)
  end

  def nearby?(threshold, roid)
    return false if roid === self
    distance_from(roid) < threshold and within_fov?(roid)
  end

  def within_fov?(roid)
    v1 = self.velocity - self.position
    v2 = roid.position - self.position
    cos_angle = v1.inner_product(v2)/(v1.r*v2.r)
    Math.acos(cos_angle) < 0.75 * Math::PI
  End

  def draw
    @slot.oval :left => @position[0], :top => @position[1], :radius => ROID_SIZE,
        :center => true
    @slot.line @position[0], @position[1], @position[0] - @velocity[0],
        @position[1] - @velocity[1]
  end
```

```
  def move
    @delta = Vector[0,0]
    %w(separate align cohere muffle avoid).each do |action|
      self.send action
    end
    @velocity += @delta
    @position += @velocity
    allow_fallthrough and draw
  end
end
```

Each roid has two attributes, `velocity` and `position`. The `velocity` of the roid describes the speed and direction it's moving, while the `position` of the roid tells us where it is at that moment. The main application window has a coordinate system that starts with 0 for *x* and *y* at the top-left corner of the window. The `position` of the roid (and anything else on the window, for that matter) is described within this coordinate system (Figure 7-2).

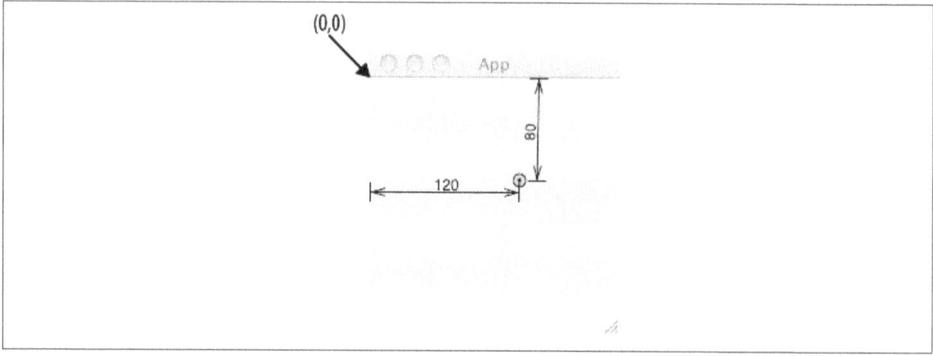

Figure 7-2. Shoes coordinate system

The attributes represent different things, but we can use the same class to describe them: the `Vector` class, which is part of the `matrix` library from the standard Ruby distribution. Although it's probably easy to understand that the `position` vector is represented by (*x*,*y*), the `velocity` vector is slightly different from the standard definition of velocity in physics that you are used to. In physics, velocity represents speed and direction. Our application runs along the same lines, but the numbers can be thought of as (*dx*,*dy*) and describe how far the roid has moved within the span of a frame in our simulation. For example, if the current position is (120,80) and the velocity is (25,35), the position of the vector in the next unit of time will be calculated using vector graphics:

$$\begin{pmatrix}120\\80\end{pmatrix} + \begin{pmatrix}25\\35\end{pmatrix} = \begin{pmatrix}145\\115\end{pmatrix}$$

As you might have guessed, the addition (+) operator for vectors is not the same operator you're used to, and we need to include the `matrix` library, which is a part of the Ruby standard library. The standard library in Ruby, unlike the core library, is not automatically included every time you run Ruby. In other words, although you don't need to install any gems or download any additional scripts, you will have to manually `require` the library that you want—in this case, `matrix`.

However, Shoes is designed in such a way that it bundles its own set of Ruby gems and its own distribution of the Ruby standard library. Normally this is OK, but under certain circumstances, especially when you need a specific version of the standard library, it can create pretty thorny issues. In our case, the `Vector` implementation in Ruby 1.9.1 does not include vector division (the reason is a mystery to me, since it has every other operation), while Ruby 1.9.2 does. Unfortunately, as Murphy's Law goes, the most current version of Shoes as of this writing, Shoes 3 "Policeman," is bundled with Ruby 1.9.1.

To evade the entire issue, I used a fairly standard Ruby technique, which some call *monkey-patching* and others call, much more diplomatically, *open classes* (Example 7-3).

Example 7-3. Adding vector division to the Vector class

```
class Vector
  def /(x)
    if (x != 0)
      Vector[self[0]/x.to_f,self[1]/x.to_f]
    else
      self
    end
  end
end
```

I've just added the division operator to the `Vector` class. If you're new to Ruby but have experience in some other languages like Java, you might be surprised to read about this trick, because in the other languages you would need to subclass a parent class in order to add new methods. In contrast, the open classes technique, which allows you to simply *open* up a class and add in your own method, is quite commonly used in Ruby. In this case, I opened up the `Vector` class and defined an additional method that allows a `Vector` to be divided by a scalar number. We'll see how this is used in a while.

Let's get back to the `Roid` class in Example 7-2. If you take a closer look at the constructor (the `initialize` method), you will see that we pass an argument called `slot` when we create an instance of `Roid`. This is the `Shoes::Slot` class. A slot is like a canvas upon which we can lay out images, text, and other things. The Shoes main application window is a kind of slot too. We pass the main application window into the `Roid` instance because we want to draw the roid on this window.

The next few methods in the listing are all about finding out how far a given roid is from this particular one. We use a simple two-dimensional model, so we can determine the distance between the two roids (known as the *Euclidean distance* or the *Pythagorean distance*) using Pythagoras's theorem (Figure 7-3).

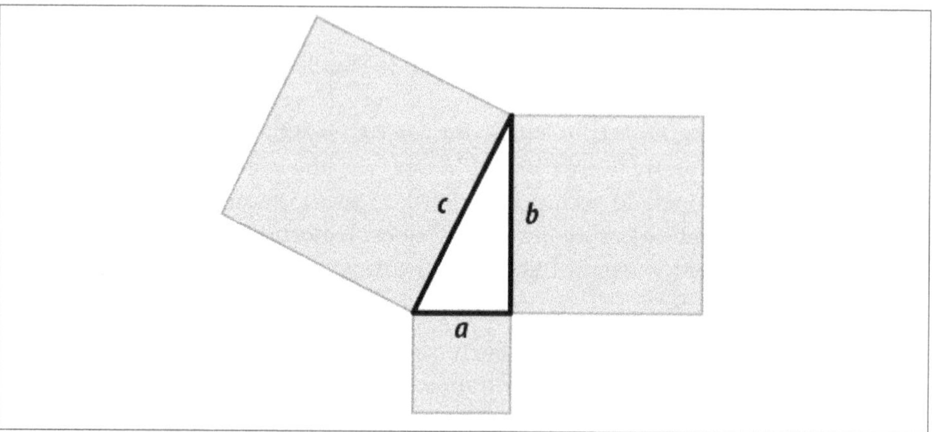

Figure 7-3. Pythagoras's theorem

As illustrated in Figure 7-3, in order to find the distance *c* between two points, we find the square root of a^2 and b^2. Thus, the distance between two points, $(x1, y1)$ and $(x2,y2)$, is shown by:

$$\sqrt{(x_1 - x_2)^2 + (y_1 - y_2)^2}$$

The formula is translated into code as follows:

```
def distance_from_point(vector)
  x = self.position[0] - vector[0]
  y = self.position[1] - vector[1]
  Math.sqrt(x*x + y*y)
end
```

We also defined a `nearby?` method that will return true only if a roid is within a specific threshold away from the current roid. This lays the foundation for the three rules later that need to find roids that are near a specific roid. In addition to lying within a certain radius of another point to be considered nearby, the roid also needs to fulfill a method called `within_fov?`:

```
def nearby?(threshold, roid)
  return false if roid === self
  distance_from(roid) < threshold and within_fov?(roid)
end
```

The `within_fov?` method is an interesting one. The acronym FOV stands for *field of vision*, which is the roid's observable world at any given moment. In other words, this is what the roid can "see" around itself. In our implementation, we assume that the roid has an FOV of 270 degrees or 1.5π radians. If we imagine that the roid is a triangle with the direction of the arrow being the direction the roid is moving, the FOV is as shown in Figure 7-4.

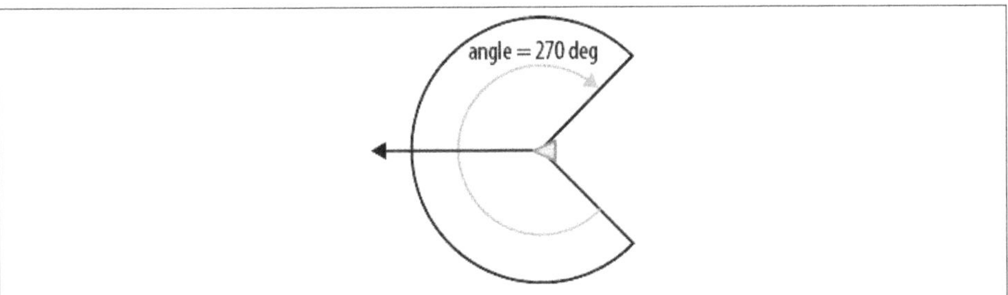

Figure 7-4. Roid's field of vision (FOV)

To find out if a roid is within its FOV, we find the angle θ between the `velocity` vector (v1) of our roid and the `position` vector (v2) of the roid we are checking. If this angle θ is less than half of its FOV—that is, if θ is less than 135 deg or 0.75π—the roid is within its FOV. We divide the angle in half because half of the FOV extends on each side of the `position` vector.

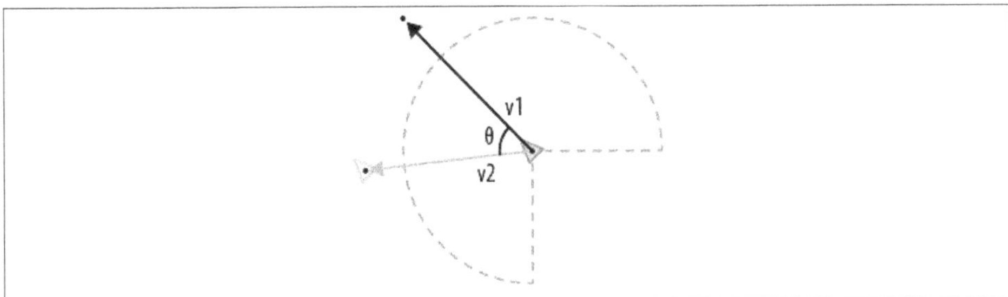

Figure 7-5. Angle between velocity vector v1 and position vector v2

To find the angle θ, we use the formula for finding the angle between two vectors in a Euclidean plane, using the *inner product*:

$$v1 \cdot v2 = \cos(\theta)\ \|v1\|\ \|v2\|$$

Because we're looking for the angle, we convert this equation to:

$$\cos(\theta) = \frac{v1 \cdot v2}{||v1|| \; ||v2||}$$

The · is the inner product between two vectors, while the two vertical bars refer to the scalar length of the vector (just the length of the line drawn between the start and end). To state the above equation in words, the cosine of the angle between the two vectors can be derived from the inner product of the vectors, divided by the product of the lengths of the two vectors.

Fortunately for us, the `Vector` class in the `matrix` package provides us with two methods that ease this calculation. The first is the `inner_product` method, which obviously does the inner product operation for the two vectors. The second is the `r` method, which returns the Pythagorean distance of the vector (this is the scalar value we need).

The result of the calculation provides us with the cosine of the angle we want (in radians, not degrees). We use the `Math.acos` method to convert the cosine of the angle into the actual angle in radians, and if it is less than 0.75π radians, it is within the roid's FOV. Note that `cos_angle` can be a negative number: this just means that v2 is on the other side of v1. The final angle is always positive, of course:

```
def within_fov?(roid)
  v1 = self.velocity - self.position
  v2 = roid.position - self.position
  cos_angle = v1.inner_product(v2)/(v1.r*v2.r)
  Math.acos(cos_angle) < 0.75 * Math::PI
end
```

Let's move on to the `move` method, which is the core method of the `Roid` class because it determines where and how the roid moves. This is the brains behind the entire logic of moving the roids, so let's look at it carefully:

```
def move
  @delta = Vector[0,0]
  %w(separate align cohere muffle avoid).each do |action|
    self.send action
  end
  @velocity += @delta
  @position += @velocity
  allow_fallthrough and draw
end
```

First, we set up a `delta` instance variable that accumulates information about the roid's velocity (which, as we've seen, includes the direction).

Then, in succession, we call the three rules defined by Reynolds: `separate`, `align`, and `cohere`, each implemented as a method in the `Roid` class. Each method will change the `delta` variable. Following that, we call two more methods that adjust the movement of the roids to fit within the window, `muffle` and `avoid`, and these adjustments also change the `delta` variable.

The roid's `velocity` is then modified by `delta`, and the `position` is in turn modified by `velocity`. This leaves the roid's new velocity and position in place at the end of the method. After we have the new `position` of the roid, we check whether the roid is beyond the boundaries of the application window, and if it is, we allow it to fall through to the other side of the window.

Finally, of course, we draw the roid.

The `draw` method is simple: it just draws the roid on the application window. In this simulation, for simplicity's sake, we made the roid look a bit like a tadpole. It consists of a circular head and a line drawn from the center of the head to the coordinates of its previous location (which is the `velocity` vector). In the simulation, this will result in a rather lifelike, tadpole-esque creature (Figure 7-6):

```
def draw
  @slot.oval :left => @position[0], :top => @position[1], :radius => ROID_SIZE,
      :center => true
  @slot.line @position[0], @position[1], @position[0] - @velocity[0],
      @position[1] - @velocity[1]
end
```

Now that we've gotten an overview of how roids move, let's dive deeper into each of the methods we mentioned earlier. Let's start with Reynolds's three boid rules.

The Boid Flocking Rules

To recap, the `separate` rule tells each roid to keep its distance from other roids. Let's see how this is implemented in our Roids simulation (Example 7-4).

Example 7-4. Separate rule

```
def separate
  distance = Vector[0,0]
  $roids.each do |roid|
    if nearby?(SEPARATION_RADIUS, roid)
      distance += self.position - roid.position
    end
  end
  @delta += distance/SEPARATION_ADJUSTMENT
end
```

For each roid in the system (this is where we use the `$roid` global variable where we kept all the roids in the system), we check whether it's within the `SEPARATION_RADIUS` of our roid, and if it is, we move it away. The amount of distance to move is the current

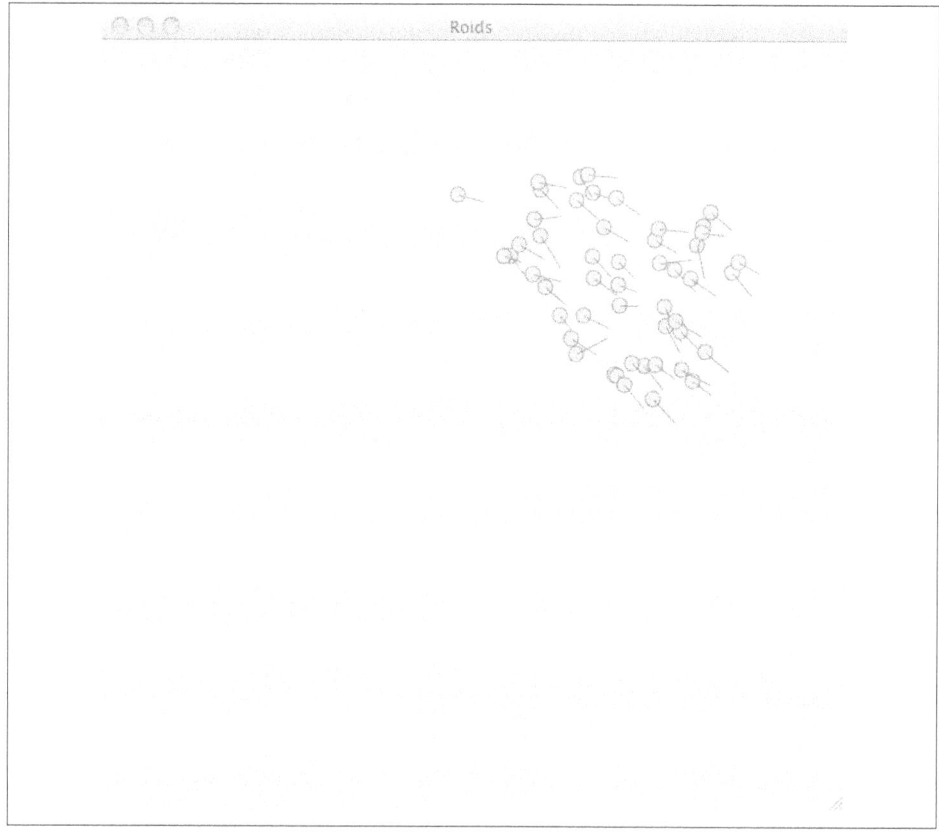

Figure 7-6. Roids in action

distance between our roid and that roid. We start with a `Vector` that is (0,0) and accumulate the difference in position for each of the nearby roids. After going through all the nearby roids, we modify the `delta` accordingly. What does this mean? It means that if the roid is close to our roid, it will move away slowly; and if it is relatively farther away, it will move away more quickly. You might notice that we divide the distance with a `SEPARATION_ADJUSTMENT` constant. This is to reduce jerky movements when this rule modifies the `velocity` of the roid.

Next is the `align` rule, which tells the roids to move in the same general direction as the roids that are near it (Example 7-5).

Example 7-5. The align rule

```
def align
  nearby, average_velocity = 0, Vector[0,0]
  $roids.each do |roid|
```

```
    if nearby?(ALIGNMENT_RADIUS, roid)
      average_velocity += roid.velocity
      nearby += 1
    end
  end
  average_velocity /= nearby
  @delta += (average_velocity - self.velocity)/ALIGNMENT_ADJUSTMENT
end
```

Just as with `separate`, we check for nearby roids, but here we use a much larger radius to check more distant roids. We add up their `velocity` values and divide the result by the number of nearby roids found to get the average velocity. We subtract our roid's `velocity` from this average velocity and, as with the `separate` rule, adjust the result by dividing it with an `ALIGNMENT_ADJUSTMENT` constant in order to make the `velocity` changes more gradual.

The last boid-related rule is `cohere`. This tells our roid to move toward the center of mass of the nearby roids (Example 7-6).

Example 7-6. The cohere rule

```
def cohere
  nearby, average_position = 0, Vector[0,0]
  $roids.each do |roid|
    if nearby?(COHESION_RADIUS, roid)
      average_position += roid.position
      nearby += 1
    end
  end
  average_position /= nearby
  @delta +=  (average_position - self.position)/COHESION_ADJUSTMENT
end
```

The implementation is quite similar to that of the `align` rule. Instead of getting the average velocity, we add up the positions of the nearby roids and divide that total by the number of nearby roids to get the average position. As before, we subtract the roid's `position` from the average position and adjust it to make the positional changes more gradual, using the `COHESION_ADJUSTMENT` constant.

Each of the three rules refers to specific parameterized values that allow us to tweak what constitutes being nearby. For example, in the `separate` rule we have the `SEPARATION_RADIUS`, in the `align` rule we have the `ALIGNMENT_RADIUS`, and in the `cohere` rule we have the `COHESION_RADIUS`. Let's look at these values here:

```
SEPARATION_RADIUS = ROID_SIZE * 2
ALIGNMENT_RADIUS  = ROID_SIZE * 15
COHESION_RADIUS   = ROID_SIZE * 15
```

In this implementation, we have used the comparative size of the roid as the base multiplier to determine how far away a roid would have to be in order to influence another roid. The radius used for the `separate` rule is much smaller than the other two rules because we don't want roids that are far away to be repelled even further. The radii for the `align` and `cohere` rules are relatively larger, as we want the roids to collect in a single group rather than many small groups.

There you have it—these three rules make up the original Boids flocking algorithm created by Craig Reynolds.

Supporting Rules

While Reynolds's three rules suffice to make a rather compelling simulation, we need a couple more rules to make the simulation run smoothly:

- Muffle the speed of the roid. We don't want roids to randomly speed up as a result of flocking. Real birds can't speed up too much, so we must slow down the roids if they move too fast as a result of our flocking rules.
- Allow the roid to fall through from one side of the application window into the other. The alternative is to make the roids bounce around the application window. I personally dislike that—it makes the roid look like it's a bouncing ball, and birds don't bounce.

Let's look at the `muffle` rule first, shown in Example 7-7.

Example 7-7. The muffle rule

```
def muffle
  if @velocity.r > MAX_ROID_SPEED
    @velocity /= @velocity.r
    @velocity *= MAX_ROID_SPEED
  end
end
```

This rule is simple enough. If the Pythagorean distance of the velocity is more than a maximum that we set, `MAX_ROID_SPEED`, we cap the speed of the roid, then set it to `MAX_ROID_SPEED`. This ensures that the roid will never go faster than this speed.

The `allow_fallthrough` rule is also quite straightforward, though a bit verbose, as shown in Example 7-8.

Example 7-8. The allow_fallthrough rule

```
def allow_fallthrough
  x = case
  when @position[0] < 0             then WORLD[:xmax] + @position[0]
  when @position[0] > WORLD[:xmax] then WORLD[:xmax] - @position[0]
  else @position[0]
  end
  y = case
  when @position[1] < 0             then WORLD[:ymax] + @position[1]
  when @position[1] > WORLD[:ymax] then WORLD[:ymax] - @position[1]
```

```
  else @position[1]
  end
  @position = Vector[x,y]
end
```

If the roid's position falls outside the boundary of the application window, we make it appear on the other side of the window. This rule has a rather interesting side effect. If the roids cohere loosely, the tail end of the flock might be attracted to the head of the flock appearing on the other side of the window!

With this, we've wrapped up our simple bird flocking simulation, following Reynolds's classic Boids algorithm. I strongly encourage you to try this out on your own and change the various parameters to see how they affect the simulation. The differences can be quite startling. Changing the various radii for the three rules might make the roids run amok on the screen, darting everywhere; or, at the other extreme, make them lounge lethargically, unwilling to move. They might even crash into each other in mad races around the application window.

A Variation on the Rules

While the Boids algorithm implemented three rules that made its motion surprisingly realistic, only recently was there any solid research to verify that real birds follow these rules when they are flocking. The next iteration of our simulation will take a look at some of that recent research and implement the new rules it produced.

Over a period of three years, 2004–2007, during the Starlings in Flight (or STARFLAG) project, researchers from various institutes in Italy, France, Germany, Hungary, and the Netherlands gathered empirical data about starlings in flight to develop insights into the flocking behavior of birds. Their research produced some interesting results. A 2008 paper,[1] based on a study conducted by European researchers in the STARFLAG project on starlings, suggested that the interaction between flocking birds is not between one bird and *all birds* within a specific distance (as suggested by the Boids algorithm and subsequent simulations), but rather only six to seven nearby birds. This means that for our simulation, instead of getting all roids within a certain radius, we would want to get only the six or seven nearest roids.

How does this change our simulation code? Nothing too drastic—the only change is really in modifying the three flocking rules to reflect this behavior. As before, let's look at the `separate` rule first (Example 7-9).

1. M. Ballerini et al., "Interaction ruling animal collective behavior depends on topological rather than metric distance: Evidence from a field study," *Proceedings of the National Academy of Sciences of the United States of America* 105, no. 4 (2008): 1232–1237.

Example 7-9. Alternate separate rule

```
def separate
  distance = Vector[0,0]
  r = $roids.sort {|a,b| self.distance_from(a) <=> self.distance_from(b)}
  roids = r.first(MAGIC_NUMBER)
    roids.each do |roid|
      if nearby?(SEPARATION_RADIUS, roid)
        distance += self.position - roid.position
      end
    end
  @delta += distance/SEPARATION_ADJUSTMENT
end
```

Instead of just getting all the nearby roids, we first sort the roids by their distance from our roid. Then we get the first `MAGIC_NUMBER` of roids, the `MAGIC_NUMBER` constant being 6 or 7 as in the research mentioned earlier. The rest of the code remains the same.

The next rule, `align`, has similar changes, as shown in Example 7-10. Note that in each place where we used to refer to the number of nearby roids, we now simply use `MAGIC_NUMBER`.

Example 7-10. Alternate align rule

```
def align
  alignment = Vector[0,0]
  r = $roids.sort {|a,b| self.distance_from(a) <=> self.distance_from(b)}
  roids = r.first(MAGIC_NUMBER)
  roids.each do |roid|
    alignment += roid.velocity
  end
  alignment /= MAGIC_NUMBER
  @delta += alignment/ALIGNMENT_ADJUSTMENT
end
```

The `cohere` rule, shown in Example 7-11, changes in similar ways to the `align` rule. As before, the changes are minimal.

Example 7-11. Alternate cohere rule

```
def cohere
  average_position = Vector[0,0]
  r = $roids.sort {|a,b| self.distance_from(a) <=> self.distance_from(b)}
  roids = r.first(MAGIC_NUMBER)
  roids.each do |roid|
    average_position += roid.position
  end
  average_position /= MAGIC_NUMBER
  @delta +=  (average_position - @position)/COHESION_ADJUSTMENT
end
```

So how does this minor change affect the behavior of the flock? An immediate effect is that the whole simulation runs a lot slower. This is because the calculations are more intensive now, especially when each call to a rule requires a sort of all the roids in the system. However, the observer perceives no differences between the old and new simulations. Both appear to be a realistic representation of flocking birds.

Going Round and Round

One effect of our implementation is that the roids seem to be in an infinite loop, entering one side of the window and going out the other like the *Portal* puzzle platform game created by Valve Corporation. Unless flocks of birds exist in the Enrichment Center for Aperture Laboratories,[2] this doesn't seem very realistic. One way to prevent this effect is to bounce the roids off the walls, but we already rejected that as also being unrealistic. Another solution, shown in Example 7-12, is to create an additional rule—`center`—that in essence tells the roids to circle the center of the application window.

Example 7-12. The center rule

```
def center
  @delta -= (@position - Vector[WORLD[:xmax]/2, WORLD[:ymax]/2]) / CENTER_RADIUS
end
```

We take the roid's `position` and subtract from it a `Vector` representing the center of the application window. Then we divide this value by `CENTER_RADIUS`, which will limit the radius of the circle that the roids follow around the center of the application window. The result is then subtracted from the delta that modifies the `velocity` of the roid.

To include `center`, we add it to the list of rules to be followed by each roid. The effect will be to make the group of roids circle the center of the application window, with the radius of orbit being `CENTER_RADIUS`.

Ideally, `CENTER_RADIUS` should not be too large; otherwise, some roids will again fall through the boundary of the application window and appear on the other side. When a good `CENTER_RADIUS` is chosen, the resultant simulation can look startlingly like a school of fish going around in an endless loop or a flock of birds circling in the air before roosting for the evening.

2. In case you're not clued in, this is the fictional setting for *Portal*.

Putting in Obstacles

Having the roids fly around and even go in infinite loops is great fun to watch, but so far we've not done anything that can affect the roids directly. We've only been observers until now, so it's time to do something more interactive. In this section, we'll put in some obstacles and see how the roids react to them.

First let's add the obstacles, as shown in Example 7-13.

Example 7-13. Obstacles

```
Shoes.app(:title => 'Roids', :width => WORLD[:xmax], :height => WORLD[:ymax]) do
  stroke blue
  fill lightblue
  $roids = []
  $obstacles = []
  POPULATION_SIZE.times do
    random_location = Vector[rand(WORLD[:xmax]),rand(WORLD[:ymax])]
    random_velocity = Vector[rand(11)-5,rand(11)-5]
    $roids << Roid.new(self, random_location, random_velocity)
  end

  animate(FPS) do
    click do |button, left, top|
      $obstacles << Vector[left,top]
    end

    clear do
      $obstacles.each do |obstacle|
        oval(:left => obstacle[0], :top => obstacle[1],
             :radius => OBSTACLE_SIZE, :center => true,
             :stroke => red, :fill => pink)
      end
      $roids.each do |roid| roid.move; end
    end
  end
end
```

We add an `$obstacles` global variable, just as we did with the roids. This gives us access to a global list of obstacles on the screen. Then we add a callback to any mouse click so that clicking on the application window will create an obstacle. The click creates a new `Vector`, with the coordinates of the click's position serving as the center of the obstacle.

In the animation loop, just as with the roids, we loop through each obstacle and draw a filled circle with the radius of `OBSTACLE_SIZE`.

Now that we have the obstacles, we need to get the roids to take them seriously and avoid smashing into them. To do this, we add an `avoid` rule, as shown in Example 7-14, that tells all roids to avoid obstacles.

Example 7-14. Avoid rule

```
def avoid
  $obstacles.each do |obstacle|
    if distance_from_point(obstacle) < OBSTACLE_SIZE + ROID_SIZE*2
      @delta += (self.position - obstacle)/1.5
    end
  end
end
```

If the roid is near the obstacle (remember that the obstacle has a radius of `OBSTACLE_SIZE` and the roid has a radius of `ROID_SIZE`), we subtract the `position` of the obstacle from the roid's `position`, apply a small adjustment to make the change less abrupt, and then apply it to the `delta`. This will result in the roid avoiding the obstacle and moving away from it (Figure 7-7).

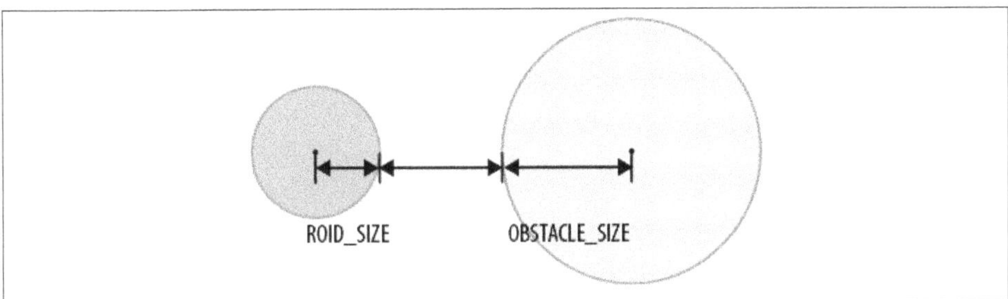

Figure 7-7. Avoidance distance between the roid and the obstacle

Wrap-up

That's it!

The simulation we've gone through in this chapter is a lifelike representation of coordinated animal movement, usually called flocking (in birds) or schooling (in fish). Flocking or schooling is an emergent behavior, meaning that complex behavorial patterns can arise from the interaction of many components following simple rules.

We built a model consisting of agents, called roids, that coordinate their movement through a number of simple rules. We started off with the implementation of the classic rules from the Boids flocking algorithm created by Craig Reynolds: separation, alignment, and cohesion. We also added some supporting rules to show a smoother simulation. Then we tweaked the rules a bit to incorporate some recent research findings from the STARFLAG project, mainly that the birds (or roids, in our case) interact with a fixed number of neighboring birds instead of taking into account all birds within a specific radius, as suggested by the Boids algorithm.

Next, instead of having the roids fall through from one side of the application window to the other, we made them circle the center of the application window. This creates a startlingly lifelike simulation of birds flocking before roosting in the evening. The final tweak to our simulation in this chapter allowed us to click on the application window to create obstacles that the roids need to avoid.

The simulation in this chapter is meant for you to play around with, so change the parameters and rerun it to see the differences. Increase the number of roids, change the radius of influence for the three rules, change the magic number. A word of warning, though—it can get quite addictive!

CHAPTER 8
Money, Sex, and Evolution

When I was young I used to drive my father up the wall by bombarding him with exasperating questions like "Why am I here?", "Why is the sky blue?", "Why am I Chinese?", and the classic "Are we there yet?" It was frustrating for him to come up with an answer that was simple enough for me to understand yet informative enough to be marginally educational.

Of course, the great wheel of karma turns, and inevitably it was my turn to try to answer my son's similar questions.

What struck me as I deftly fielded my son's constant barrage was the same question that I always asked and to which I never really got a good answer (except in *The Hitchhiker's Guide to the Galaxy*, but that's another story): "What makes the world go round?"

Many attempted to answer this question. Charles Dickens said it's love. According to Michael Jackson, it's people. The 1960s musical *Cabaret* claimed it's money. Plenty of songs say it's music. The answer I like best, though, is from the 1963 Disney animated film, *The Sword and the Stone*:

> You see, my boy, it's nature's way. Upon the weak the strong ones prey. The human life, it's also true. The strong will try to conquer you. And that is what you must expect. Unless you use your intellect. Brains and brawn, weak and strong. That's what makes the world go round.

As you might have guessed, this is the chapter where we will make our own attempt at answering it. When we left Chapter 7, we had a functioning simulation of a Boids clone, called Roids. In this chapter, we're going to expand upon that simulation and build an entire artificial world populated by roids.

It's a Good Life

Some of what I describe in this chapter is inspired by original research conducted by Joshua Epstein and Robert Axtell from the 2050 Project, a joint venture of the Santa Fe Institute, the World Resources Institute, and the Brookings Institution. The research is covered in detail in Epstein and Axtell's excellent book *Growing Artificial Societies: Social Science from the Bottom Up* (Brookings Institution Press/MIT Press). What I've done here is to reimplement and elaborate on some of Epstein and Axtell's ideas using the Roids simulation.

The roids we built in Chapter 7 have the good life. First, they are immortal and free to roam their world with any cares or worries. Sure, occasionally you'll drop nasty obstacles around them, but that's about it. They don't need to eat or sleep, and since they are immortal, they don't need to procreate to continue their species either. All they do is to wander around in flocks in an infinitely wide space. It's a veritable Garden of Eden.

That's not much of a world, though, and as a simulation, quite uninteresting after a while. What we'll do is, starting from this basic simulation, increasingly add behavior to the roids and the world they live in. As we run the simulation, we'll gather different types of data and run some analysis on it, asking certain questions along the way, and hopefully, finding the correct answers.

Let's start simple in our Garden of Eden by doing what the serpent did—offer food to the roids.

Money

Starting with the basic Roids simulation in Chapter 7, we will add on some interesting features to create our new simulation, which I will call Utopia.[1] In this new simulation, each roid has an energy level that is randomly assigned at its creation. At every tick, each roid loses some energy; if the roid loses all his energy, it will die. To survive, each roid continuously seeks out food, which it eats to replenish its energy. That's quite a fall from absolute immortality, but the roids are still *potentially* immortal—if they can find enough food at all times, they will live forever.

Naturally, we will also need to add food in Utopia. To do so, we will create a random amount of food and scatter it throughout the world. More food will be constantly and miraculously created at another random location at random intervals.

1. The term *utopia* originally comes from Greek, meaning literally "no place." The idea of an ideal society was satirized in Thomas More's book *Utopia*, which brought the word into mainstream usage. More's book described a fictional island state in the Atlantic Ocean that had an unusual (at that point in time) society. As you will see later, this name is rather apt for our simulation.

To create this simulation and also to ease simulations down the road in this chapter, we will streamline the base code from Chapter 7. What this really means is that we'll break down *roids.rb* from Chapter 7 into a number of smaller files. The main file will be called *utopia.rb*, while the rest will be broken down into logical pieces.

First, let's look at *utopia.rb*, which is the main file we're going to run for the simulation (Example 8-1).

Example 8-1. The main Utopia simulation code

```
Shoes.app(:title => 'Utopia', :width => WORLD[:xmax], :height => WORLD[:ymax]) do
  background ghostwhite
  stroke slategray

  $roids = []
  $food = []
  data = []
  populate
  scatter_food

  time = END_OF_THE_WORLD

  animate(FPS) do
    randomly_scatter_food FOOD_PROBABILITY
    clear do
      d = Array.new(POPULATION_SIZE, 0)
      para time
      fill yellowgreen
      $food.each do |food| food.tick; end
      fill gainsboro
      $roids.each do |roid|
        roid.tick
        d[roid.uid] = roid.energy
      end
      data << d
    end

    time -= 1
    close & write(data) if time < 0
  end
end
```

All code examples may be downloaded from GitHub (*https://github.com/sausheong/everyday*).

If you've gone through Chapter 7, this should be familiar to you. There are some subtle differences, though. First, we have a `time` variable, which is initially set to a constant called `END_OF_THE_WORLD`. The simulation essentially loops indefinitely until the end of the world is reached, which is 2,000 ticks.

Besides the `$roids` global variable, we also have a `$food` global variable, which is an array of all the food objects in Utopia. When we fire up the simulation, we populate the world with roids and also scatter food randomly all over Utopia by calling the `scatter_food` method, as shown in Example 8-2.

Example 8-2. Scattering food initially

```
def scatter_food
  FOOD_COUNT.times do
    $food << Food.new(self, random_location)
  end
end
```

We scatter a number of food objects, fixed by the constant `FOOD_COUNT`. However, `FOOD_COUNT` is only the seed number of food objects. As we pass each tick in the animation loop, we randomly add new food objects into Utopia by calling the `randomly_scatter_food` method, as shown in Example 8-3.

Example 8-3. Scattering food randomly

```
def randomly_scatter_food(probability)
  if (0..probability).include?(rand(100))
    $food << Food.new(self, random_location)
  end
end
```

The scattering of new food objects at each tick is determined by a probability that is set by the constant `FOOD_PROBABILITY`. Also at each tick, all the food in Utopia is drawn on the screen, and is filled with the color yellow-green. Each food object is drawn as a circle, with the radius of the circle indicating the amount of food it contains. In other words, the larger a food object appears, the more food it has. When a roid "eats" at the food object, it will reduce the food object's size, which, of course, makes plenty of sense.

Finally, we want to gather data from this simulation for analysis. What we want to find out in this first simulation is how many roids survive and how much energy the surviving roids have over the period of 2,000 ticks. To determine this, we need to record, at each tick, how much energy each roid has.

At the start of the simulation, we create an array the size of the entire population and set it to 0. At the first tick, this will be replaced by the initial randomly set energy levels of all the roids. As each tick passes, we record the energy level of each roid (even if it's dead) in an array and accumulate that information in the overall `data` variable. Finally, we write this data into a CSV file named *money.csv*, as shown in Example 8-4.

Example 8-4. Writing data to a CSV file

```
def write(data)
  CSV.open('money.csv', 'w') do |csv|
    data.each do |row|
      csv << row
    end
  end
end
```

That's it for *utopia.rb*. Now let's look at the `Roid` class in the *roid.rb* file. Most of the code is the same, except for a few additions. First, instead of calling `move` every tick, the main Shoes application calls the `tick` method. This method is quite simple—it moves the roid, lets the roid lose energy, and if the roid runs out of energy, makes the roid remove itself from `$roids` (Example 8-5).

Example 8-5. Actions at every tick

```
def tick
  move
  lose_energy
  if @energy <= 0
    $roids.delete self
  end
end
```

The `move` method, shown in Example 8-6, is almost exactly the same, with the exception that in addition to the other various rules, we now add in a `hungry` method, which is quite self-explanatory.

Example 8-6. Moving the roid

```
def move
  @delta = Vector[0,0]
  %w(separate align cohere muffle hungry).each do |action|
    self.send action
  end
  @velocity += @delta
  @position += @velocity
  fallthrough and draw
end
```

The `hungry` method, defined in Example 8-7, allows the roid to get attracted to food. When it is near enough to a food object (in this case, 5 pixels away), the roid will eat some of the food.

Example 8-7. Getting attracted to food

```
def hungry
  $food.each do |food|
    if distance_from_point(food.position) < (food.quantity + ROID_SIZE*5)
      @delta -= self.position - food.position
    end
```

```
    if distance_from_point(food.position) <= food.quantity + 5
      eat food
    end
  end
end
```

Eating food, as shown in Example 8-8, will reduce the amount of food in the food object, and increase the roid's energy level by a fixed amount determined by the constant METABOLISM.

Example 8-8. Eating the food

```
def eat(food)
  food.eat 1
  @energy += METABOLISM
end
```

Next, losing energy really means reducing the energy level by 1 at every tick (Example 8-9).

Example 8-9. Losing energy

```
def lose_energy
  @energy -= 1
end
```

We're almost done with the Roids class, but there's one last change. The size of each roid now grows with the amount of energy it has, and correspondingly shrinks when it loses energy. We don't want the roids to end up monstrously sized, so we cap the size at 10 pixels in radius, as shown in Example 8-10.

Example 8-10. Changing the roid size according to the energy level

```
def draw
  size = ROID_SIZE * @energy.to_f/50.0
  size = 10 if size > 10
  o = @slot.oval :left => @position[0], :top => @position[1], :radius => size,
      :center => true
  @slot.line @position[0], @position[1], @position[0] - @velocity[0],
      @position[1] - @velocity[1]
end
```

Next is the Food class (Example 8-11), which is new in this chapter. If you remember Chapter 7, this is really a stripped-down version of the Obstacle class.

Example 8-11. The Food class

```
class Food
  attr_reader :quantity, :position

  def initialize(slot, p)
    @position = p
    @slot = slot
    @quantity = rand(20) + 10
  end
```

```
  def eat(much)
    @quantity -= much
  end

  def draw
    @slot.oval :left => @position[0], :top => @position[1], :radius => quantity,
        :center => true
  end

  def tick
    if @quantity <= 0
      $food.delete self
    end
    draw
  end
end
```

Each food object has a `quantity` and a `position`, both randomly created initially. Eating the food reduces the `quantity` of the food pile, and at each tick we will check if the `quantity` has dropped to nothing. If it has, we will remove it from `$food`.

We're done with the code. Unlike Chapter 7, where the code is given in full, I have provided only snippets here. You should download the code from GitHub (*https://github.com/sausheong/everyday*) and try it out yourself! A typical session looks like Figure 8-1.

Now that we have data for the simulation, let's analyze it.

First, let's look at the CSV data that was generated (Figure 8-2). It consists of 50 columns, one for each roid, and 2,000 rows, one for each tick.

Scrolling down, you will notice that as time passes, more and more of the roids "die," and only a few roids remain by the end of the simulation. Surprisingly, the surviving roids have a large amount of energy left. Let's run this through an R script and investigate closer (Example 8-12).

Example 8-12. Plotting histogram of roid energy levels over time

```
library(ggplot2)
data <- read.table("money.csv", header=F, sep=",")
samples <- data.frame(roid=1:51)
points = c(1,5,15,30,50,75,100,125,150,200,300,500)

pdf("money.pdf")
grid.newpage()
pushViewport(viewport(layout=grid.layout(4,3)))
vp_layout <- function(x,y) {viewport(layout.pos.row=x, layout.pos.col=y)}

row <- 1; col <- 1
for (i in points) {
  point <- data.frame(t(data[i,]))
```

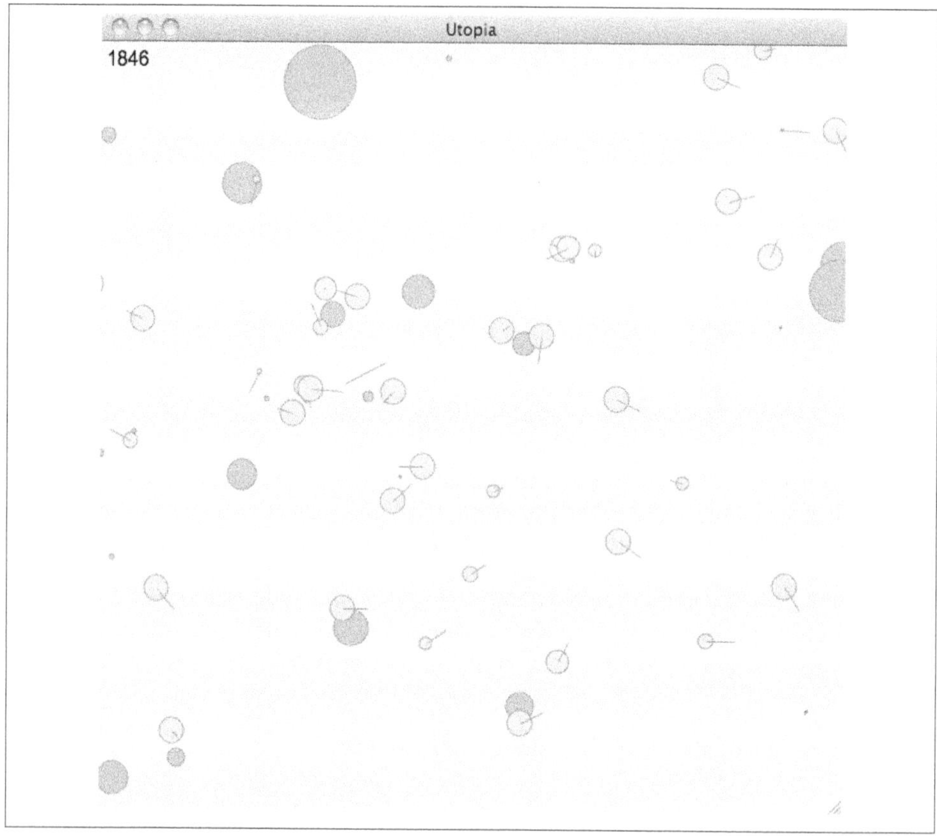

Figure 8-1. First simulation

```
  colnames(point) <- 'energy'
  p <- qplot(energy, data=point, geom="histogram", binwidth=5,
      main=paste("time=",i,sep=""))
  print(p, vp=vp_layout(row,col))
  if (col == 3) {row <- row + 1}
  col <- (col %% 3) + 1
}
dev.off()
```

The first two lines of the script should be familiar by now. However, we cannot possibly use the entire population of data we've collected, so we will take just a sample. We create a `samples` data frame to contain these samples, which are collected from different points in time. To visualize energy level changes of all roids over time, we take snapshot histograms of the energy levels of all roids at different points in time. In the script, we do this at tick 1, 5, 15, 30, and so on. Notice that we don't go all the way to the 2,000th tick—you'll see why in a short while.

56	79	66	74	96	54	91	59	70	95	65	82	64	80	63	68	69	69	72	89	64	53
55	78	65	73	95	53	90	58	74	99	64	86	63	79	62	72	78	73	71	93	63	52
54	77	69	72	104	52	89	57	73	98	63	90	62	78	61	76	87	77	75	92	62	51
53	76	73	71	113	51	88	56	77	97	62	89	61	77	60	80	91	81	79	91	61	55
52	75	77	70	122	50	87	55	76	101	66	88	60	76	59	84	95	85	78	95	60	54
51	74	81	69	131	49	86	54	80	100	70	92	59	75	58	88	99	89	77	99	59	58
50	73	80	68	140	48	85	53	84	99	74	91	58	74	57	92	98	93	81	103	58	62
49	72	79	67	149	47	84	52	83	103	78	90	57	73	66	96	102	97	80	107	57	61
48	71	83	66	158	46	83	51	82	102	77	89	56	72	70	105	101	101	79	111	56	65
47	70	82	65	167	45	82	50	86	101	81	93	55	71	79	109	100	105	83	110	55	69
46	69	81	64	171	44	81	49	85	105	85	92	54	70	83	118	104	109	82	114	54	68
45	68	85	63	180	43	80	48	84	104	89	91	53	74	92	122	108	113	81	113	53	67
44	67	84	62	179	42	79	47	88	103	93	95	52	73	96	131	107	112	80	112	52	71
48	66	83	61	188	41	78	46	87	107	92	94	51	77	105	135	106	116	79	111	51	70
52	65	87	65	187	40	77	45	86	106	91	93	50	76	109	139	105	115	78	110	50	69
51	64	86	69	196	39	76	44	90	105	90	97	49	75	118	143	104	114	77	109	49	73
50	63	85	73	195	38	80	43	89	109	89	96	48	79	122	152	103	118	81	108	48	72
49	62	84	77	204	37	84	42	88	108	88	100	47	78	126	156	102	117	80	107	47	71
48	61	83	81	203	36	88	41	92	107	87	99	46	77	130	160	101	116	84	106	46	75
47	60	87	85	207	35	92	40	91	111	86	98	45	81	134	164	100	120	83	110	45	74
46	59	86	84	206	34	96	39	90	110	85	102	44	80	133	163	99	119	82	114	44	73
45	58	85	83	215	33	100	38	94	109	84	101	43	79	132	167	98	118	81	118	43	77
44	57	89	87	214	32	104	37	93	113	83	100	47	83	131	166	97	122	80	122	42	76
43	56	88	86	218	31	103	36	92	112	82	99	46	82	130	170	96	121	79	126	41	75
42	55	87	85	217	30	107	35	96	111	91	98	50	81	129	169	95	120	78	130	40	79
41	54	86	84	226	29	106	34	95	115	90	97	54	85	128	173	94	124	77	129	39	78
40	53	85	83	225	28	105	33	94	114	94	96	53	84	127	172	93	123	76	128	38	77
44	52	84	82	229	27	109	32	93	113	93	95	52	83	126	171	92	122	75	132	37	76
43	51	83	81	228	26	108	31	92	112	92	94	56	82	125	170	91	126	74	131	36	75
42	50	82	80	232	25	107	30	96	111	96	93	55	81	124	169	90	125	73	130	35	74
46	49	81	84	231	24	106	29	100	115	95	92	54	80	123	168	89	124	72	134	34	73
45	48	80	83	235	23	105	28	99	114	99	91	53	79	122	167	88	123	71	133	33	72

Figure 8-2. Data collected from simulation

To display all the histograms at once, we will use *grid*, the underlying graphics system used by ggplot2. Because it is part of the R distribution, we don't need to include grid as a library. What we will need to use from grid is the *viewport*: a rectangular subregion of the display. The default viewport takes up the entire display, but with a bit of tweaking we can lay out plots the way we want by specifying multiple viewports and their positions in the display.

Viewports are created with the `viewport()` function. To create a plot in a rectangular grid, we use `grid.layout()`, which sets up a regular grid of viewports. `grid.layout()` creates a grid with four rows, each with three columns. The `viewport()` call that follows fills those rows and columns. After being created, a viewport must be pushed into a viewport tree before it can be displayed. To do this, we use the `pushViewport()` function. In Example 8-12, we first create a viewport with a grid of four rows and three columns and push it to the viewport tree. Next, we create a simple function that will be reused in a later loop. This function, `vp_layout()`, simply creates a viewport at the given row and column.

With this, we're ready to go through each point in time that we want to sample. First, we create a data frame by transposing the data at a given time using the `t()` function, and assign the data frame to a variable point. We need to transpose the data first because our data is written by row, but data frames need the data by column. We change the name of the column to `energy` to make it more obvious that we're dealing with the energy levels of the roids.

After that, we plot a histogram with the `binwidth` of 5 and slap a title on it, telling us which tick we are plotting. This plot is then printed on a viewport of the correct row and column. The last two lines help us to loop over all 12 sample points. As I noted earlier, we do not go all the way to the 2,000th tick; we stop at the 500th. This is because going any further doesn't give us much more information, as you can see from the plot in Figure 8-3.

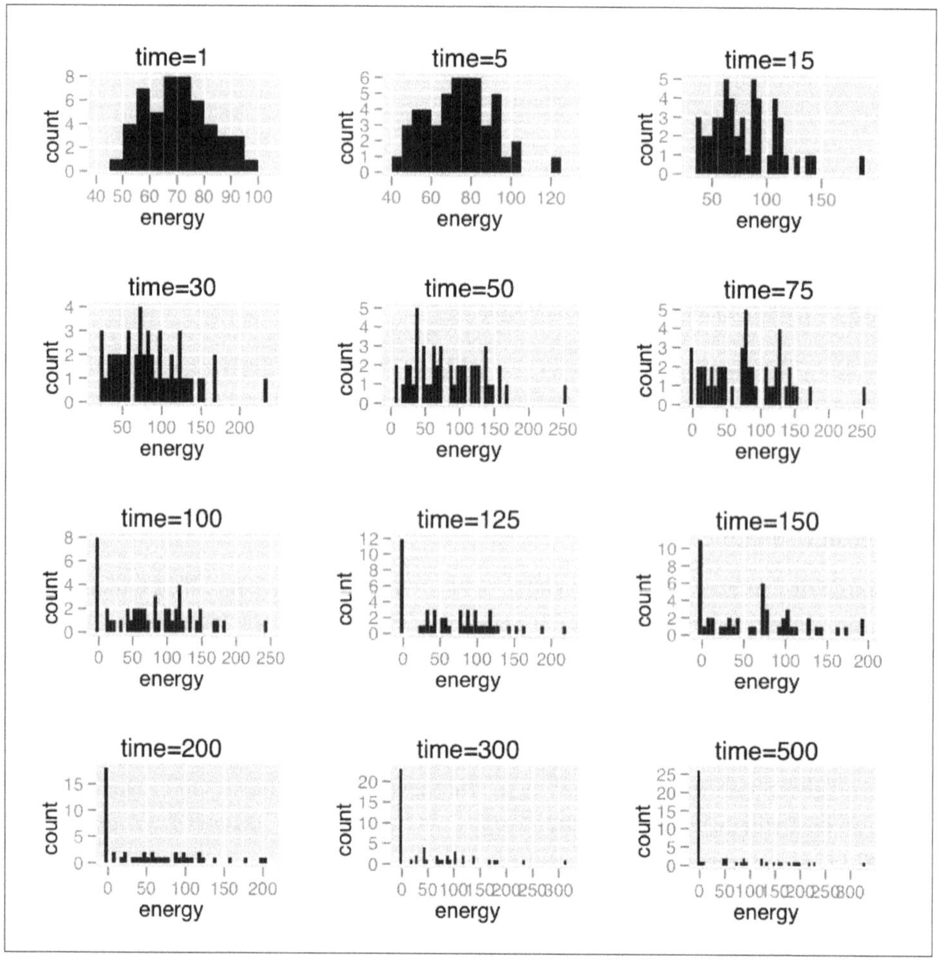

Figure 8-3. Energy levels of roids over time

A quick glance of the histograms tell us a clear story. At the beginning, the distribution is normal since it's random. For more on this topic, see the next sidebar, "Checking for Normal Distribution".

Checking for Normal Distribution

Let's check if the distribution of the initial population is really normal. R has a number of normal-distribution testing functions. For our purposes, we'll be using one of the more popular tests, the Shapiro-Wilk test. Without going in depth into the mathematics of this test (which would probably fill up a whole section, if not an entire chapter, on its own), let's examine the initial population by assuming that the population is normally distributed and running the Shapiro-Wilk test on it:

```
> data <- read.table("money.csv", header=F, sep=",")
> row <- as.vector(as.matrix(data[1,]))
> row
 [1] 56 79 66 74 96 54 91 59 70 95 65 82 64 80 63 68 69 69 72 89 64 53 87 49
[47] 68 66 80 89 57 73 72 82 76 58 57 78 94 73 83 52 75 71 52 57 76 59 63 ...
> shapiro.test(row)

  Shapiro-Wilk normality test

data:  row
W = 0.9755, p-value = 0.3806

>
```

As you can see, the *p*-value is 0.3806, which (on a a scale of 0.0 to 1.0) is not small, and therefore the null hypothesis is not rejected. The null hypothesis is that of no change (i.e., the assumption that the distribution is normal). Strictly speaking, this doesn't really prove that the distribution is normal, but a visual inspection of the first histogram chart in Figure 8-3 tells us that the likelihood of a normal distribution is high.

The initial histogram chart roughly follows a nice bell curve. As time goes by, though, the histogram starts to skew toward the left as more and more roids lose energy. Over time, we end up with a lot of dead roids or roids with very little energy, while only a few roids survive. The surviving roids, however, have one very surprising attribute—all of them are clustered on the left side with very high energy levels!

So what does this tell us? It definitely couldn't be that some roids are simply better than others (e.g., smarter, braver, or better looking) because all roids are exactly the same.

Could the results be totally random? A few lucky roids survived simply because they were at the right place at the right time? Intuitively, it sounds correct, but it's actually not. If it's truly random, the histogram should remain the same—that is, totally random behavior should have a normal distribution as well, but you can see clearly in the final histogram that it does not.

So how can we explain this?

One plausible explanation is that the Utopia simulation shows an emergent behavior (complex behavior arising from simple entities), much like the base simulation's movement, which created the illusion of flocking by just following a few simple rules. Given that all roids are the same, our Utopia simulation simply shows that over time, the rich get richer and the poor get poorer (in this case, the poor die), and the gap of inequality widens.

Isn't this simply guessing? Let's do a second analysis. Inequality is frequently measured using the Gini coefficient, so we'll analyze the distribution of energy levels with the Gini coefficient and Lorenz curves (for more information, see the sidebar "Gini Coefficient and Lorenz Curve").

Gini Coefficient and Lorenz Curve

The Gini coefficient is a measure of statistical dispersion developed by the Italian statistician and sociologist Corrado Gini and published in his 1912 paper "Variability and Mutability." It is a measure of the inequality of a distribution, a value of 0 expressing perfect equality and a value of 1 expressing perfect inequality. Although commonly used as a measure of inequality of income or wealth, the Gini coefficient has also been applied in many other fields, including ecology, health science, and chemistry.

Associated with the Gini coefficient is the Lorenz curve, a graphical representation of the cumulative distribution function of a probability distribution. It was developed by Max O. Lorenz in 1905 to represent inequality of the wealth distribution. If there is perfect equality, the curve will be a line $y = x$. If there is perfect inequality, it will be a line $y = 0$ (i.e., a horizontal line). The Gini coefficient is the area between the line of perfect equality and the Lorenz curve, as a percentage of the area between the line of perfect equality and the line of perfect inequality.

For this analysis, we'll use the ineq library, which conveniently provides all the necessary functions for us to do this analysis. Let's apply the same data points we used for graphing to some new R code that calculates the coefficience of inequality (Example 8-13).

Example 8-13. Analyzing inequality over time

```
library(ineq)
data <- read.table("money.csv", header=F, sep=",")

points = c(1,5,15,30,50,75,100,125,150,200,300,500)

pdf("inequality.pdf")
par(mfcol=c(4,3))
for (i in 1:12) {
  p <- Lc(as.vector(as.matrix(data[points[i],])))
  ie <- ineq(data[points[i],])
  plot(p, main=paste("t =", points[i], "/ Gini = ", round(ie, 3)), font.main=1)
}
dev.off()
```

Although we use the same data as before (of course) and the same sample points, instead of generating histograms, this time we generate Lorenz curves and print out the Gini coefficient in the title of the chart as well (Figure 8-4).

As expected, inequality increases over time—that is, the rich get richer and the poor get poorer. This is a simple simulation, so how does it reflect the real world?

One of the major catchphrases in the "Occupy Wall Street" protest movement that started in 2011 is "We are the 99%," which refers to the unequal distribution of wealth in America. The protesters have also accused Wall Street and corporations of risky lending practices that eventually caused the economic crisis of 2008, and have protested against corporate money in politics.

These claims are not without merit. A report from the Congressional Budget Office (CBO) pointed out that income inequality in America has risen dramatically over the past 20 years. Between 1979 and 2007, the incomes of the top 1% of Americans grew by an average of 275%. During the same time period, the 60% of Americans in the middle of the income scale saw their income rise by 40%. By 2007, the top 20% of Americans owned 85% of the country's wealth, and the bottom 80% of the population owned 15%. However, after 2007, the share of total wealth owned by the top 1% of the population grew from 34.6% to 37.1%, and wealth owned by the top 20% of Americans grew from 85% to 87.7%.

However, the culprits might not be the fat cats on Wall Street alone, nor the stereotypical dirty-money politicians. In fact, the phenomenon of wealth inequality has been around for a while in America. In 1922, the top 1% owned 36.7% of the wealth, and this number jumped to 44.2% by the time the stock market crashed in 1929.

From our Utopia simulation, it seems that this phenomenon might be a natural one. This argues for an alternative to a pure free-market solution—for example, regulations to prevent a concentrated accumulation of wealth in a small portion of the

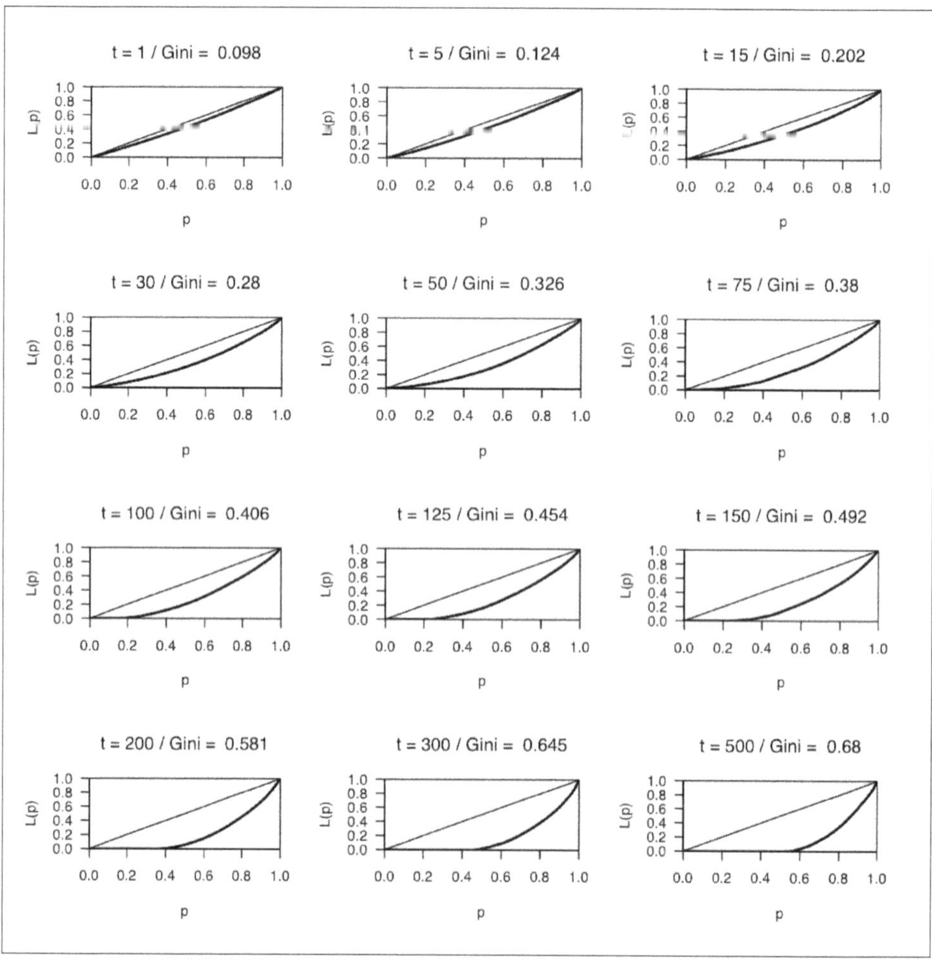

Figure 8-4. Lorenz curves showing inequality over time

population. Of course, the reality is much more complicated than a simple simulation such as the one that we've done here. However, it's interesting to realize that there's no totally black and white answer to the question of why the rich get richer and the poor get poorer.

Sex

Next, let's spice things up a bit with a little sex. By that, I mean now allowing the roids to procreate (what else did you think I meant?). The reason for doing this is because we want to observe changes in the roid population and find patterns in procreation. In this section, we'll investigate the pattern of changes in the roid population over a period of time.

Birth and Death

First of all, we will have male and female roids. Both male and female roids are almost the same except for three aspects. First, only the females of the species can and will initiate procreation and can give birth. Second, we're introducing the concept of *metabolism*, which determines how much of the food the roid consumes is turned into energy. Female roids have a slightly higher metabolism than the male roids. Finally, males are blue and females remain gray.

In addition, as a result of increased population, we can't afford to allow roids to be immortal anymore and need to introduce the Grim Reaper into the population. Much like the mythological Fates controlling the thread of life for every living person, once the roid is born, its lifespan is predetermined; once that lifespan is up, Atropos comes in to cut its thread and the roid dies.

In other words, we will introduce the idea of a maximum lifespan. Each roid will age at every tick and when its maximum lifespan is reached, it will die. Of course, as before, if the roid loses all its energy, it will also die.

In this simulation, instead of collecting data on energy level, we'll be collecting data on the population size over a period of time. What we want to do is to observe the pattern of population size—is it constant or does it fluctuate? It is entirely possible, of course, that the population dies out altogether as well.

The Changes

Most of the changes for this enhancement, as you can imagine, happen in the `Roid` class, although the `Roid` class itself actually changes very little (Example 8-14). First of all, we change the constructor method of the `Roid` class such that when a roid is created, it will have a randomly assigned sex. We'll change Utopia to include both male and female roids. Again, there isn't much difference between male and female roids except for their color, their metabolism, and their reproductive abilities.

Example 8-14. Changes in the Roid class to introduce sex, lifespan, and age

```
class Roid
  attr_reader :velocity, :position, :energy, :sex, :lifespan, :age

  def initialize(slot, p, v)
    @velocity = v
    @position = p
    @slot = slot
    @energy = rand(MAX_ENERGY)
    @sex = rand(2) == 1 ? :male : :female
    @lifespan = rand(MAX_LIFESPAN)
    @age = 0
  end

  def male?
    @sex == :male
  end

  def female?
    @sex == :female
  end
```

We added three new attributes to the `Roid` class here:

`sex`
: Either male or female, obviously.

`lifespan`
: The maximum lifespan of the roid. Each roid is randomly assigned a lifespan up to a `MAX_LIFESPAN`.

`age`
: The current age of the roid.

We also have two convenience methods to help us check whether the roid is male or female. Notice that for this simulation, we no longer need the unique ID, so we simply dropped it from the code.

As mentioned earlier, the female roid has a higher metabolism than the male roid, so we need to modify the `eat` method to cater to this difference (Example 8-15).

Example 8-15. Sex-aware eat function

```
def eat(food)
  amt_consumed = (male? ? MALE_METABOLISM : FEMALE_METABOLISM)
  food.eat amt_consumed
  @energy += amt_consumed
end
```

Next, we add the `procreate` method into the `Roid` class to allow the roids to procreate and have babies (Example 8-16).

Example 8-16. How roids procreate

```
def procreate
  if attractive and female?
    r = $roids.sort {|a,b| self.distance_from(a) <=> self.distance_from(b)}
    roids = r.first(MAGIC_NUMBER)
    roid = roids.delete_if{|r| female? and not attractive}.first
    if roid
      baby = Roid.new(@slot, @position, @velocity)
      $roids << baby
      reduce_energy_from_childbirth
      roid.reduce_energy_from_childbirth
    end
  end
end
```

The `procreate` method is the main focus of this current simulation. Let's get into the details a bit. First, only the female roids actively seek out mates for procreation. If the female roid is attractive enough (which we'll define shortly), she will look nearby for attractive male roids. Once she selects the nearest attractive male roid, they will mate and create a baby roid. The baby officially enters Utopia by inserting itself into the `$roids` global array, and once "born" this way, is randomly assigned a `sex` and `life span`. After the act of procreation, both the male and female roids lose some energy.

Let's look at what it means to be an attractive roid (Example 8-17).

Example 8-17. What constitutes an attractive roid

```
def attractive
  CHILDBEARING_AGE.include? @age  and @energy > CHILDBEARING_ENERGY_LEVEL
end
```

Unromantically, the attractiveness of a roid depends on its age (whether it is of childbearing age) and if it has enough energy to actually procreate. If you feel that this smacks of age discrimination, consider that the definition of attractiveness in our simulation is based on ability to reproduce and not any aesthetic property (since there is no aesthetic difference between roids of the same sex).

Reducing the female roid's energy after she gives birth is a simple formula that takes a small amount of her energy, as shown in Example 8-18.

Example 8-18. Reducing energy due to childbirth

```
def reduce_energy_from_childbirth
  @energy -= CHILDBEARING_ENERGY_SAP
end
```

At every tick, a few actions are taken, as shown in Example 8-19.

Example 8-19. Actions at every tick

```
def tick
  move
  lose_energy
  grow_older
  procreate
  if @energy <= 0 or @age > @lifespan
    $roids.delete self
  end
end
```

Moving should be familiar to us after Chapter 7, and losing energy every tick is straightforward. Growing older is simply increasing the age at every tick. We covered procreation earlier, so all that is left is to check if the roid has enough energy or if it has lived beyond its lifespan. If either is the case, it's the end of the line for the roid, and it is removed from the `$roids` global array.

That's really about it for the changes in the `Roid` class. Now let's look at *utopia.rb*. The main change is in the `animate` loop, as shown in Example 8-20.

Example 8-20. Changes in the animate loop to get population data

```
animate(FPS) do
  randomly_scatter_food 40
  clear do
    males = 0
    females = 0
    fill yellowgreen
    $food.each do |food| food.tick; end
    fill gainsboro
    $roids.each do |roid|
      males =+ 1 if roid.male?
      females =+ 1 if roid.female?
      roid.tick
    end
    data << [$roids.size, males, females]
    para "countdown: #{time}"
    para "population: #{$roids.size}"
    para "male: #{males}"
    para "female: #{females}"
  end

  time -= 1
  close & write(data) if time < 0 or $roids.size <= 0
end
```

The differences here are just in the way data is being collected. Instead of getting the energy levels of each roid, we now do a count of the number of roids in Utopia as well as the number of male and female roids.

It might come as a surprise to you that running this simulation is not straightforward. This is because the emergent behavior of the population can cause it to take sudden dives from which it cannot recover, and the whole population can be wiped out. Therefore, choosing the correct set of parameters (as configured in Example 8-21) is very important in maintaining a stable population throughout the duration of the simulation.

Example 8-21. Parameterized constants used in the simulation

```
END_OF_THE_WORLD = 10000
MAX_LIFESPAN = 100
MAX_ENERGY = 100
CHILDBEARING_AGE = 15..55
CHILDBEARING_ENERGY_LEVEL = 12
MALE_METABOLISM = 6
FEMALE_METABOLISM = 10
CHILDBEARING_ENERGY_SAP = 3
```

To analyze the simulation, we'll turn once again to an R script to generate the necessary data (Example 8-22).

Example 8-22. Analysis of population changes over time

```
library(ggplot2)
library(mgcv)

data <- read.table("sex.csv", header=F, sep=",")
pdf("sex.pdf")
colnames(data) <- c('population','male','female')
time = 1:nrow(data)
ggplot(data=data) +
  geom_smooth(aes(time,population),color='gray',method='gam',formula=y~s(x)) +
  geom_smooth(aes(time,male),color='blue',method='gam',formula=y~s(x)) +
  geom_smooth(aes(time,female),color='pink',method='gam',formula=y~s(x))
dev.off()
```

The general syntax should be quite familiar now. Because we have a lot of data points in the chart, it makes more sense to show just the smoothed line instead of every data point. The default method for a smooth geom in `ggplot2` is the *LOESS* algorithm, which is suitable for a small number of data points. LOESS is not suitable for a large number of data points, however, because it scales on an $O(n^2)$ basis in memory, so instead we use the `mgcv` library and its `gam` method. We also send in the formula `y~s(x)`, where `s` is the smoother function for GAM. GAM stands for *generalized additive model*, which is a statistical model used to describe how items of data relate to each other. In our case, we use GAM as an algorithm in the smoother to provide us with a reasonably good estimation of how a large number of data points can be visualized.

In Figure 8-5, you can see that the population of roids fluctuates over time between two extremes caused by the oversupply and exhaustion of food, respectively.

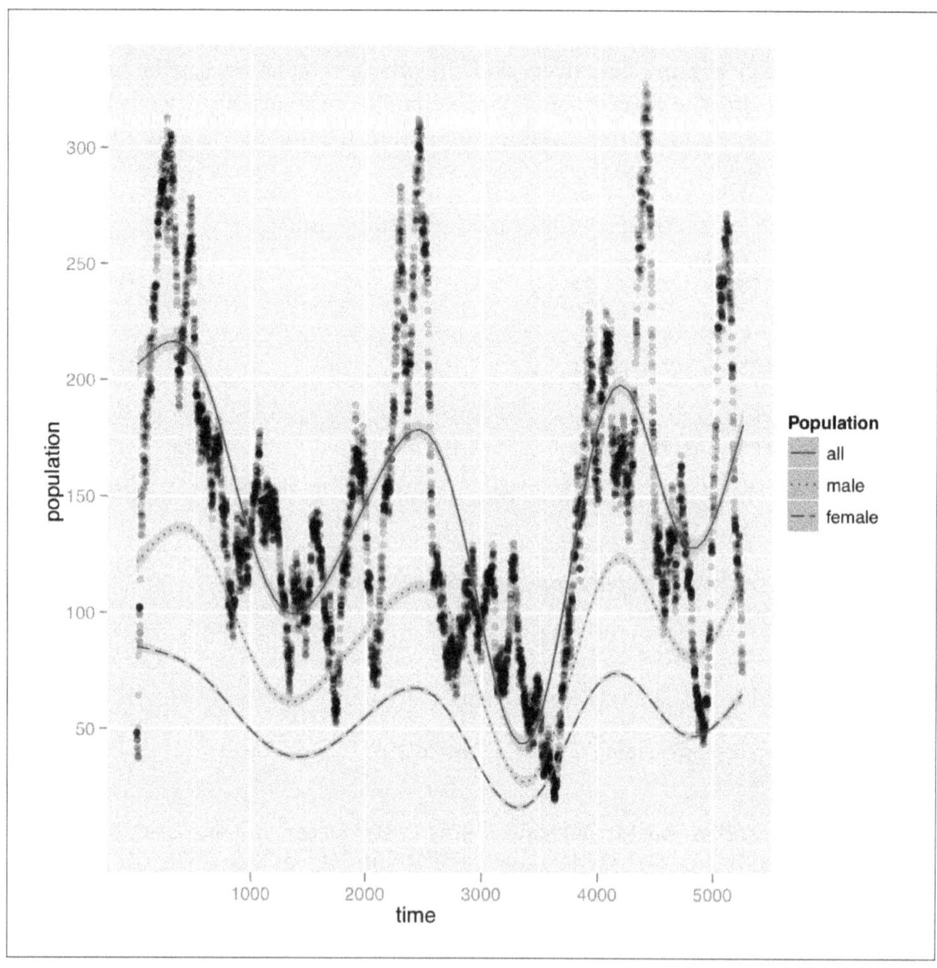

Figure 8-5. Population fluctuation over time

As the population matures, roids start to produce offspring. This causes a population explosion at regular intervals, and Utopia pretty soon runs out of food because the amount of food our program generates cannot keep up. This results in a mini-famine in which the weaker roids (the ones with less energy) die off. Very soon, the population numbers drop to a level where food can appear faster than the roids can consume it. This in turn causes a revival of the population numbers until the next famine. And so the wheel turns.

If you happen to hit upon the right combination of parameters, a sort of stable state can be achieved for a long time (in Figure 8-5 we ran the simulation for more than 5,000 ticks). However, more often than not, a fluctuation can swing so wildly that the bottom drops out and the whole population dies off, as shown in Figure 8-6. *This happens even if we start off with the same parameters*! Why does this happen? We have discussed emergent behavior, where small local rules result in complex, macro-level, group behavior. The pattern we have observed here, rather than emergent behavior, can be classified as a kind of "butterfly effect"; see the sidebar "Butterfly Effect" (page 218).

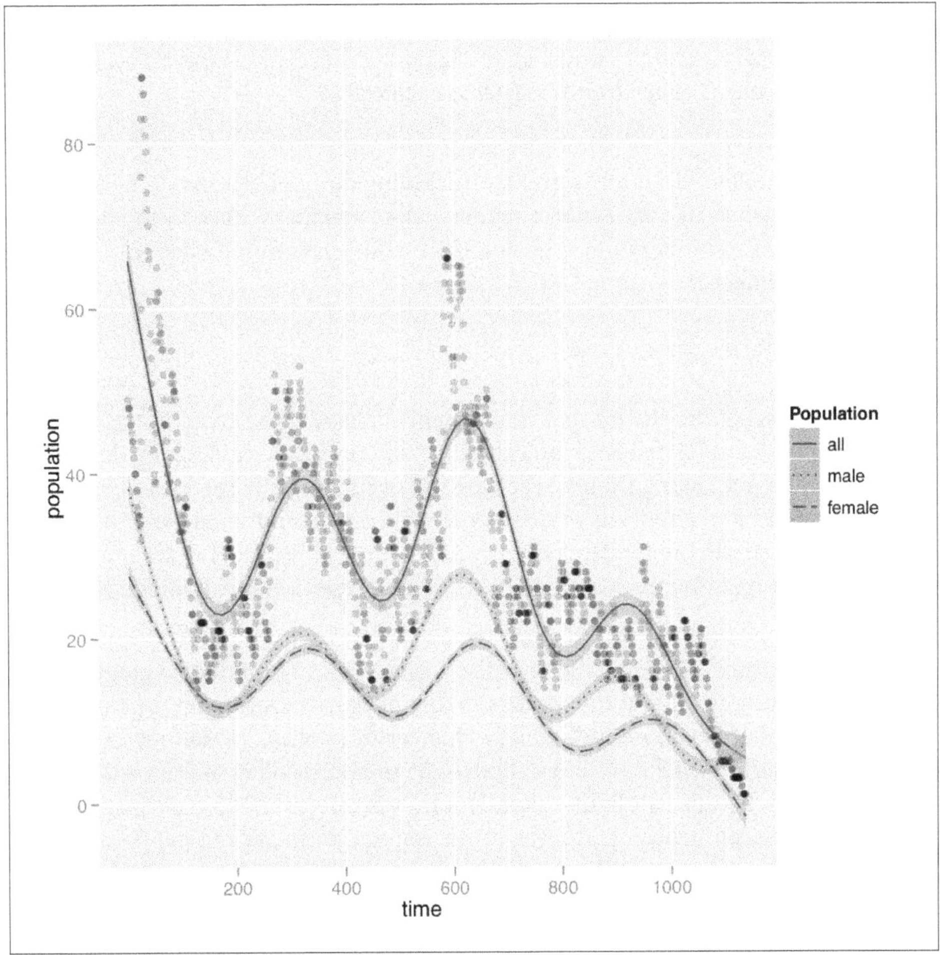

Figure 8-6. Population fluctuation swings, resulting in extinction of the roids

Butterfly Effect

In chaos theory, the butterfly effect is the sensitive dependence on initial conditions, where a small change somewhere in a nonlinear system can result in large differences at a later stage. This name was coined by Edward Lorenz, one of the pioneers of chaos theory (and no relation to Max Lorenz of the Lorenz curve fame).

In 1961, Lorenz was using a computer model to rerun a weather prediction when he entered the shortened decimal value .506 instead of entering the full .506127. The result was completely different from his original prediction. Lorenz later published his findings in a 1963 paper, saying that "one meteorologist remarked that if the theory were correct, one flap of a seagull's wings could change the course of weather forever." This reference was later changed from a seagull to a butterfly.

What does this tell us? In many systems—including our global ecosystem, and some manmade constructs like the American financial system that we briefly touched upon earlier—internal stability is not a given. Small and unassuming changes can often have dramatic effects.

Evolution

Evolution is a scientific theory that most scientists have come to accept as the only possible explanation for the enormous biodiversity on Earth. It basically describes a process of change in living things over a period of time. While the idea of evolution has been around in some form or another since the time of the ancient Greeks, it's really Charles Darwin (and independently, Alfred Russell Wallace) who came up with a scientific argument for evolution through natural selection, the familiar theory we know today.

Evolution by natural selection is one of the cornerstones of modern biology. Variations occur naturally among individuals in any population of living organism, and such differences affect those individuals' chances of survival. A famous example is the peppered moth, which is found in both light and dark colors in the United Kingdom. Originally, because the light-colored moths were better at hiding from predators on the light-colored lichens and trees of the region, dark-colored peppered moths were rare.

During the Industrial Revolution, however, many of the trees that the moths rest upon were blackened by soot generated by the coal-burning factories. This reversed the fortunes of the dark-colored moths, giving them a better chance to survive and produce dark-colored offspring. About 50 years from the time the first dark peppered moth was reported, nearly all moths in Manchester, an industrial city, were dark. However, due to current laws that have reduced the amount of pollution, the number of light-colored peppered moths has risen again.

Our last simulation will demonstrate natural selection, but instead of the light and dark peppered moths, we'll be using roids. Originally, the concept of natural selection was developed without knowledge of genetics. In our simulation, however, we'll introduce a simple genetic inheritance mechanism and investigate whether natural selection really works.

What We Will Be Changing

In the two previous simulations, all the roids had the same attributes, except for their maximum lifespan and starting energy level. Every roid aged the same way and had equal opportunity to procreate and produce offspring. In this simulation, we'll add two more attributes that introduce some unfairness into the equation:

`metabolism`
: A measurement of how well the roid converts food into energy

`vision_range`
: A measurement of how far the roid can see when it is looking for food

While the concept of metabolism was introduced in the previous section, it was a fixed value—that is, all male roids had the same metabolism, and all the female roids had the same metabolism. In this simulation, I'll call both metabolism and vision range "traits" because each roid can have a different metabolism and vision range.

Every roid baby born from the second generation onward will inherit these genetic traits from its parents. To simulate heredity, we will use a mechanism adapted from a simplified form of Mendelian inheritance.

If we consider the male roid to have a metabolism and vision range of values (M,V) and the female roid to have the values (m,v), we assume that the newborn baby will have one of four possible values, as shown in Table 8-1.

Table 8-1. Possible values inherited by the child roid

	metabolism m	metabolism M
Vision range v	(m,v)	(M,v)
Vision range V	(m,V)	(M,V)

To simplify the whole mechanism, we'll randomly pick one of the four values. In other words, no trait is dominant or recessive.

Why are these traits important? As you will see in a short while, these traits affect the roid's survivability. The roid's metabolism—that is, how efficiently it can convert food to energy—affects its odds of surviving to old age. The roid's vision range determines its chances of noticing, and therefore moving toward and consuming, food. If natural selection works, we should observe that the roids will, over time, have better metabolism and vision range.

Implementation

Now let's look at how the roid code is changed to implement our simple evolutionary traits. As before, let's look at the changes in the constructor for the `Roid` class first, as shown in Example 8-23.

Example 8-23. Changes to Roid class for evolution simulation

```
class Roid
  attr_reader :velocity, :position, :energy, :sex, :lifespan, :age, :metabolism,
              :vision_range

  def initialize(slot, p, v)
    @velocity = v
    @position = p
    @slot = slot
    @energy = rand(MAX_ENERGY)
    @sex = rand(2) == 1 ? :male : :female
    @lifespan = rand(MAX_LIFESPAN)
    @age = 0
    @metabolism = (male? ? rand(MAX_MALE_METABOLISM*10)/10.0 : \
                  rand(MAX_FEMALE_METABOLISM*10)/10.0)
    @vision_range = rand(MAX_VISION_RANGE*10.0)/10.0
  end
```

These changes reflect the addition of the `metabolism` and `vision_range` attributes to the `Roid` class. These are initialized randomly.

Next let's look at the `procreate` method in the `Roid` class (Example 8-24).

Example 8-24. How roids procreate and pass on their traits

```
def procreate
  if attractive and female?
    r = $roids.sort {|a,b| self.distance_from(a) <=> self.distance_from(b)}
    roids = r.first(MAGIC_NUMBER)
    roid = roids.delete_if{|r| female? and not attractive}.first
    if roid
      baby = Roid.new(@slot, @position, @velocity)
      crossovers = [[@metabolism, @vision_range],
                    [@metabolism, roid.vision_range],
                    [roid.metabolism, @vision_range],
                    [roid.metabolism, roid.vision_range]]
      baby.inherit crossovers[rand(4)]
```

```
      $roids << baby
      reduce_energy_from_childbirth
      roid.reduce_energy_from_childbirth

  end
end
```

The only change here is to create a `crossover` array from the male and female roids' traits, then allow the newborn baby to randomly inherit one of the four possible choices. The `inherit` method is simply copying the parents' traits to the child's traits, as shown in Example 8-25.

Example 8-25. Inheriting traits from the parents

```
def inherit(crossover)
  @metabolism = crossover[0]
  @vision_range = crossover[1]
end
```

Metabolism and vision range affect the survivability of the roid because they increase or decrease the chances of the roid finding food and turning it into energy. To add these traits into each roid's daily life, we modify the `hungry` and `eat` methods, as shown in Example 8-26.

Example 8-26. Modifying the hungry and eat methods

```
def hungry
  $food.each do |food|
    if distance_from_point(food.position) < (food.quantity + @vision_range)
      @delta -= self.position - food.position
    end
    if distance_from_point(food.position) <= food.quantity + 15
      eat food
    end
  end
end

def eat(food)
  food.eat 1
  @energy += @metabolism
end
```

As you can see, the `vision_range` variable modifies how far away the roid can see food. The `metabolism` variable, on the other hand, modifies how well the roid digests and converts food to energy.

Let's move on to see how we collect data. Remember that we want to find out whether natural selection really works, so we need to determine the average metabolism and average vision range at every tick and plot those values over a period of time. To do this, we need to modify the main file, *utopia.rb*, and change the `animate` loop (Example 8-27).

You may ask why we don't compare the roids' metabolism and vision range to their life expectancy (i.e., the roids with better metabolism and vision range survive better). It's not our goal here to prove that better metabolism and vision range improve life expectancy (although we can guess that the correlation would hold true on average). Instead, we're looking at evolution—at whether roids' metabolism and vision improve over the generations.

Example 8-27. Collecting data in the animate loop

```
animate(FPS) do
  randomly_scatter_food 30
  clear do
    fill yellowgreen
    $food.each do |food| food.tick; end
    fill gainsboro
    $roids.each do |roid|
      roid.tick
    end
    mean_metabolism = $roids.inject(0.0){ |sum, el| sum + el.metabolism}.to_f /
                      $roids.size
    mean_vision_range = $roids.inject(0.0){ |sum, el| sum + el.vision_range}.to_f /
                        $roids.size
    data << [$roids.size, mean_metabolism.round(2), mean_vision_range.round(2)]
    para "countdown: #{time}"
    para "population: #{$roids.size}"
    para "metabolism: #{mean_metabolism.round(2)}"
    para "vision range: #{mean_vision_range.round(2)}"
  end

  time -= 1
  close & write(data) if time < 0 or $roids.size <= 0
end
```

The average metabolism is simply the sum of the metabolism of all the roids, divided by the total number of roids. The average vision range is calculated the same way. The data that we end up with is three columns of numbers and a number of rows equal to the number of ticks the simulation has run. The first column shows the current roid population; the second column shows the average metabolism, rounded to two decimal places; and the last column shows the average vision range, also rounded to two decimal places.

Armed with this data, let's look at how the average metabolism and average vision range change over time, using R (Example 8-28).

Example 8-28. Plotting changes in average metabolism and vision range over time

```
library(ggplot2)

data <- read.table("evolution.csv", header=F, sep=",")
colnames(data) <- c('population','metabolism','vision_range')
pdf("evolution.pdf")
time = 1:nrow(data)

grid.newpage()
pushViewport(viewport(layout=grid.layout(1,2)))
vplayout <- function(x,y) {viewport(layout.pos.row=x, layout.pos.col=y)}

p <- qplot(time, metabolism, data=data, geom=c("point", "smooth"),
     main="Evolution in metabolism")
print(p, vp=vplayout(1,1))
p <- qplot(time, vision_range, data=data, geom=c("point", "smooth"),
     main="Evolution in vision range")
print(p, vp=vplayout(1,2))

dev.off()
```

This script is quite similar to the one in Example 8-12. Both scripts use a grid and create viewports to lay out multiple plots on the same chart. We create two plots on the chart: the first shows the average metabolism over a period of time, and the second shows the average vision range over a period of time. Results are shown in Figure 8-7.

You will notice straightaway that both the average metabolism and the average vision range increase over time and reach a stable maximum after a while. This shows that, thanks to natural selection, roids with better metabolism and vision range survive longer and therefore are more able to pass on their traits to the next generations. This is evolution in action.

Why do both the average metabolism and vision range values reach a maximum? This is because the simulation does not include random mutations. Therefore, the maximum possible metabolism and vision range are predetermined randomly at the beginning of the simulation, and no amount of evolution can cause any roids to exceed that.

You might notice that for the evolution of both traits, but especially in vision range, the journey wasn't all that smooth. In real life, as in this simulation, evolution is not always a smooth, orderly progression. Regression sometimes occurs, but in the larger scheme of things, natural selection moved the roids toward traits that enable them to survive longer.

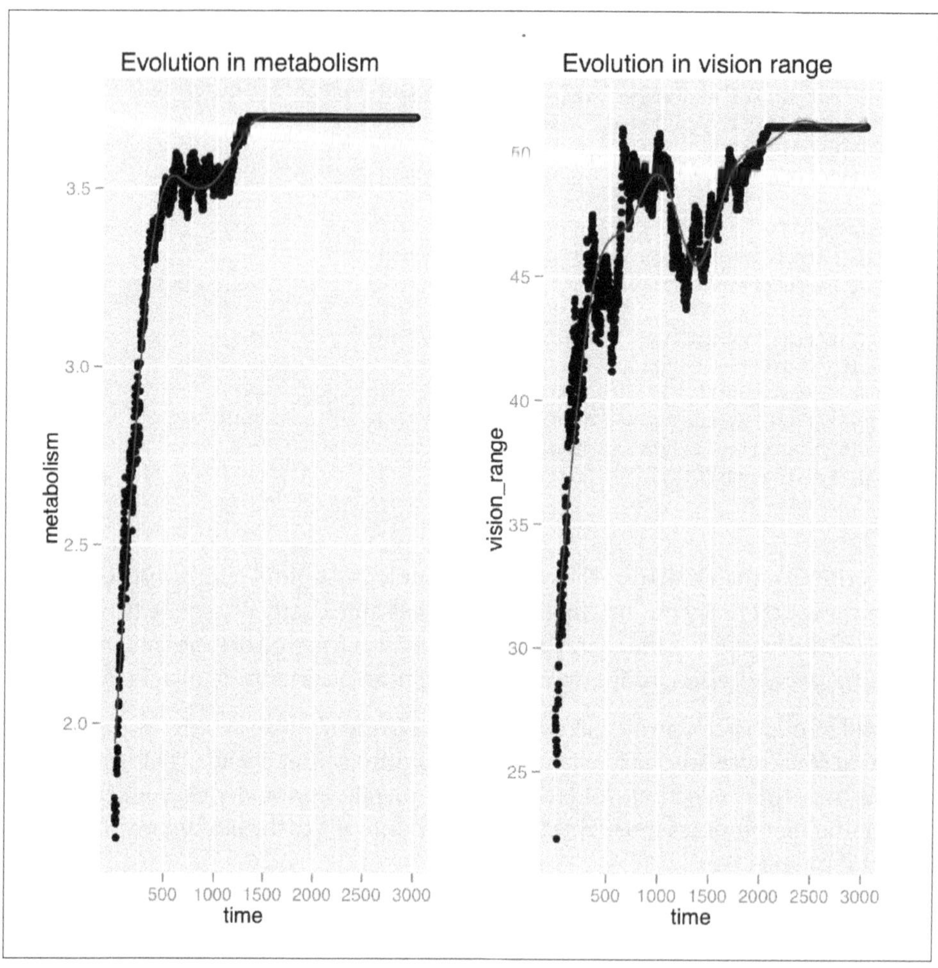

Figure 8-7. Evolution in action

Wrap-up

This chapter was a continuation of Chapter 7, where we implemented a bird flocking simulation, called Roids, with Ruby and Shoes. In this chapter, we took our Roids simulation further by building an entire artificial society called Utopia.

We ran through three different scenarios in simulating an artificial society populated by roids. In the first simulation, we introduced the idea that roids need to continually consume food in order to gain energy and avoid dying due to a lack of energy. From our basic observation of the energy levels over time, we reached the interesting conclusion that "the rich get richer and the poor get poorer"—a reflection of how our artificial society shows emergent behavior.

In my commentary, I associated energy levels with wealth and drew comparisons to the sorry but common state of affairs in the real world. Even our simple simulation revealed much complexity and emergent behavior, and therefore we concluded that the real world, being much more complex, cannot be easily explained.

The next scenario introduced sex and death into our artificial world. We created male and female roids, and had them procreate. We prevented total overcrowding by assigning random maximum lifespans to each roid. Our focus in this simulation was on population patterns over a period of time. We observed that it is difficult to reach a state where a population is stable enough to survive for a long time. Very often, population fluctuations involve crazy swings that eventually end with the extinction of the society, even with identical starting parameters. We observed that a small effect can ripple down, causing unexpected changes—a phenomenon known as the butterfly effect.

The final scenario dealt with evolution. We simulated natural selection by getting the offspring of the roids to inherit traits of their parents. These traits were specially designed to influence the survivability of the roids over a period of time. We anticipated that, if natural selection occurred, the traits of the roid population would move toward those that allow it to best survive. That was our exact observation, and we ended the final simulation by concluding that evolution through natural selection is valid.

So have we found out the answer to what makes the world go round?

Index

Symbols

A

We'd like to hear your suggestions for improving our indexes. Send email to index@oreilly.com.

B

C

D

E

F

G

H

I

J

L

M

N

O

P

Q

R

S

T

U

V

W

X

About the Author

Sau Sheong Chang has been in software development—mostly web applications and recently cloud- and data-related systems—for more than 17 years, and is still a keen and enthusiastic programmer. He has been active in Ruby programming for more than six years, and has worked with R for more than a year. He is active in the local developer communities, and is an active speaker at various technology conferences, especially Ruby conferences.

He has published two books, *Ruby on Rails Mashup Projects* in 2008 and *Cloning Internet Applications with Ruby* in 2010 (both Packt Publishing). Sau Sheong Chang is currently the Director of Applied Research for HP Labs Singapore, with research focusing on cloud computing, big data, and urbanization. His previous roles include stints as the CTO of a popular online gaming company and as the director of engineering for Yahoo! Southeast Asia. More detailed information can be found at *http://www.saush.com/profile*.

Colophon

The animal on the cover of *Exploring Everyday Things with R and Ruby* is the hooded seal (*Cystophora cristata*), a finned mammal native to the North Atlantic Ocean. Its scientific name is Greek for "bladder-bearer," so named for the large inflatable hood that develops on the head of the males when they are around four years old. This hood is used for courtship, as well as to intimidate rivals and enemies—hooded seals are one of the most aggressive seal species. When deflated, the bladder hangs down the forehead and between the eyes. Males also have a red secondary sac inside one nostril, which they can inflate by closing their other nostril valve.

Females are not as distinctive (or as large): they are around 7 feet long and 440 pounds, while males average 8 feet long and 660 pounds. However, both sexes have silvery fur with dark irregular spots. As with other semi-aquatic mammals, they have sleek clawed flippers that efficiently move them through water, but are clumsier on land.

Hooded seals are highly migratory, and will travel long distances throughout the year for food (generally by themselves), only to regroup at breeding grounds in late winter to mate and in summer to molt. They hunt in the water, able to dive almost 2,000 feet and stay underwater nearly an hour. Their diet changes depending on their location, but generally consists of fish, squid, shrimp, octopus, and mussels.

In their first 14 months, hooded seal pups have a blue-grey coat and pale bellies, giving them the nickname "bluebacks." They nurse for an average of 4 days, the shortest period of any mammal. However, the pup will nearly double in weight during this time, gaining around 10–15 pounds a day—their mother's milk is 60%–70% fat.

The cover image is from *Riverside Natural History*. The cover font is Adobe ITC Garamond. The text font is Minion Pro by Robert Slimbach; the heading font is Myriad Pro by Robert Slimbach and Carol Twombly; and the code font is UbuntuMono by Dalton Maag.

Lightning Source UK Ltd.
Milton Keynes UK
UKHW031307140521
383721UK00006B/224

9 781449 315153